Foundations of Cognitive Therapy

Theoretical Methods and
Practical Applications

Foundations of Cognitive Therapy

Theoretical Methods and Practical Applications

Edited by
Nicolas Hoffmann

The Free University of Berlin
Berlin, Federal Republic of Germany

Translated from German by
Elizabeth Lachman

Plenum Press • New York and London

Library of Congress Cataloging in Publication Data

Grundlagen kognitiver Therapie. English.
  Foundations of cognitive therapy.

  Translation of: Grundlagen kognitiver Therapie.
  Includes bibliographies and index.
  1. Cognitive therapy. I. Hoffmann, Nicolas. II. Title.
RC489.C63G7813   1984   616.89'14   84-4853
ISBN 0-306-40681-0

The present edition is a translation of *Grundlagen kognitiver Therapie,* originally
published by Hans Huber Verlag, Bern and Zurich

©1984 Plenum Press, New York
A Division of Plenum Publishing Corporation
233 Spring Street, New York, N.Y. 10013

Printed in the United States of America

Contributors

Aaron T. Beck, *Department of Psychology, University of Pennsylvania, Philadelphia, Pennsylvania*

Peter A. Fiedler, *Psychologisches Institut, Abteilung für Klinische Psychologie, West. Wilhelms Universität, D-44 Münster, Bundesrepublik Deutschland*

Michael Frese, *Technische Universität Berlin, Gesellschaftswissenschaften, D-1 Berlin 10, Bundesrepublik Deutschland*

Ruth L. Greenberg, *Department of Psychology, University of Pennsylvania, Philadelphia, Pennsylvania*

Nicolas Hoffmann, *Institut für Psychologie, Freie Universität Berlin, D-1 Berlin 41, Bundesrepublik Deutschland*

Ferdinand König, *Institut für Psychologie, Freie Universität Berlin, D-1 Berlin 41, Bundesrepublik Deutschland*

Evelyn Krautzig, *Institut für Psychologie, Freie Universität Berlin, D-1 Berlin 41, Bundesrepublik Deutschland*

Michael Linden, *Delbrückstrasse 13·17, D-1 Berlin 33, Bundesrepublik Deutschland*

Jürgen Otto, *Institut für Psychologie, Freie Universität Berlin, D-1 Berlin 41, Bundesrepublik Deutschland*

Thomas Bernhard Seiler, *Technische Hochschule, Hochschulstrasse 1, D-61 Darmstadt, Bundesrepublik Deutschland*

Norbert Semmer, *Büllowstrasse 90, D-1 Berlin 30, Bundesrepublik Deutschland*

Preface

Cognitive therapy is one of the newest and most promising developments in the psychotherapeutic field. Following the basic proposals of Beck, Ellis, and Frankl, an increasing amount of work is being done which shows a strong interest by behavior therapists in cognitive strategies. An increasing number of outcome studies show that cognitive methods are effective in many disorders, and it can be predicted that they will have a growing part to play in the practice of psychological therapies.

In spite of this, the development is only in its beginnings. Especially from a theoretical standpoint, many of the proposed techniques lack a sufficient foundation, and the implications of important results from different areas of psychology for providing a theoretical basis for cognitive intervention have not yet been sufficiently recognized.

To investigate these developments is the main purpose of this book. The intention of the authors is not to give a summary of the present status of cognitive therapy but to try to show its possibilities for future development.

A number of areas of psychological research have been selected as being the most important for future development of cognitive therapeutic techniques: the genetic theory of Piaget, the investigations of attitude theory, attribution theory, and psychological action theory, and the psychology of problem-solving.

After a description of the latest developments in these areas, the authors attempt to extract the theoretical implications for cognitive therapy and, on this basis, to make a few initial proposals for practice.

As the most finely elaborated form of cognitive therapy, and the one with the firmest theoretical foundations, the approach of Beck could not have been omitted. Beck and Greenberg give a description of the therapy of depression, which, thus far, constitutes the area most extensively encountered in practice.

The chapter by Fiedler also has a more practical orientation; he shows the impact of cognitive elements on behavior therapy.

In the final chapter, Krautzig and Linden warn that the increased usage of cognitive terminology may lead, if the terms are used imprecisely, to the loss of their meaning.

Many aspects of these various themes could not be discussed as extensively as they deserve; but the authors hope to provide some useful suggestions and to help clarify certain problems.

NICOLAS HOFFMANN

Contents

Chapter 3
Attitude Change and Cognitive Therapy............................ 51

Nicolas Hoffmann

Chapter 4
The Problem of Attribution and Cognitive Therapy.................. 73

Jürgen Otto

Cognitive Therapy

Introduction to the Subject

NICOLAS HOFFMANN

One of the latest developments in the area of psychological therapies concerns the increasing significance which "cognitive therapy" is gaining in both theoretical discussions and in practice. At the present time, one can identify numerous therapeutic approaches which are given this designation but which are quite distinctive in their foundations and procedures. Examples include Frankl's "logotherapy" and Ellis's "rational-emotive therapy," which have been known for a long time, and also more recent techniques that lend a strong "cognitive" flavor to behavior therapy and behavior modification.

In this chapter, the common features of cognitive therapies, their distinction from other approaches, and some problems regarding their theoretical foundation will be treated briefly, as an introduction to the chapters that follow.

1. Definitions

A. T. Beck, who has certainly made the largest contribution toward spreading the concept of "cognitive therapy," suggests the following definition: "In a broad sense, any technique whose major mode of action is the modification of faulty patterns of thinking can be regarded as cognitive therapy" (1970, p. 187).

As Beck (1970) notes, however, all therapeutic operations which indirectly affect thought processes may also be included in this definition.

NICOLAS HOFFMANN • Institut für Psychologie, Freie Universität Berlin, D-1 Berlin 41, Bundesrepublik Deutschland.

Seen in this fashion, it is scarcely possible to find a therapeutic approach that could not be considered "cognitive therapy."

Beck (1970) also states: "However, cognitive therapy may be defined more narrowly as a set of operations focused on a patient's cognitions (verbal or pictorial) and on the premises, assumptions, and attitudes underlying these cognitions" (p. 187).

This more specific definition identifies several therapeutic approaches which can readily be distinguished from others with regard both to goals and procedures. A brief characterization of the most important cognitive approaches follows.

2. Cognitive Therapy

The forms of cognitive therapy which are at present most relevant to theoretical discussion and practice may roughly be divided into two groups. The earliest approaches were based on the psychoanalytic methods of their founders and developed into independent therapies, whereas more recent work constitutes a development within the field of behavior therapy.

2.1. Cognitive Therapy as a Result of a Turnabout from Psychoanalysis

The three protagonists of the first significant systems of cognitive therapy, Frankl, Ellis, and Beck, with all the differences in the results of their work, show certain parallels with regard to their points of departure. All three view their approaches as renunciations of the psychoanalytic position which they originally assumed.

Frankl sees in his "logotherapy" a decisive extension to the Freudian theory of psychopathology, with far-reaching therapeutic implications. He also asserts that Freud was influenced too strongly by the mechanistic conceptions of the nineteenth century and, in consonance with this ideology, ignored an important dimension of man beyond the somatic and the psychic realms: the realm of the spirit (i.e., the noetic or intellectual).

Thus, Frankl advocates the view that, besides illnesses of a somatic or of a psychic origin, a problem of conscience—an ethical conflict or existential crisis—often lies at the root of the disorder. He calls these neuroses "noögenic" and provides a place for them alongside the somatogenic and psychogenic.

The therapy which Frankl (1969) considers advisable in this case goes considerably beyond the central concepts of Freudian psychoanalysis:

namely, repression as the cause of the disorder, and transference as the fundamental therapeutic process.

The approach, which he called "logotherapy," represents the attempt at a psychotherapy from the "spiritual" aspect; it constitutes the specific therapy for noögenic neuroses, and is also a valuable general aid in somatogenic and psychogenic illnesses, as a supplement to other forms of therapy.

This form of therapy tries to provide the patient with an "education for responsibility" (Frankl, 1969, p. 119). Through new interpretation and mediation of values it seeks to fill the existential vacuum in which Frankl believes neuroses and other psychic illnesses typically originate. It employs numerous techniques, such as "dereflection" and "paradoxical intention," which extensively modify emotions and behavior by influencing the cognitive level.

Ellis, who also comes to terms critically with psychoanalysis, though by another path, arrives at the growing realization of the significance of cognitive factors in psychic disorders, which leads to the attempt to influence them systematically.

With increasing experience in his analytic work, which he practiced first in an orthodox way and later more and more eclectically, his doubts about the correctness of the method grew. Soon he saw this method as only a passive waiting for "insights," a method which usually linked current problems in an arbitrary fashion to some past events, and which, when these insights occurred, often failed to lead to the desired changes. Regarding the passivity imposed on the therapist by this conventional role, Ellis (1962) asked why, after clearly understanding what the patient's problem was, the therapist then had to wait inactively for weeks, until the patient let it be known through his own interpretive attempts that he was fully ready to accept new insights. Why was the therapist not allowed to help the patient further by asking a few pertinent questions or making a few direct comments?

Regarding the etiological factors, Ellis came more and more to the conviction that the critical, currently virulent conditions of disorders lie not so much in the repressed memories of earlier traumas, or in the repressed drive impulses, but rather in the fact that these pathogenic experiences from early childhood are reflected in irrational thoughts and convictions that are maintained by pertinacious verbal self-indoctrination and that have become an integral component of the patient's "philosophy of life." According to Ellis, these irrationalisms are at the root of the psychic disorders, and the constant, active way in which the patient keeps them alive through his inner monologue is responsible for their persistence.

Ellis (1962) identified a number of these irrational beliefs, which he recognized in most of his patients, and came to see the therapist's task in convincing his patients that their difficulties are predominantly the result of distorted perception and illogical thinking. He believed in a relatively simple method requiring the patient's active involvement for the improvement of his perceptive capacity and for the reorganization of his thinking in such a way that the main causes of the personal difficulties cease. Ellis's method consists in convincing patients of the fallacy of their internalized assumptions and imparting to them more rational views which change their emotions and their behavior.

The cognitive restructuring implied in this is not unjustly designated "philosophical conditioning"; it requires the client to adopt completely the view of life which the therapist considers rational.

Beck takes a similarly rationalistic view of man as the basis for his therapeutic approach. Originally he also experimented in the main with the problem of depression, looking for empirical validation of psychoanalytic concepts (Beck & Valin, 1953; Beck & Hurvich, 1959), and, influenced by the difficulty of supporting these hypotheses, he began to think about etiology in cognitive terms.

Referring to the terminology of Harvey, Hunt, and Schroder (1961), Beck developed a new theory of depression. According to his theory (1963, 1967), typically depressive cognitive "schemata," which become virulent subsequent to a juncture with particular elicitors, have an increasingly strong influence on the patient's total thinking and can condition the other phenomena of the depressive syndrome. Beck (1976) later extended his cognitive theory to include the other most important disorders.

The goal of Beck's therapeutic approach is to correct these mental distortions and misperceptions by applying a great number of techniques (for a detailed description, see Chapter 7).

Thus, Beck, like Frankl and Ellis, abandoned the central principles of psychoanalytic therapy in favor of a cognition-centered, active, and more direct procedure.

2.2. Cognitive Therapy as a Development within Behavior Therapy

As Mahoney (1974) notes, the era has ended in behavior therapy during which the attempt to exclude "mentalistic" phenomena had almost the character of an inquisition; the expressions "mental" and "nonobservable" had, as he asserts, acquired, with the passage of time, classically conditioned connotations through their connection with expressions such as "indefinite," "unscientific," and "not sufficiently simple," and the processes that designate them were considered unsuitable objects for a scientific approach.

For some time, embittered controversies flared up concerning whether practical behavior therapy, following its claimed strictly behavioral point of view, can get along without mentalistic concepts in analyzing problems and describing therapeutic interventions, or whether it must inevitably have recourse to a cognitive terminology (see, for example, the controversy between Locke, 1971, and Eysenck, 1972).

Many debates referred mainly to the extent to which cognitive processes are *implicitly* influenced by the current behavioral-therapeutic procedures, and the extent to which "unspecific" therapeutic effects such as the client's expectation of positive therapeutic results, that is to say, cognitive factors, are responsible for the successes of behavior therapy. Relatively soon, another development was already getting under way which, in contrast to these more theoretical questions, was supposed to have great practical relevance.

Influenced by basic research, which inspired the development of behavioral therapeutic techniques, strategies of intervention originated in which the manipulation of environmental conditions and the initiation of learning-processes directly in the problem situation played a prominent part. The originality of behavior therapy consisted to a great extent in the fact that it offered a very immediate, action-oriented form of therapy in contrast to the more verbally and interactionally oriented approaches.

Moreover, due to the pressures arising from the effort to organize the therapeutic situation in the most economic way possible (perhaps from the standpoint of time), therapists increasingly saw the necessity for replacing the usually very extravagant interventions in the real-life situation by other interventions, for example, by "cognitive rehearsal," that is, by practicing under simulated conditions and by provoking learning processes in the presence of symbolic stimuli that represent the *in-vivo* situation.

Many authors tried rather awkwardly at the beginning (and in part still do today) to maintain, in spite of this development, the appearance of a strictly "scientific" behavioristic procedure. Thus, Pavlov's "second signalling-system," and Hull's "fractional antedating reaction," etc., were arbitrarily employed, so that it would not occur to anyone that the safe ground of "modern learning theory" had been abandoned (see, e.g., Cautela, 1970). Others now explicitly welcome the increasing inclusion of cognitive factors and see this as a positive development which breaks away from much of the ideologically dependent one-sidedness of the past (Kanfer & Grimm, 1976; Lazarus, 1971; Mahoney, 1974). In connection with sharp critiques of behavior therapy such as that by Breger and McGaugh (1965), with the ever more certain cognitive trend in the psychology of personality (Mischel, 1973; Rotter, Chance, & Phares, 1972) and with an increasing consideration of central factors in recent theories of psychopathology (Beck, 1967, 1976; Seligman, 1975)—and also, in my opinion, relative to the necessities of practice—there emerged a "cognitive behavior therapy" (for a review of the process, see Mahoney, 1974), the development of which is still in full progress and which, in addition to the techniques developed outside of behavior therapy, forms the most important methods summarized under the label "cognitive therapies."

3. The Common Elements of Cognitive Therapies

Frank (1973) suggested subdividing the profusion of existing therapies into evocative and directive approaches. Both forms have the goal of changing inadequate attitudinal systems and behavioral models. Evocative therapy attempts this in a more indirect way, by creating favorable conditions, but leaving the actual change to the client. The intention is to encourage emotional growth by offering a relatively unstructured, permissive therapeutic situation in which the client is free to change and develop his accustomed ways of thinking, feeling, and behaving (see p. 235).

Cognitive approaches, on the other hand, are included under directive therapy. The directive therapist endeavors to structure the situation as strongly as possible. His function consists mainly in directly influencing the client's symptoms in order to effect necessary changes.

In this sense, the manner of proceeding used by cognitive therapists is very similar to that employed by behavioral therapists. Both conduct a series of diagnostic interviews to obtain a detailed description of the client's current difficulties. Subsequently, a synthesis of the problems is made, formulated in the therapist's respective theoretical language, which provides the client with an explanation for the emergence of his difficulties. The therapist, in order to eliminate the target symptoms, gives precise instructions about the procedures during the sessions and for the time between. On the basis of the therapist's personal and professional authority, the patient commits himself to adherence to these instructions.

The cognitive therapies are distinguished without exception by their preference for mediating behavioral models. As a justification, one is referred both to the growing significance of cognitive theories within experimental psychology (Lazarus, 1966; Miller, Galanter, & Pribram, 1960; Neisser, 1967) and to studies emphasizing the significant part that such factors play in behavioral disorders (Beck, 1976; Seligman, 1975).

In this sense, cognitive therapy, like behavior therapy, is to be understood as a technology[1] which builds upon the findings of basic research

---

[1]For a discussion of the problem of what part basic research plays in the origin of therapeutic techniques, using behavior therapy as an example, see Westmeyer and Hoffmann, 1977.

concerning the part played by cognitive factors in the regulation of behavior, both in general and in the origin and maintenance of specific disorders, and which develops strategies of intervention whose effectiveness must be established through follow-up investigations.

4. The Present Theoretical Status of Cognitive Therapy

As one of the newest developments in the field of psychotherapy, cognitive therapy plays an ever more important part in practice, particularly when used in combination with behavioral-therapeutic measures. To an increasing extent, therapeutic techniques are described which, as initial investigations show (Beck, 1976), can be employed after a rather short training period, so that a uniform and consistent therapeutic behavior results. The effectiveness of cognitive therapies within a relatively wide range of disorders has been verified in analog studies, in controlled case studies, and in control-group experiments (see, for instance, Beck, 1976; Mahoney, 1974).

Nevertheless, the current theoretical status of cognitive therapy must be viewed as highly unsatisfactory. The assumptions which its advocates use in its support often have more of the character of ideologically and philosophically inclined world-views than of coherent, empirically founded theories. In some other viewpoints, the "cognitive approach" represents an extension of laws which have a completely different jurisdiction in the area of basic research. The only exception is Beck's "cognitive model," which has been submitted to a number of empirical examinations, at least in the area of depression (see Chapter 7).

Thus, Ellis, for example, must concede that his rational-emotive therapy, based on a "theory" of the significance of "irrational beliefs" as the mediation between stimulus and response, has, to say the least, a certain originality in contrast to what is known from social psychology about the part that attitudes play in regulating behavior.

According to his view, practically all behaviors—at least those that have relevance on the level of disorders—are finally determined by very global "internal beliefs." They reflect environmental influences from the past, particularly from the most important phases of socialization, but in the current situation lend the individual an enviable degree of environmental independence (if one accepts Ellis's point of view).

Although in social psychology widely differentiated models relative to the interaction of internal and external behavioral determinants are considered necessary in order to do justice to the empirical data (see Chapter 3), and, moreover, much more modest successes are reported when it comes to changing such attitudinal and value systems through communication, nevertheless rational-emotive theory shows little sign of orienting itself to these results and of further development.

In this sense, it is more than questionable whether Ellis's approach is to be seen as based on cognitive theories at all; perhaps it comes from the area of attitude research. (The same observation can be applied to a greater extent to Frankl's therapy.) In contrast to these approaches, most procedures in the direction of "cognitive behavioral therapy" make explicit reference to basic psychological research.

Starting from the thesis that the "change of thought processes" influences overt behavior in a predictable way (Cautela, 1970), the attempt is made to modify this cognitive process according to principles that are valid in behavioral therapy for the area of "overt behaviors."

Thus, Homme (1965) directly labels hypothetical "covert verbalizations," such as "I absolutely need a cigarette," which he assumes "functionally activate smoking," mere "coverants," and postulates that they obey the principles of operant conditioning; whereas Cautela (1970) assumes a "functional equivalence of external and covert stimuli," under certain conditions, as he adds in clarification.

In attempting to change the cognitive behavioral determinants, Homme (1965) proceeds in such a way that these "coverants," which promote adequate behavior "according to the Premack principle," are "reinforced" by a behavior with a high frequency (thus completely misinterpreting this Premack principle, as Mahoney, 1972, 1974, pointed out). Cautela (1970), for his part, asks his client to visualize a desired behavior which is then "reinforced" by imagining an arbitrary pleasant activity within the framework of a technique which he calls "covert reinforcement."

Although there are scarcely any data about the clinical effectiveness of these procedures (for a survey, see Mahoney, 1974), and some investigations into the effect of the "theoretical principles" assumed by the initiators grossly contradict the hypotheses (Kingsley, 1973), these procedures are part of the standard repertoire of many therapists, and are considered to be methods of cognitive influence "founded in basic science."

Nevertheless, the assumptions underlying them are more than problematic. Thus Mahoney (1972, 1974) points out that the "continuity assumption," which postulates that covert behavior obeys the same principles as overt behavior, exceeds by far the existing data, and that the "automaticity assumption," which states that a reinforcer has an effect, although the antecedent behavior does not produce it, is disputed, and is called into question by Skinner (1974) as well.

Along with Beck's work, the experiments of Meichenbaum in changing internal monologues seem to have better theoretical foundation. In connection with the classical models of Luria (1961, 1963) and Vygotsky (1962) concerning internalized behavior control, the significance of verbal self-instruction for complex behaviors has been shown in several investigations (Hartig & Kanfer, 1973; Meichenbaum, 1969, 1974; O'Leary, 1968), and Meichenbaum has demonstrated how behavioral changes can be produced for many disorders by systematic training in internal monologues (Meichenbaum, 1973; Meichenbaum & Cameron, 1973).

Certainly the point is not to deny all practical relevance or directive effects for the procedures in question. Nevertheless, it becomes clear that cognitive therapy is only at the beginning of its development. The most important thing seems to be the establishing of a theoretical basis. For this purpose, the attempt to start from already existing theoretical models is promising. Preliminary studies suitable for this have been performed in various areas of psychology, and efforts to base procedures of cognitive therapy on them have already been set in progress, even though only recently.

The essential theories on the basis of which further development of cognitive therapy seems possible, as well as the first concrete reflections upon these theories, will be described in the chapters that follow.

References

Beck, A. T. Thinking and depression: 1. Idiosyncratic content and cognitive distortions. *Archives of General Psychology,* 1963, *9*, 324–333.

Beck, A. T. *Depression: Causes and treatment*. Philadelphia: University of Pennsylvania Press, 1967.

Beck, A. T. Cognitive therapy: Nature and relation to behavior therapy. *Behavior Therapy,* 1970, *1*, 184–200.

Beck, A. T. *Cognitive therapy and the emotional disorders*. New York: International Universities Press, 1976.

Beck, A. T., & Valin S. Psychotic depressive reactions in soldiers who accidentally killed their buddies. *American Journal of Psychology,* 1953, *110*, 347–353.

Beck, A. T., & Hurvich, M. S. Psychological correlates of depression: 1. Frequency of "masochistic" dream content in a private practice sample. *Psychosomatic Medicine,* 1959, *21*, 50–55.

Breger, L., & McGaugh, J. I. Critique and reformulation of "learning theory" approaches to psychotherapy and neurosis. *Psychological Bulletin,* 1965, *63*, 338–358.

Cautela, J. R. Covert reinforcement. *Behavior Therapy,* 1970, *1*, 33–50.

Ellis, A. *Reason and emotion in psychotherapy*. New York: Lyle Stuart, 1962.

Frank, J. D. *Persuasion and healing*. Baltimore: The Johns Hopkins University Press, 1973.

Frankl, V. E. *The will to meaning*. New York: New American Library, 1969.

Frankl, V. E. *Theorie and Therapie der Neurosen*. Munich: Reinhardt, 1970.

Harvey, O. J., Hunt, D. E., & Schroder, H. M *Conceptual systems and personality organization*. New York: Wiley, 1961.

Hartig, M., & Kanfer, F. H. The role of verbal self-instructions in children's resistance to temptation. *Journal of Personality and Social Psychology,* 1973, *25*, 259–267.

Hoffmann, N. Einführung in den Problembereich. In M. Westmeyer & N. Hoffmann (Eds.), *Verhaltenstherapie: Grundlegende Texte*. Hamburg: Hoffmann & Campe, 1977.

Homme, L. E. Perspectives in psychology: XXIV. Control of coverants, the operants of the mind. *Psychological Record,* 1965, *15,* 501–511.

Kanfer, F. H., & Grimm, L. G. Promising trends toward the future development of behavior modification: Ten related areas in need of exploration. In W. E. Craighead, A. E. Kazdin, & M. J. Mahoney (Eds.), *Behavior modification: Principles, issues, and applications.* Boston: Houghton Mifflin, 1976.

Kingsley, R. E. *An evaluation of contingency content in covert conditioning.* Unpublished master's thesis, Rutgers University, 1973.

Lazarus, A. A. *Behavior therapy and beyond.* New York: McGraw-Hill, 1971.

Lazarus, R. S. *Psychological stress and the coping process.* New York: McGraw-Hill, 1966.

Locke, E. A. Is "behavior therapy" behavioristic? *Psychological Bulletin,* 1971, *76,* 318–327.

Luria, A. *The role of speech in the regulation of normal and abnormal behavior.* New York: Liveright, 1961.

Luria, A. Psychological studies of mental deficiency in the Soviet Union. In N. R. Ellis (Ed.), *Handbook of mental deficiency.* New York: McGraw-Hill, 1963.

Mahoney, M. J. Research issues in self-management. *Behavior Therapy,* 1972, *3,* 45–63.

Mahoney, M. J. *Cognition and behavior modification.* Cambridge, Mass.: Ballinger, 1974.

Meichenbaum, D. The effects of instructions and reinforcement on thinking and language behavior in schizophrenics. *Behaviour Research and Therapy,* 1969, *7,* 101–114.

Meichenbaum, D. Cognitive factors in behavior modification: Modifying what clients say to themselves. In C. M. Frank & G. T. Wilson (Eds.), *Annual review of behavior therapy theory and practice* (Vol. 1). New York: Brunner/Mazel, 1973.

Meichenbaum, D. *Cognitive behavior modification.* Morristown, N. J.: General Learning Press, 1974.

Meichenbaum, D., & Cameron, R. Training schizophrenics to talk to themselves: A means of developing attentional controls. *Behavior Therapy,* 1973, *4,* 515–534.

Miller, G. A., Galanter, E. H., & Pribram, K. H. *Plans and the structure of behavior.* New York: Holt, Rinehart & Winston, 1960.

Mischel, W. Toward a cognitive social learning conceptualization of personality. *Psychological Review,* 1973, *80,* 252–283.

Neisser, U. *Cognitive psychology.* New York: Holt, Rinehart & Winston, 1967.

O'Leary, K. D. The effects of self-instruction on immoral behavior. *Journal of Experimental Child Psychology,* 1968, *6,* 297–301.

Rotter, J. B., Chance, J. E., & Phares, E.J. *Application of social learning theory to personality.* New York: Holt, Rinehart & Winston, 1972.

Seligman, M. E. P. *Helplessness.* San Francisco: Freeman, 1975.

Skinner, B. F. *About behaviorism.* New York: Knopf, 1974.

Vygotsky, L. S. *Thought and language.* Cambridge: M. I. T. Press, 1962.

Westmeyer, H., & Hoffmann, N. (Eds.). *Verhaltenstherapie: Grundlegende Texte.* Hamburg: Hoffmann & Campe, 1977.

2

Developmental Cognitive Theory, Personality, and Therapy

THOMAS BERNHARD SEILER

In modern psychology, cognitive theories are considered progressive. One speaks of cognitive development, cognitive functions, cognitive structures, cognitive styles, cognitive attitudes, cognitive dissonance, cognitive balance, cognitive needs, cognitive learning theory, cognitive personality theory, etc. Yet, the term "cognitive" is probably just as ambiguous as it is popular. Although presumably the word is always meant to express a relationship to internal conscious or unconscious processes of cognition, thought, or decision, cognitive theories deal not only with the phenomenon of cognition but also with the most varied problems and fields of psychology. A cognitive theory, therefore, need not be a theory of cognition. Beyond the consideration of internal processes, most of which are postulated to be conscious, cognitive approaches are also characterized by a preference for global explanations, complex solutions, and system-theory lines of thought.

Consequently, we find cognitive theories where the concerns are to investigate and explain not only human thought and judgment, but also perception and learning. Cognitive interpretations are especially popular in social psychology and in the psychology of personality. But even in areas which formerly were the exclusive domains of behavioristic research more and more cognitive interpretations are being applied; cognitive attitudes influence and determine reaction time, and the individual's cog-

THOMAS BERNHARD SEILER • Technische Hochschule, Hochschulstrasse 1, D-61 Darmstadt, Bundesrepublik Deutschland.

nitive strategies are drawn upon to explain the learning of concepts and of probability. Cognitive viewpoints also find increasing consideration in the areas of theory and methods that relate to application. This holds true also for therapeutic methods. Even in behavioral therapy, which owes its approach primarily to a behavioristically oriented learning theory, cognitive aspects and processes are being introduced into the therapeutic methods and their explanations. No specialist in this area will dispute the fact that the technological arsenal of behavioral therapy today contains numerous elements whose theoretical substantiation is to be sought in cognitive processes. Scheele and Groeben (1976), among others, have demonstrated this in refined form. Is this a matter of paradigm-change (Scheele & Groeben, 1976) in the sense of a displacement of theoretical basis, whether conscious or unnoticed? Is it not true that many further cognitive assumptions are actually incompatible with the original theoretical approach and its implications? We shall comment on this question in Section 4.

In recent years, moreover, a whole series of approaches to therapy has arisen, built basically on cognitive assumptions and consistently drawing on conscious processes to explain personality disorders and abnormal behavior. The comprehensive presentations by Meichenbaum (1976a, b), McFall (1976), and Valins and Nisbett (1976) may be pointed to as evidence of this. On closer consideration, it certainly becomes obvious that although they systematically build on internal processes of information-processing and although their methods have been formulated according to such viewpoints, most of these therapeutic approaches lack an explicit theoretical foundation. The basis of their conceptual endeavors often seems more to lie in thoroughly justifiable and meaningful general considerations and commonsense truths than in a coherent theory of cognition deserving of the name. Only rarely does one find well-based explanatory approaches which go beyond the requirement to consider internal conscious processes and to take into account the individual's active and autonomous processing of hypotheses in learning and thinking. Often it is only the use of the term "cognitive" that links the representatives of this new paradigm of psychological explanation. Thus, for most of these authors this term seems to have acquired the meaning of conscious information-processing.

In what follows, therefore, I should like to present some considerations which may perhaps be fit to contribute to the development of a theory of cognition—a task that has of late grown increasingly more urgent. This epistemology is of a developmental or genetic kind. What we can present today is certainly nothing more than some general principles forming a kind of guiding theory, which could serve to direct the working out of precise models that would have greater explanatory and predictive value. From this, I derive some principles in an attempt to explain reaction patterns, which differ both inter- and intraindividually in the processing of internal and external experiences. Finally, general directives for therapeutic measures and methods based on these considerations will be discussed.

1. Principles of a Genetic Theory of Cognition

The following principles are founded on Jean Piaget's genetic epistemology. The claim is not made that they coincide in all points and shades of emphasis with Piaget's assumptions. Fundamental to this approach is the assumption that cognitive structures determine both the action and perception, and especially the thinking, reasoning, and judging of each human subject. They direct his intake and processing of information; they bring order to the stimulus supply through selection and classification, and they represent the foundation for and control of motivational and affective impulses. In the language of artificial intelligence, cognitive structures are labeled as the programs for information processing.

The construct of *cognitive structure* stands, therefore, at the center of this developmental theory of cognition. In the following sections, I shall attempt to clarify this concept and its implications and to work out the fundamentals of the theory.

1.1. Cognitive Structures

Cognitive structure is a theoretical concept combining a great number of psychological constructs and everyday concepts which are all intended to extract particular uniformities from the mass of human actions and operations, and of human learning and thinking. Such "unities" are, for example, not only complex processes of perception and problem solving on the level of external action, but especially ideas, concepts, intellectual operations and hypotheses, rules and strategies in intellectual problem solving and in concept formation. All these complex human activities and their results are embraced within the theoretical concept of cognitive structure. This designation did not result from the widespread tendency in scientific discussions to label familiar things with new names and to rearrange them into unusual classifications. On the contrary, the construct of cognition structure accentuates and names essential aspects common to all these human activities, seemingly so different.

In our first attempt to describe cognitive structures, we may designate them generally as alternative programs of categorization, problem solving, and goal-directed action which the organism has at his disposal and can consciously and deliberately activate within certain limits and according to the situation. These patterns of categorization and problem solving are neither genetically established nor unchangeable. They are the result of past categorizations and reactions, that is, of the individual's history of activity and experience relative to specific area (cf. Seiler, 1973a,b, 1977).

Generally speaking, cognitive structures are the means by which the organism masters its environment. For the human subject, this means, in particular, the possibility of coming to terms with his social environment. As we shall see, cognitive structures are at the same time the medium through which (material and social) reality is internally represented or, better yet, in part reconstructed. It is further implied in the concept of cognitive structure (as distinguished from the S–R concept) that the organism does not react to a situation of physical stimulus occurring independently of his action patterns or his conceptual means of cognition. The objects of the environment and their characteristics and perspectives are not known directly, but only through the individual's self-developed cognitive structures; therefore, they are founded on these structures in his active and cognitive confrontation with and adaptation to the physical and social pressures of the environment.

The developmental process of the building of cognitive structures does not start from a void; it begins in established patterns of activity of a reflexlike kind. We know that the newborn infant already carries with it a great number of highly differentiated capabilities for perception and reaction. We have only to think of the so-called sucking reflex: a predominantly established reaction schema of the newborn infant, which consists of a highly complex pattern of muscular movements and sensations of touch that work together organically and systematically and direct each other. When this reflex pattern connects with a corresponding stimulus, it begins to function after a period of hesitation in which the sensory and the motor elements must adapt to each other. The survival of the child is ensured. And when the child sucks on more and more new objects, the reflex develops into a differentiated sensorimotor action schema which adapts to the most varied situations. The sensorimotor behavioral schemata, which animals and small children use to come to terms with their environment and to solve their survival problems in an intelligent way, originate, therefore, out of the change and extension of established, reflexlike reaction patterns and their reciprocal connection to integrated systems. All these so-called sensorimotor action schemata contain sensori-perceptive acts as essential components that are embedded within the performance of muscular movements.

Since these sensorimotor schemata account for specific aspects of external situations and objects, the subject uses them to represent these situations and objects. Thus, over the course of time, they become increasingly simplified, schematized, economized, and internalized. On the basis of this process, which cannot be analyzed more closely here (see Seiler, 1978), internal cognitive structures of a mental or intellectual kind emerge, corresponding to what one experiences in introspection as images, concepts, thoughts, and acts of reasoning and will. It could perhaps be said that the subject uses this schematic and internalized performance of sensorimotor acts as an abbreviation for the corresponding situations or objects and their qualities, that is, refers to them as representations of the environment.

Internal images, concepts, and operations do not, however, arise only from external acts; they always remain incorporated within a performance of a supplementary sensorimotor activity, from which they proceed and which they direct.

This initial description implies a dual thesis: Human motor and cognitive action is executed, first of all, by means of programs which the individual himself has developed and stored. Second, it is not only environmental objects and events, affecting the organism as such, that determine his perceiving and thinking, acting and learning. These theses are to be explained further.

Now we can define the concept of cognitive structure somewhat more precisely as a relatively lasting, interference resisting, and systemlike pattern of actions and reactions, of an organism that serves his cognition and mastery of the environment. It was developed by means of the differentiation and integration of already existing structures and can be activated by the organism whenever necessary.

From the numerous aspects that are implied in this definition of cognitive structure, a few are given more precise explanation subsequently. In particular, however, we have to deal with the conditions of the emergence and change of cognitive structures, that is, with their development.

1.2. Cognition and Meaning—Functions of Cognitive Structures

The most important and most fundamental characteristic of cognitive structures is their cognitive function. Not only the cognitive structures of a higher or intellectual kind, that is, our images and concepts, but also the simplest behavioral schemata of a sensorimotor kind serve in the representational reconstruction of our environment. Cognition, therefore, is not based on a separate intellectual ability by means of which the human mind directly and completely comprehends, represents, or reflects the essence and characteristics of real things. Cognition is bound up with the activity of particular cognitive structures. Each of these structures has its own representational content, which originated in a complex developmental process and can be traced back to a great number of elementary substructures. Cognition never occurs in the form of an isolated and

passive act of perception. As already mentioned above, the first sensorimotor patterns already consist of numerous motor actions and perceptual
acts, which are combined to form one mutually complementing and directing unit. Thus, the baby, who picks up a perforated wooden block
with his hand, imperfectly delineates or recreates the shape of the object,
its surface quality, its hardness, weight, and form by the mold of his
grasping and adjusting hand, the sensations of touch, and the proprioceptive muscular sensations combined with these muscular movements.
The pattern of grasping is not completely established right away; rather
it proceeds developmentally. Through continuous changes and a gradual
progression in the functioning of this reaction pattern in confrontation
with different objects and their given features, various grasping patterns
are created with different cognitive contents.

Similarly, in each concept and in each image a great number of internalized (in the meaning indicated above) patterns of perception and
action exist which combine to form a more or less thoroughly constructed
complex. Consequently, one can say that all the sensorimotor experiences
which the subject has had with a particular class of objects in similar
situations are concentrated in the respective representational structures.
The subject then applies these crystallized experiences to new objects
and situations as a reference or as a measuring device, checks whether
and to which of these reference systems a particular object corresponds,
and brings the structure, if necessary, to a better "fit" by means of a
change or an integration of several structures. This adaptation and integration is made possible exclusively through the interplay of various structures and structural elements among themselves; it does not presuppose
any other kind of mental faculty. The process is, however, most likely
directed by some superior goal-schema. (This process has been analyzed
elsewhere [Seiler, 1978].) At the same time, one can say that inherent in
this process is a tendency to reconstruct the things, events, and situations
of the environment in an ever more perfect and complete way, as will be
seen.

What was already said in the preceding sections has again become
clear in this analysis; namely, that the characteristics and the relationships
can be recognized of only those things for which the corresponding structures are available or can be made available by means of a process of
differentiation and integration executed ad hoc. In this perspective, the
concept and the process of imitation or of imitative learning are also to
be relativized. The concept of imitation does not actually explain new
performances, but rather labels a few complex situations in which the
subject step by step successfully adjusts certain behavioral and/or representational structures at his disposal to the action pattern of a model.
Therefore, one can also say that the imitator already has a fundamental

command of the behavior which he is imitating. Piaget and Chomsky formulate these facts in a pointed manner as follows: The child imitates only what he is already capable of doing; or, expressed another way, imitation does not explain learning; rather it characterizes situations in which learning takes place. This thesis is to be supplemented and explained in more detail.

The meaning function of cognitive structures is closely linked with the representational function. Meaning is a relation. Depending upon the level of analysis, different relations of meaning are to be ascribed to cognitive structures. On an abstract level the cognitive structure mediates between the object and the recognizing subject. (The term "recognizing subject" is an abstract construct for the totality of the cognitive processes and structures of an individual.) The meaning of the structure is thus the qualities which it selects and emphasizes. On this abstract level one can also say that each cognitive structure, as a part of the total activity of the organism, serves the goal of survival and mastery of the environment and thus has meaning for him in this very global sense. In a less abstract approach, a structure has as many meanings as it has relationships to the subject's other structural systems and, among other things, can be employed as a possible means of realizing his goals. Moreover, each sensory or motor subaspect of a structure, considered by itself, can be taken as a reference to the entire structure or to its effect. Thus, in particular, verbal signs can also stand for concepts and images with which they have become systematically connected. In this case, one can speak of these corresponding structures as the meaning of the verbal signs.

When we spoke of the cognitive or representational function of cognitive structures, "cognitive" and "conscious" were not meant to be equated. The concept cognitive in the sense used here implies that the subject recognizes reality, in that by selectively reconstructing and representing reality in his sensorimotor action schemata and in his internal or mental structures, he confers meaning to events, subordinates them to the goals of his activity, and through them places things in relation to each other. Many authors (especially the Russians) call this the "process of consciousness." However, this does not mean that the individual structures and processes, or even the elementary subacts contained within them, are at all times conscious to the acting and recognizing person. Therefore, I prefer to label cognitive structures or their subelements "conscious" only after they have been represented in their performance by other structures ranked beside or above them. In this sense, consciousness always presupposes a duplication. Here it is important to point out that in this accompanying grasp of cognitive processes by adjacent or higher processes, it is always only individual sections from the conceptual processing of information or from problem-solving processes that are duplicated, that is, consciously experienced. This conscious self-perception and, even more, the conscious triggering and control of cognitive processes can be, and is, gradually learned. It also represents an essential condition for generalizing cognitive structures and for solving complex problems, as we shall demonstrate.

1.3. The Memory Function of Cognitive Structures

The cognitive structure does not have only a cognitive or representational function; beyond this, it can be regarded as a plan stored in memory for perceiving, acting, and thinking which has been acquired over a long period of time and can be called forth again in comparable situations. It thus supersedes the concept of memory as a comprehensive capability, or as a place where perceptions, decisions, knowledge, meanings, words, and sentences are deposited. One does not have a memory, but rather just as many memories as one has structures. For this reason, one also does not have a good or a bad memory, although one can actualize memories more easily in a subject area in which one is equipped with very many complementary structures, and where these structures are, on the one hand, well differentiated from each other, but, on the other hand, also systematically coordinated by higher rules (structures). Here it should be mentioned that research in modern learning and memory theory has contributed enormously to the clarification of the processes and conditions which regulate not only the consolidation and resistance to interference, but also the recall of stored experiences. In the view taken here, learning theory has its place in the area of the economization, consolidation, and strengthening of cognitive processes and structures; whereas memory research deals with the higher conscious or unconscious processes by means of which the subject actively ensures the reactualization of cognitive structures in many situations.

I do not wish to conclude this point without one qualification which to me seems important: Although cognitive structures are stored plans for action and thought, nevertheless each actualization of a structure always demands at least a minimum of change, adaptation, and mobility.

1.4. The "Systems" Aspect of Cognitive Structures

In the previous statements, it has been explicitly expressed several times that no cognitive structure exists in isolation. Each is ranked within the complex establishment of a great number of such structures or activities of the subject in his relations to the objects, situations, and persons of the environment. There we have already addressed the systems aspect of cognitive structures.

The concepts of structure and system are, to a great extent, synonomous. The mutual basis in meaning is characterized by the fact that both structure and system are defined as a multitude of elements and of relations between these elements. Therefore, both contain an ordered collection of individual elements which are not further broken up on the specified level of analysis.

In principle, however, it is always possible to reduce these elements further, to comprehend them as systems or subsystems. Thus, the concept of a triangle contains among others the conceptual aggregates, as structural elements: surfaces, sides, and angles, which themselves may be traced back in turn to a multitude of schematic acts of perception.

The structure also possesses, as does the system, the characteristic of closure or totality, whereby the degree of closure alloted to a system or a structure depends, in a formal sense, on the relationships between the elements and, in a dynamic sense, on the laws which regulate the interaction or the interplay of the elements among one another. When looked at in psychological terms, the unity or closure of a structure also depends on its resistance to interference and thus on the degree of its availability under changing situations and circumstances. The aspect of structure is thus also closely connected to the memory function, as previously noted. Considered developmentally, the ''systems'' aspect of cognitive structures is not only the result of the economization and schematization of situationally relevant external or internal acts of processing information, but also of their simultaneous consolidation or fixation.

This analysis does not presuppose an absolute contrast between structure and content. Whether one has to speak of structure or content depends on the level of consideration. The elements and the relations between these elements can be labeled as the content of the structure. The content or the meanings of ''house'' (as image, concept, or word) are the sum of the general characteristics, their relationships, and the personal experiences that are condensed in them. Thus, the content of a particular grasping schema is the totality of all motor adjustments and perceptual acts necessary for grasping a particular object, and which thus selectively represent certain characteristics of this object, and their relationships.

Not only do cognitive structures possess the characteristic of structure when each is considered individually; in addition, many of them unite to form more and more complex systems. The numerous relations determining such systems, their adjacent, superior, or subordinate ranking, cannot be analyzed in detail here. I should like, however, to indicate the complex means–end relationships, which are contained in problem-solving processes, and certain fundamental logical laws on which "adult" thinking is based (see Section 1.7. and Seiler, 1978).

1.5. The Dynamic Character of Cognitive Structures

Cognitive structures are not to be thought of as static formations, but as dynamic processes. They are actions, perceptions, activities, images, classifications, and operations of thought or plans for such actions. The concepts of schema and action, on the one hand, and structure and operation, on the other, are only intensionally different, but extensionally identical, that is, they refer to the same things. Action or operation expresses the quality of process; whereas schema or structure signifies the network of relationships of these recognitive activities. What we wish to show in more detail later is already becoming clear: namely, that a structurally analytic way of viewing the human personality is not opposed to a dynamic view, but on the contrary includes and requires the latter.

With regard both to this dynamic character and to the developmental one still to be discussed, the character of system discussed in the preceding point differs from a Gestalt-psychology analysis. The problem situation is not directly comprehended by means of "Gestaltlike" impressions. Cognitive structures must be understood as complex systems of control, within which numerous individual sensory and/or motor acts regularly mesh, influence, and direct each other, as indicated above by way of the examples of the sucking reflex and the grasping schema. Nor are they simple mechanisms for converting information into behavior: It is not just a case of one stimulus acting on a sensor which conducts it in converted form to a transformer, from which point a corresponding muscular activity is released by way of a corresponding efferent path. The very kind and intensity of stimulation are determined and regulated by the organism through the activities which belong to this structure. Thus, each cognitive structure forms a system of reference expressed in a control-system language. The environment's supply of stimulation is, in a sense, measured by means of this reference system (cf. Miller, Galanter, & Pribram, 1960; Powers, 1973). The "systems" character of cognitive structures is emphasized even more through the fact that cognitive structures of parallel or higher rank often enter into a process of perception or experience as conditions of estimation or expectation.

Beyond this, however, the dynamic character needs to be considered in terms of motivation and emotion. When we spoke about cognitive structures as the subject's means of recognition, this was not meant to imply that human experience, behavior, and thought possess only cognitive or structural characteristics. The construct of cognitive structure is supposed to express, above all, the function of recognizing and reconstructing the reality of human actions, perceptions, images, and concepts. Nevertheless, cognitive structure is in no way merel a "rational" formation or instrument of knowing; it is at the same time and always a dynamic formation determining the actions of the human subject and qualifying them affectively or emotionally. In this interpretation, therefore, the motivational aspect is separated from the cognitive aspect only in the theoretical analysis. In contrast to other theories of motivation, the factor which stimulates and advances cognition and action is not assigned to a separate structure. Motivation represents only another aspect of these units. At least three distinct aspects can be differentiated in the motivational composition of cognitive structures.

First of all, one could assign to each structure a hypothetical tendency to actualize itself anew and to further differentiate itself over against all objects with which it is confronted. Beyond this tendency to reactualize, one could also speak of the stimulative character of cognitive structures, or of their intrinsic motivation (in contrast to extrinsic). In this respect, the theory of cognition and motivation presented here clearly differs from an interpretation according to drive theory. It is held that no singular or general drives, however one chooses to name and characterize them, determine behavior and development. Drives are always only a general interpretation label of a highly abstract kind, unifying a great number of individual perceptual and action structures, by means of which the individual person comes to terms with specific situations and thereby acquires new structures for perception and action.

Besides this inherent dynamic, which determines the developmental process by which cognitive structures are built up, each cognitive structure has a particular affective or emotional quality. Depending on the circumstances present at its formation, in particular the individual's affective condition during the situation in question, each cognitive structure has its own emotional tone, its entirely specific pleasant or unpleasant (repellent) feeling quality, which colors what is perceived and what is done. This emotional quality also makes the object or the act a delightful or, on the other hand, an unpleasant and repellent activity or perception which one would prefer to avoid. The process of affective or emotional qualification of cognitive structures can be explained by the principle of contiguity, as follows. The affective quality of other activities, perceptions, and concepts actualized at the same time has an effect on the new structure that is formed or changed in a process of differentiation and integration.

Neither the individual dynamic of cognitive structures nor their affective disposition is, however, sufficient to contain all of what customarily enters into a motivational analysis of human behavior and human personality. Still another aspect is essential for this, namely, the accumulation of cognitive structures in a particular object area. This "multi-plication" of similar and complementary cognitive structures in an object area is not to be confused with the systematic formations of groups from which cognitive operational systems of a logical kind originate. In the latter case, it is a matter of a systematic or structural interaction estab-lishing and guaranteeing logical or rational procedures during the pro-cessing of information or while solving problems. In the former case, it is due rather to an accumulation of cognitive structures—in part by chance and in part dependent on the affective element discussed above—that is related in both affect and content within an object area. This process of "content accumulation" explains an individual's state of interests, atti-tude, and effectivity in coming to terms with the problems and information of a particular object area.

The explanatory approach taken by cognitive theory is, therefore, not undynamic, or averse to drives and emotions. On the contrary, it offers an entirely new, fundamentally different approach to the analysis of the motivation or impulse of human behavior. This approach differs from conventional drive theories in that it does not reify the motivational aspects, which are perceived by an outside observer on the basis of an abstracting and generalizing approach, to the level of drives and makes them into general sources of impulse for human action, but rather assigns a separate need in a specific way to each individual structure. This ap-proach thereby avoids the mistake of overgeneralization that is inevitably connected with every attribution to a drive, and from the start does not expect the individual to react on the basis of the same drive dynamic in each situation and relative to a great variety of object areas.

1.6. The Generality and Specificity of Cognitive Structures

Is there not, however, another kind of overgeneralization connected with the concept of structure? Does it not lend permanence (see aspect of memory) and generality covering many objects and situations to human perceptions, actions, and conceptual considerations that often last but a moment?[1]

---

[1]As a side note, the concern here is the question of generality and not of the recognitive theoretic problem of reification, as is often wrongly claimed (cf. Seiler, 1973b). Naturally, it is claimed that a psychological and also physiological or neurological concept corresponds to an individual cognitive structure; whereby the question, to what degree the assumed structure corresponds to or coincides with the reality which it attempts to represent, nat-urally always remains open. However, this holds true in the same way for every theoretical concept. The problem of generality can be separated well enough from this epistemological problem.

It is certainly correct that a multiple assertion of generality is connected with the assumption of a cognitive structure. One assumes that a particular perception, action, and conceptual behavior can be repeated in the same or in a similar manner at different times, that the same aspect in a great number of objects is accentuated by the structure in question, and that the act or operation corresponding to the structure can be performed in the same way in different situations.

Beyond this threefold intraindividual postulate of generality, one also assumes that, for a designated series of individuals in comparable situations, identical or at least similar and consistent operational and behavioral systems can be distinguished when similar objects or events are presented. An example of structures to which one ascribes a relatively extensive generality in the stated dimensions and in a broad scope are conceptual and logical invariances, without which neither communication nor noncontradictory speech and thought nor in general any form of meaningful social interaction is possible. This form of generalization which is always necessary for every scientific analysis, and the pitfalls and problems connected with it, have been discussed in another place (Seiler, 1973a,b), where it was pointed out, in particular, that many theorists of cognition, Piaget among them, often tend to make problematical claims about generality which inevitably lead to contradictory findings and to consequences that are dangerous for practice. As an upshot to the discussion presented there, it should here be emphasized in summary that the generality implied in the concept of structure is limited in principle. An individual's cognitive structures are, to state it in an oversimplified manner, specific to particular objects and situations, even when their theoretical analysis in general concepts does not allow this limitation to show up. Therefore, the observer and the theoretician often tend to ascribe to them the nonrestricted generality contained in the theoretical description. As we shall see, this process of generalization beyond the original objects and situations from which it arose occurs only very gradually and is subject to laws and conditions with which we are still scarcely acquainted. In conclusion, we maintain that the extent of generality of an individual structure can never be decided other than empirically.

In this connection, the question arises, on the basis of which indices can the conclusion be made that particular comprehensive and consistent structures exist? In general, this conclusion is comparatively obvious and unproblematical in the area of sensorimotor behavioral structures. However, where internal structures, images and concepts, and rules and operational systems are concerned, the scientist is dependent on the individual's always fragmentary communication of internal experiences, and on the interpretation of actions coinciding with them. In each case, however, both in the observation of external actions and in the interpretation of the communicated personal experiences and the corresponding external consequences, the scientist is dependent on theoretical concepts which he takes from a historically evolved, socioculturally determined vocabulary and from the level of scientific discussion. In structuring his introspective experience, the individual is dependent on these historically evolved interpretations and their verbal labels which he has developed in continuing social interaction. At a later point, I shall speak about this socially conditioned character of cognitive structures.

1.7. The Genesis and Development of Cognitive Structures

Up to this point, we have dealt with a few characteristics of cognitive structures. Within the framework of a developmental cognitive theory, however, the question of their origin and the explanation of the ongoing building of new cognitive structures is more important. As the word "building" expresses, cognitive structures are not preprogrammed in the genetic structure of the individual, but are gradually developed anew by the individual himself in his coming to terms with the environment. This building begins with a few established reflexlike patterns of activity, as was stated in Section 1.1, and is based on the activity of the structures themselves, that is, on their reactualization in ever-new situations.

In simplified form, one could characterize this process in the following way. In coming to terms with an object or a problematic situation in the environment, the subject activates certain sensorimotor or conceptual structures that are available to him. In another terminology, one could say that he processes the accruing information with the help of previously acquired recognitive resources. In so doing, it repeatedly happens that the subject applies structures to a situation that do not fit on the first attempt. In this way, the subject generates his own problems, both on the behavioral and on the conceptual levels. These structures represent the goals which are to be achieved by making available other structures, whether actions or conceptual operations. They then activate other more or less appropriate structures or substructures. Such structures or substructures are perceptual schemata, activities, concepts, or conceptual operations, depending on the particular situation. While being tested out, they are continually being measured against the goal structures. If they yield no approximation, they are dropped. To the degree to which they lead to or promise success—even if it is only partial—the aspects adequate to the goal are worked out more distinctly step by step, and are gradually integrated with the goal pattern to form a new structure. In this way a new structural system arises as a step in the direction of mastering the problematic situation created by the individual. Problematic situations on the level of actions or concepts are, therefore, not simply presented by objects, but rather originate through the attempt of the acting and recognizing subject to integrate new or old environmental situations into existing structural systems.

This explanation, presented here in a very abbreviated and simplified form, of the construction of new cognitive structural systems, in particular, that is, of new ideas, concepts, rules, and operations, has a whole series of implications, some of which are as follows:

1. The formative process of cognitive structures is never concluded. The more concepts developed, the more new ones become possible, because the individual can create all the more problems.

2. In the process just described, the statement that the recognizing subject creates the recognitive means himself is not synonymous with an idealistic interpretation. On the contrary, the subject reaches this goal only to the degree that he attempts to subordinate things, characteristics, events, and situations of the environment to his systems of structure, that is, to apply concepts to new objects and, in the case of failure, to draw on other more or less well-suited structures and combine them in a new, integrated structural system. In this way, ever new aspects of reality are recreated through the structural system.

3. This construction can, at the same time, be understood as a process of solving conflicts or problems. The behavioral or conceptual structure, which is to be applied to an immediately present situation and the lack of success of which is reported back to the intrastructural criteria of estimation or reference by means of the intrastructural processes of perception, creates in the individual a cognitive conflict combined with more or less strong emotional loading. From this, one can assume that through self-activation and stimulation the conflict has an effect on the subject's other sensorimotor or conceptual structures of activity (possibilities for action) (Seiler, 1975, where the possibilities and limits of creating such conflicts in a controlled manner and of actively promoting the process of cognition are also discussed).

4. Such an interpretation further implies that cognitive progress, and thus learning, is possible only to the extent that the individual is already equipped with corresponding behavioral possibilities or conceptual catgories that are compatible with the fixed goals.

5. For the same reason, imitation is, as already stated, also possible only to the extent that the individual has behavioral patterns and categories at his disposal that are similar to the model behavior. For example, the infant can imitate voiced sounds only when he has spontaneously produced one or another voiced sound, even if only in an imperfect way. This restriction regarding imitation naturally acquired prominent significance in cognitive development, because cognitive development, as we shall see, can take place only in processes of social intercourse, and

because the individual can develop higher strategies of control (see No. 7) in the systematic imitation of model behaviors in particular areas.

6. It could easily be shown—although this will not be explained in more detail here—that the generalizing process of sensorimotor behavioral patterns and of conceptual structures and, even more, the transfer to and use of learned behavioral patterns and concepts in new situations and in the setting of practical goals is to be understood in the same way as a process of further differentiation and integration of the available cognitive structures.

7. Of decisive importance in this connection is the subject's capacity for forming higher structures and structural systems in the course of progressing development—often referred to as strategies—with which he is able more or less systematically to influence and control the building of new structures. This point deserves detailed discussion. In analyzing the concept of consciousness, the thesis was supported that the subject is in the position of duplicating his cognitive structures and processes, that is, of re-creating them by means of other adjacent or higher conceptual systems of structure, and is all the more able to do this the more conceptual structures he has developed. The partial duplication of structures, in the sense of their conscious intellectual comprehension, represents, however, only one of the possibilities. As the subject partly perceives himself, in the act of cognition and of solving problems, he learns at the same time to extract certain general and repetitive characteristics of this process (Piaget's "*Abstraction de l'action*") and to put them into controlled and directed use in new attempts. In other words, he learns in this way how to learn (cf. Harlow's learning set). He learns how one can generate and systematically try out hypotheses more or less consciously and under control—both in the formation of concepts and in the problem-solving process. In this way it becomes possible for higher forms of human learning, concept formation, and problem solving to represent, even if only in part, a consciously controlled process. The creative element in this process lies in the summoning of experiences that are unusual and unfamiliar in the particular context but indeed correspond to essential expectations in the process of verification.

8. To be brief, in this building process, cognitive structural systems are developed which obey particular logical or formal laws. They can be explained on the basis of comparable regularities, as in the strategies above. The subject finds even in the simplest structural systems some fundamental regular and repetitive relationship and applies them as expectations or conditions of control more or less consciously in the building of new structural systems. We must, of course, mention that this important and fundamental process in the building of thought-structures does not lead to the acquisition of a strictly logical system or to a strong formalism.

In other words, the "natural" logic of thinking has little in common with the stringency of a formalized logic. It is determined to a large extent by semantic factors.

1.8. Social Conditions in the Development of Cognitive Structures

A further aspect in the process of building cognitive structures is their social conditionality. This aspect is so basic that it deserves separate emphasis. No recognizing subject stands totally alone in coming to terms with actuality. He is not only embedded in a social unit and in an environment which is socially and culturally determined in a multiplicity of ways, but he comes to terms with this world only under the influence of a stimulating and controlling interaction with concrete social partners. Four essential conditions characterize this process:

1. Even in its material constitution, the reality confronting the child is predominantly of a social-historical origin. His environment was formed by and is continually changed through social conditions and the influence of concrete persons.

2. An individual's actions and perceptions are at all times complementary to the actions and perceptions of one or several social partners who interact with him. It has been sufficiently proved that neither a normal development nor—in the extreme case—the survival of a child is ensured without this complementarity.

3. Seen in terms of developmental psychology, this complementarity gradually changes over into an explicit process of interaction, and finally into a process of communication. From the child's original complementary schemata of action and perception, action patterns become differentiated through which the child meaningfully interacts with his constant social partners—he looks in the direction that his mother looks; he hands things to her and takes them back from her. These patterns of interaction soon take on an important function in the further differentiation relative to control and goal-orientation and in the constructive integration of complex cognitive behavioral patterns. Through them, new goals are set and corresponding conflicts are touched off.

4. Through the internalization of sensorimotor behavioral structures and through the process of linkage with linguistic symbols, the prerequisites for a conceptual communication are produced, which influence the further development of cognitive structures in a similar but much more intensive and fundamental way than the sensorimotor interactions.

The process of social exchange and communication is, therefore, one of the essential factors in the development of cognitive structures. By this means, new goal systems are conveyed to the subject. In the process

conflicts are created, through confrontation with new concrete and intellectual situations, that lead to further differentiations and new integrations
of the individual structures of meaning. At the same time, however, a
constant adaptation and adjustment of these structures to social standards
is achieved. In other words, the cognitive structures are socialized. The
meanings of words gradually function in terms of culturally and socially
established contents. This socialization process of cognitive structures is
not to be seen as detached from the developmental conditions previously
discussed. It proceeds according to the same regularities.

2. Personality and Personality Disorders from the Viewpoint of the Theory of Cognition

2.1. Personality

If by personality we mean the characteristic individuality of a human
subject, which determines his particular form of social interaction, through
which he comes to terms with impressions, influences, and demands of
the environment, and by means of which he differentiates himself from
others, then a corresponding cognitive theory of personality also follows
from the theory of cognition advocated here. Accordingly, personality is
based on the cognitive structures and structural systems specific to the
individual in question, which he has developed in the course of his life
history on the basis of internal and external influences and laws. It could
be, for example, that individuals with higher linguistic ability differ primarily from those who are linguistically less fluent in that they can, on
the basis of effective searching processes (i.e., corresponding structures
or programs), more quickly grasp the information stored in the phonemic
structures (of the long-term memory); as investigations by Hunt, Frost,
and Lunneborg (1973), Hunt, Lunneborg, and Lewis (1975), and Goldberg,
Schwartz, and Stewart (1977) seem to support. Therefore, such an interpretation does not understand by personality a static formation consisting
of unchangeable abilities or layers. Nor does it attempt to differentiate
particular individuals on the basis of fewer but all the more ambiguous
typological characteristics. Rather, it comprehends personality as the way,
specific to each individual, of actively coming to terms with the environment. This interpretation of personality also contrasts strongly with a
drive-theory interpretation (the disadvantages of which have already been
pointed out). Cognitive theories of personality are no longer new and
unusual today. They are supported by a number of authors, in particular
since Kelly (1955). Despite many individual differences and particularities,

these authors have this in common: they understand personality as the sum of all the cognitive structural systems of the individual.

The differences refer chiefly to the question of where the differential features are to be placed within the cognitive structural system. In my opinion, three main directions may be distinguished in the cognitively oriented, differential exploration of human behavior, learning, and thinking:

1. First, one could speak of a stronger orientation toward the investigation of structures (or programs of information processing) specific to the individual, and their particularities. Through which structures or programs of a higher order do individuals, or groups of persons, differ from one another? (Here one could incorporate the orientation from the research both of Hunt and of Goldberg and their colleagues. For which situation and content areas are particular structures specific to an individual or group of individuals, which in principle imply, according to their theoretical and abstract formulation, an unlimited claim to validity (see the discussion of generality and specificity of cognitive structures, p. 20)? In which content areas do characteristic "accumulations" of cognitive structures appear in one or a series of individuals, and which is their preeminent emotional or evaluative content? (Examples for the latter orientation are interest tests and cognitive value analyses.)

2. A second orientation concentrates more intensively on the nature of the connection between the structures, operations, and operational systems; that is, for example, a viewpoint characteristic of Piaget. From the lack of connections between the individual structures on the one hand, or their specific sorts of coordinations on the other, he derives essential personality features of individuals of different ages. The concepts of egocentrism, other-directedness, moral realism, moral relativism, and concrete and formal operations, have today become general and are not confined to the analyses of developmental psychology. In this respect, Kohlberg's model of role behavior and moral judgment could also be cited.

3. One could speak finally of a comparative structural analysis. In this research approach, characteristic of theories of cognitive style, one formulates certain common features of a large number of perceptions, images, concepts, evaluative categories, or problem-solving processes and makes distinctions between individuals based on the preeminent characteristic feature of their way of processing information (cf. Seiler, 1973a). The theory of cognitive complexity, for example, which goes back to Bieri and to Harvey and Schroder, could be classed here. In this theory, the differentiation, discrimination, and integration of cognitive structures are viewed as the conditional basis for a characteristic way of processing information, of solving problems, and of evaluating others socially. Thus, for example a low degree of differentiation and integration with regard to

the cognitive structures in a particular field is associated with the tendency toward overgeneralization, with the inclination to stereotyped judgments, with a high claim for absoluteness, with a low tolerance for ambiguity, and with the inability to interpret situations in different ways and to settle the conflict between these interpretations by thinking.

Though we shall not discuss further these three different kinds of analysis, two comments seem appropriate. First, the three kinds of analysis are not independent of each other; on the contrary, there are important relationships and dependencies between them. Second, the differing meanings and uses of the terms "differentiation" and "distinctiveness" must be pointed out. Whereas in Section 1 differentiation was understood as a general process advancing the development of individual structures, here individuals are to be differentiated according to the degree of distinctiveness (and degree of integration) attained by their structures for a particular area or task. Since I have set myself the task of showing the relationships between a developmental cognitive theory and certain basic therapeutic principles, the problem of the disturbed personality, in this context, is preeminent. For this reason, possible consequences of this epistemology for the analysis and explanation of personality disorders will now be discussed.

2.2. Explanations of Personality Disorders by Cognitive Theories

The terms "personality disorders," "behavioral disorders," "emotional disorders," and "neurotic behavioral patterns" are used almost interchangeably. Their common feature is that the behavior and experience of individuals are measured according to certain norms. When individuals deviate from these norms, their behavior and experience are labeled *inappropriate, maladaptive, retarded,* or simply *disturbed.* Neurotic behavioral disorders or emotional disorders of any kind are, therefore, always determined with respect to cultural or social norms. The distribution of such norms and the obligation they impose vary, of course, very greatly. Certain norms can be very general, for example, sex roles; other norms can be specific for particular cultures, societies, or societal subgroups, for example, homosexual behavior considered as abnormal behavior. Without a doubt, there are emotional disorders which at extreme degrees are perceived as maladaptive or even pathological in all societies, for example, deep depressions. One can also make an objective connection between this norm and certain necessities of human behavior and survival, or even simply of the human quality of life. "Neurotic" is, therefore, never a structure unto itself but rather only a structural system which has its relation to others.

Furthermore, the concept of emotional disorder also expresses that the person in question experiences feelings of which the mode and the degree go beyond the "normal" and prevent the person from processing information objectively in certain situations. To this category for example, belongs intense anxiety, be it diffuse anxiety, a specific anxiety such as fear of examination, or anxiety about particular situations and objects, as, for example, in phobias of a great variety of forms. We may also include a high level of arousal, as, for example, in particular situations of social interaction that lead either to blocking or to intense aggression. As already indicated, the question may be asked whether one can speak at all about behavioral disorders that are not connected with emotional disorders. Above all, if we consider as emotional disorders not merely intense emotional levels of a positive or a negative kind but also emotional deficits, we shall have no difficulty including such personality disorders as deprivation, inability to form attachments, etc., in this category.

Many authors associate personality disorders with characteristics of the content and/or structure (in the meaning discussed above) of behavior. Beck (1976), for example, advocates the thesis that the highly anxious, the highly excitable, and the depressive all prove, in the behavioral areas in question, to be poorly differentiated and poorly integrated in their processing of information. Personality disorders can, therefore, also be understood and classified as extreme expressions of certain features derived from cognitive theory.

A cognitive-theory perspective on the question of the origin and development of personality disorders seems to yield more significant and more fundamental contributions. It might, of course, be a great deal easier to postulate certain general principles for the explanation of the origin of behavioral disorders than to reconstruct the development of a concrete case, with all the individual circumstances and conditions. These principles follow from the theses concerning the development of cognitive structures.

Whereas the general aspects and functions of cognitive structures discussed in Section 1.1 can be drawn upon for the descriptive characterization of personality disturbances, their origin may be attributed to the cognitive-structural laws of differentiation and of integration. Nevertheless (and this should not be overlooked), the fact that a particularly pronounced disorder affects one of the designated aspects or functions should not and must not be utilized to identify precisely the cause of its onset. I should now like to select and discuss—without claiming completeness—some of the viewpoints that seem especially fundamental and important.

1. We have advocated the thesis that the progressive differentiation and integration of cognitive structures is to be understood as a kind of

conflictive process. The advancing effect of this conflictive process depends in a certain sense, as I have indicated, upon the optimal discrepancy between the goal set by one structural schema and the structure of possible behaviors available for the attainment of this goal in a particular situation. If this discrepancy repeatedly proves too great and insurmountable in one particular area, the corresponding experience of frustration will be excessive each time, and as a consequence the structures that relate to this area or to these situations and their contents, will be quite intensely loaded with negative feeling qualities. This, in turn, will result in the individual's avoiding the activation of these structures. He will steer altogether clear of these situations as far as possible. His reaction could also be explained neurophysiologically as an overly intense, central-nervous excitation combined with an emotional stress that disturbs or prevents the organized completion of this structure and thereby also its further development.

Something like this might be contingent on negative early childhood experiences in the area of interpersonal relationships. If the toddler normally learns in numerous and varied situations that his actions and needs are generally supplemented by the actions of others and that this supplementation leads both to a better satisfaction of needs and to optimal solutions for particular problem situations, then a more or less generalized system of expectation and action of an opposite kind might develop in the individual whose experiences are negative. This system is then not only affected with a negative emotional value, but the further differentiation of its structures will be insufficient also. In other words, since these negatively loaded structures resist actualization, no meaningful process of differentiation and interaction can take place which would ensure the building of adequate structures for interactional and social evaluation. This can manifest itself in the following reaction tendencies, among others. The individual in question is incapable of understanding and empathizing with the actions and experiences of others. He relates all the statements and actions of others to himself and experiences them as threatening. He cannot convey his own feelings and thoughts to others in an appropriate way.

Precisely in this area it is clear that interactional structures can be acquired neither on the basis of given external learning situations—occasions for positive social interactions arise sooner or later for almost every human being—nor through simple imitation as such. Neither learning nor imitation is a one-dimensional process. Whether or not an individual learns, through suitable occasions or from persons as models, how he can and is supposed to express his wishes and feelings, how others perceive and experience certain situations, and how he can take this perceiving and experiencing into account, depends on whether he brings to these situations structures that are suitable and emotionally colored in a positive way. In this case, we can only expect that he will further differentiate and integrate them in accordance with the laws outlined. We can already deduce from this that isolated interventions are not enough, particularly in the area of deficits of socially normative behavior; on the contrary, new emotionally satisfying modes of interaction can be built up only very gradually. Nevertheless, on the basis of multiple and repeated experiences, we do not exclude the rare possibility that an adult under special conditions may be able to intercept and to work through negative experiences and reaction tendencies by means of a continuous process of interpretation.

2. The negative loading of cognitive structures resulting from unmastered conflicts is, however, only one form of emotional causation for behavioral disturbances. The simpler case, also analyzed by learning theory, is that, in certain situations, the burgeoning structures are so intensely filled with a negative affective content through experiences of pain, deprivation, and abstinence that the individual avoids activating them again under any circumstances. As soon as certain perceptive reactions occur, which are connected with these structures, the individual will use other activities (for example, flight) to prevent the complete activation of structures. If no other possibilities exist, the consequence is often a blocking of all motor and sensory processes in the area of this situation. Such reaction patterns are characteristic of many phobias and situations, as already described with regard to avoidance learning. It may prove that in the case of cognitive structures relating to particular situations and objects, as, for example, fire, snakes, etc., an increased readiness exists to experience them in an emotionally negative way, but to date this has not been unequivocally demonstrated (cf. Seligman, 1975).

3. Another principle seems perhaps more important for the explanation of personality disorders. In Section 1 we emphasized that the recognizing subject is capable of observing himself, at least in part, during the cognitive processing of information and during problem situations, and that in this way he gradually develops not only higher structures of conscious self-reflection, but also coherent structural systems with which he is able to direct his process of cognitive assimilation. Obviously, this may occur not only in a way which promotes cognitive information processing and social interaction, but also in a way which obstructs them. If, for example, the subject repeatedly experiences failure in attempting to solve problems either through action or mind in a great variety of situations, he will in time probably form the conceptual structure, or, as we might say, "learn the lesson," that in this area his attempts to solve problems lead to nothing, that he had better discontinue them, and that he can spare himself disappointments and unpleasant experiences if he does nothing. This tendency, which can be specific or more or less general,

is designated "learned helplessness," by Seligman, who was able to support it empirically in numerous animal studies and in observations of depressed patients. A conceptual control structure of a higher kind that is learned in this way can, but need not, be connected with internal or external verbalizations. A depressed person might then say to himself in certain situations of demand, possibly without being conscious of it himself, "It's no use, you can't do it, it will certainly fail," etc.

4. The cognitive structures underlying the emotional disorders can be analyzed in terms of content as well as of structure. A consideration of content will be oriented either toward current perceptions or toward objectively controllable circumstances. In both cases, it is a matter of comparing these contents or interpretations with a norm. This norm lies either in historically developed interpretations, which are characteristic for a particular time and society, or in knowledge that has validity only in a particular context. From a content-comparing perspective of this kind, the structures of the emotionally unadjusted appear to be a misinterpretation of events or a misunderstanding of relationships. In this context, it is to be remembered that, in our view, reality, including social reality and the reality expressed in widespread societal conceptions, is not perceived as such but is perceived only through cognitive structures. The fact that the anxious person experiences objectively harmless and neutral stimuli as threatening can thus be explained. Emotional personality disturbances are treated by such authors as Beck (1976), who interprets the anxiety of the phobic person about certain objects or situations as a misinterpretation of the situation in question. Consequently, Beck deduces that one must provide these persons with the possibility of learning alternative perceptions and interpretations and of testing them in concrete situations.

In my opinion, this viewpoint can hardly provide a satisfactory explanation. First, the origin of the misunderstanding is not clarified; second, it suggests (insinuates) a method of change or intervention that could lead, circumstances permitting, to a superficially understood concept of advice or instruction. I am not claiming that in Beck this is the case to any pronounced extent; on the contrary, I believe that he does take the essential demands of a cognitive theory into account in his therapeutic procedures.

5. A structural analysis of the cognitive structures implied in personality disorders will search for alternative structures available to the individual. The decisive question here is in which situations and under what circumstances or conditions is the individual capable of activating these alternative interpretations? With this, a therapeutic program of generalization could possibly be linked.

6. For the explanation of norm behavior and norm expectations and, possibly, of the emotional resistances connected with them, the cognitive theory outlined here offers indications that are in accord with many everyday experiences and scientific observations. Norm behavior and value conceptions do not comprise a relatively superficial, easily modifiable rational superstructure of short-term origin, but are, rather founded, in general, on comprehensive and widely ramified structural systems with a long history and heavy emotional loading. The common experience, that we do not react indifferently to the value interpretations of others with whom we are confronted, is also involved here, since we know, from our own experience and from the reports of others, that in such circumstances there is a feeling of injury and of attack on one's personal integrity which causes genuine suffering. Consequently, it is not surprising that a single insight into the groundlessness or the unsuitability (whether to a given social-historical point or to a societal situation) of moral norms and behaviors does not lead at once to a changing or overcoming of the corresponding attitudes and expectations. These kinds of structural systems can only very gradually be changed or replaced by others. On the other hand, we expect that under the pressure of certain cognitive structures or needs, as, for example, to be accepted and integrated into a social community, other structures with different norms are learned for the situations in question, which then possibly generalize—not readily, of course—to other situations.

√

3. Therapy Based on Cognitive Theory

From the theses here advanced concerning cognitive structures and processes, their conditions of origin, and their implications for personality disorders, we should first like to derive a series of general theoretical principles and then some guiding rules about the formation of the therapeutic process.

3.1. General Theoretical Principles and Considerations

In this first discussion, we refer to the relationship between origin and change. Therapy represents the attempt to change a personality structure, an attitude, an emotional experience, or a behavior in a particular direction. In the previous theoretical discussions, we have held to the interpretation that there is no difference between the laws of original formation and those of the change of cognitive structures. We use the concept of origin only to emphasize qualitatively new features in patterns of human thought and behavior. It was our intention, however, which could only be carried out by way of suggestion here, to indicate that the origin of new behavioral patterns and, in particular, of intellectual abilities is not founded in separate or developmentally preprogrammed structures. Rather (as Piaget would say), they are constructed on the basis of functionally identical processes from relatively primitive sensorimotor structures, similar to reflexes, which are present at birth. In other words, for cognitive processes and personality structures, the laws of genesis and of change are identical. Therapy, as an attempt to change personality, can therefore be meaningful and successful only if it takes these laws of change into account; that is, if therapeutic measures are derived from them.

A second observation has to do with the relationship between knowing and acting. Structures of knowledge are internal acts or operations, concentrated into systems, which are stored and can be reactivated, and which, by means of an ontogenetic analysis, can finally be traced back to external sensorimotor acts. On the other hand, from a relatively limited quantity of patterns for perception and motor action, the cognitive ontogeny allows an abundance of conceptual systems and operations to originate, of which one can no longer keep track. In this process, moreover, the human subject gradually and ever more perfectly acquires the possibility of controlling and directing external actions and internal operations through adjacent and higher structural systems, as stated above. Furthermore, since the action of an individual in a particular concrete situation can be influenced by, and be conditional to, a large number of varied cognitive structures, a necessary and reversible relationship of conditions can in no case be established between a specific action and particular structures of knowledge formulated in general concepts. Nevertheless, in each concrete situation of action some conceptual structures have, in fact, a controlling and determining influence on the corresponding speech and activity. This connection determines, among other things, the effectiveness of so-called mental training. In mental training, the subject anticipates, by means of representational imagery and conceptual emphasis, the individual aspects of the actions to be performed and the perceptions and motor innervations necessary for them, and thereby prepares their consolidation into a functioning system. It is immediately obvious that this viewpoint must be significant for every type of therapy. Therapy is concerned not only with external behavior and speech but with their structural conditions also and, particularly, with the conceptual systems capable of triggering and directing them.

The knowing-acting dimension is as it were intersected by the conscious-unconscious dimension. It has already been stated that, according to the cognitive-theory view presented here, consciousness is identical neither with activity and perceiving nor with thinking and knowing; consciousness does not even necessarily and always accompany these processes. Since the subject always represents[2] only very particular and substantially limited segments of his actions, perceptions, and thoughts in adjacent or higher cognitive structures and operations, a consciousness defined in this way is only in part parallel to these processes and structures. To speak, therefore, of unconscious thoughts, speech, and acts, is certainly meaningful. The unconscious, thus defined, has of course nothing in common with repressed drive impulses. On the contrary, the unconscious comprises essentially two areas—the entirety of an individual's structural systems not actualized at a particular point, and the action and thought structures and their subcomponents which, although newly activated, do not come under the spotlight of consciousness as just defined. Furthermore, it seems important to indicate that higher structures which influence and direct the activation and the course of behavior and thought sequences can also be conscious or unconscious. The role of consciousness with respect to action, thought, and speech is at least twofold. On the one hand, the subject can reconstruct individual substructures or aspects of an operational system into metastructures. This process obeys the same laws and is just as laborious as the development of cognitive structures as a whole, because it demands more than merely an intuitive inward search, as was believed by early theoreticians of introspection. On the other hand, the subject can direct and control the courses of thought or behavior by means of higher structural systems, triggering them and regulating their exact course while at the appropriate moment calling back the individual substructures and, at a particular point in the course, signaling them to go into action. This control function of conscious higher structures becomes habitualized through practice, thus once again losing the quality of consciousness to the extent that the conscious triggering and control is gradually omitted and even becomes obstructive to a smooth and uninhibited course of operation.

It is probable, and has been supported both by observations of individual cases and by empirically controlled investigations, that this kind of unconscious, or only partially conscious, directive process can also determine neurotic behavior, as we explained in Part 2. Thus, people who fail and those who are depressive may in particular situations of demand discouragingly persuade themselves: You can't do that, all that makes no sense, etc. This need not occur by way of internal verbalization, but can also lie in corresponding conscious or habitualized thoughts and ideas. Thus, in investigations made of children who are poor achievers, it seems to be shown that they spend a great deal of the time available to them

[2]Cf. Nisbett and Wilson, 1977.

for completing a task on self-devaluating thoughts and with conceptions about the possible consequences of failure. They not only lack orderly and effective processes of control, but in addition they reactualize paralyzing images and thoughts which prevent the actualization of concepts and measures appropriate to the task. It is doubtless important that in such cases therapy deal with precisely these points if it is to be successful. In a difficult and lengthy process of redevelopment, therapy has to make these habits of thought conscious and to gradually replace them with thought systems that will advance the process of activity and problem solving. Aside from the pertinacity of such partly unconscious habits of thought, it must not be overlooked that the goal is reached probably in this way only in the rarest cases. Moreover, in the main, it will be necessary to help the subject develop the basic behavioral and conceptual systems necessary to solve the corresponding problems of his everyday or professional life. This often calls for very simple capabilities, which one regards all too readily as given. If this second condition is not fulfilled, the client will inevitably have renewed experiences of discrepancy and failure, from which he can only draw the "conclusion" that he does not measure up to the tasks.

A last remark applies to the relationship between generality and specificity. In the context of therapy, it is particularly important to indicate what we have already strongly emphasized in the theoretical section, that newly acquired structures are specific to the situations and objects in which they were acquired. One is never justified in assuming from the start that a cognitive structure can be transferred without further adaptation to similar and related situations, even when identical structural elements between them seem to the external observer evidently to be given. Extension, generalization, and transfer of cognitive structures is itself an active process, which in principle obeys the same laws as the building of new structures. The process will run its course all the faster, the more structures the individual already possesses in the respective area, and the more he has learned to observe and to direct the generalization process in this area by means of higher structures. For the most part, however, this will not be the case under therapeutic conditions. In all cases where genuine behavioral deficits exist, therefore, it will follow that the construction and, even more, the generalization of new and adequate ways of behaving and experiencing will demand a great deal of time and practice, and that an optimal learning environment must be made available.

In this context it is interesting to point out that the learning results of behavior-therapy measures are for the most part quite specific to situations (cf. McFall, 1976; Meichenbaum, 1976). That cognitive theory can perhaps explain rather better how the measures of behavior therapy work is a point that will be taken up later. At issue here is simply the finding, confirmed in many investigations, that the goal behavior stops at the moment the external reinforcing situation has ended. This, as experience has taught, can be prevented in two ways. On the one hand, an appropriate generalization of this behavior can and must be provided for, by means of commensurate variations of the learning situation and its gradual transition to the life situation external to therapy. On the other hand, suitable self-directing programs can be imparted to the individual which permit him to transfer learned problem-solving mechanisms to new situations. In the latter case, at least, it becomes evident that such programs have nothing more to do with a behavior therapy based on behaviorism.

3.2. General Guidelines for Therapeutic Management

In the following I should like to attempt to derive a few practical principles and general guidelines for therapeutic management from the considerations and theses that have been presented. With this I do not in any way claim to be developing a new therapy. On the contrary, I believe that similar approaches are implicitly contained in many therapeutic techniques without having been worked out explicitly. One will not rarely be able to detect an inherent contradiction between the techniques put forward and the theory explicitly advanced to explain them (cf. Section 4).

As one of the most essential consequences of the theory put forward here, I should like to lay down the principle that the therapy of behavioral and experiential disorders must always begin with the individual structures of the person undergoing therapy. In other words, there is no such thing as *the* therapy, and even less is there some all-purpose technique. Even when therapy is attempted in group situations, the resulting interactions can lead to changes of individual behavior and experience, according to the principles of cognition theory, only if they take effect in the cognitive structural systems of the persons participating. But whereas in group therapy the intended effect is left to the chance situation of group events, in that one hopes the discussions and interactions initiated by the group itself will provide a conflict-generating incentive suited to the structural systems of the participants; goal-directed individual therapy, on the other hand, would be meaningful only if knowledge, as exact as possible, of the structures of thought, action, and experience of the individual in need of therapy underlies the therapeutic interventions. In his endeavors the therapist must therefore strive, both beforehand and in the event, to concentrate on the comprehension and analysis of the client's cognitive structure and structural system in the areas of behavior and experience.

Unlike the psychoanalytic way of proceeding, this is not, however, a matter of uncovering repressed drive impulses. The theoretical discussions suggest that the following questions and viewpoints above all be taken into consideration:

1. What are the sensorimotor skills, conceptual categories, problem-solving habits and their emotional composition, in the affected area of behavior and experience? What expectations does the person entertain in relation to the events and accomplishments (level of aspiration) specific to this area; by what norms are his respective performances regulated? What of the skills which would enable him to meet his expectations and norms? This latter point is not often taken into account, because it is mistakenly regarded as almost a matter of course that each individual is equipped with the behavioral possibilities and conceptual skills sufficient for his everyday tasks and in particular for his necessary or desired social interactions.

2. It will be equally important to investigate the degree of generality in the behavioral and thought structures just indicated. It often appears certain, for example, that an individual in a particular situation, in a limited social constellation, is in a position adequately to process the relevant information and to react in a suitable way; but that with only slight changes in the situation it becomes impossible for him to activate these same structures. We all know the case of someone who is able to express his opinion adequately with respect to voice, form, and content when in a small group of acquaintances, but is on the contrary no longer in a position to do so in a larger group or with people he does not know. This may, of course, be due in most cases not merely to the generalization of the corresponding structure, but to other perceptions interfering with it, and to corresponding emotional overtones (for example, anxiety). The next point is already implied within this.

3. Which adjacent or higher behavioral systems accompany, influence, and impede the activation of judgment and of reaction systems adequate to the situation? Attention is also to be paid here to missing or inadequate control systems. Thus it is here a matter of conceptual arrangements and verbalizations, discussed above, with which the individual in part consciously, in part unconsciously accompanies his internal and external reactions, particularly in socially demanding situations. Also, however, precisely in this connection it is important to point out again that, according to our theoretical considerations, the individual obviously never has at his disposal a universal and conscious potential for processing and self-control.

4. Another aspect, which relates to and builds on the previous one, is the degree of distinctiveness and integration of cognitive structures. In this regard, the therapist will not merely ask which categories of infor-

mation processing and alternatives for decision the individual has at his disposal in the relevant area, but will also inquire as to the extent these alternatives are differentiated, and the possibilities that the individual has at his disposal to bring them into relation with one another. Is he equipped with rules according to which he weighs the alternatives, coordinates them, and, depending on the particular circumstances at hand, draws on them to make a decision? (On this subject see Seiler, 1973.)

5. A further diagnostic question relates to the emotional loading of the structural systems relevant to therapy. This point is so fundamental, that we want to reserve some considerations about it for a separate section.

The objective is plain, but what means and methods are available to achieve it? One thing is certain, that conversations and inquiries above cannot suffice. This would require that the client be fully conscious of all his structures and structural aspects, his skills and habits of thought, and beyond this also be able to verbalize them in a manner intelligible to the other person. As we know, this is never the case. On the other hand, there is no single adequate scientifically researched and certain method. Here the task is set for future research to develop methods through which this goal can be reached satisfactorily and with economical application. We must content ourselves with inadequate and rather tentative suggestions.

a. An important possibility would seem to lie in instructing and leading the client step by step in self-observation, both of his actions and of the internal concepts which accompany them, in quite concrete problem situations. He must learn to observe himself exactly in such cases. He must ask himself, What has occurred within me? What have I just perceived, thought, felt? By this means, he can in time obtain important information about his capacities for action and his habits of thought.

b. A great deal of information can probably also be obtained about the individual's ways of thought and reaction through the use of questionnaires, as well as measuring instruments and tests taken over from decision theory. It is important, however, to see that a normative interpretation or comprehensive calculation of these methods of measurement is of no value in diagnosing the individual's cognitive structures and structural systems; only a detailed analysis of the structures themselves can be of use here. One should bear in mind that the attitudes and styles of thought appearing in this procedure cannot generally be classified as spontaneously conscious, having rather been expressed only reactively in response to pointed questions and demands. Therefore, one must in addition not expect the individual normally to make use of them in conscious self-directing actions.

The first demand we raised, that the therapist (as also the person who educates and teaches) start from the individual structural systems of his client, has validity beyond the diagnosis. A basic thesis of our model expressed that only the inherent activity of the already acquired cognitive structures, in coming to terms with the given facts and particularly the social-communicative influences of the environment, can guarantee the extension and new acquisition of structural and behavioral systems. Here, we emphasized, in connection with Piaget, Hunt, and Berlyne among others (cf. Seiler, 1975), that conflict is included in this self-dynamic process. The developmental constructive process can, therefore, be effectively advanced and its direction determined by appropriate dispensation and control of these conflicts. In this sense, therapy is also conflict management. In the presentation of the theory, reference was made to some essential conditions and aspects of the cognitive conflict. For this reason, only a few points relevant for practice are to be singled out here; other aspects of cognitive conflict are discussed elsewhere (Seiler, 1975). It is obvious, after all that has been said, that no cognitive conflict arises from the confrontation between a cognitive expectation and the external stimulus situation as such. This confrontation becomes possible only in the event, and to the extent, that the stimulus situation is represented by appropriate perceptual and conceptual structures. Beyond this, additional structures are involved, which either measure the incongruence between the expected and the resulting actions, or set the limits for a new integration of action or thought structures yet to be completed. How can the therapist actuate optimal conflicts which introduce the process of change? The rules can be derived from our theoretical discussions. A basic rule demands that the client be offered suitable alternative possibilities for thought and action, and that he be challenged to form new goals in his range of possibilities and then, step by step, differentiate appropriate structures and integrate them to view systems in such a way as to ensure a realization of these goals. This challenge can only be successful if it stays within the further limits of the individual's capacities for thought and action. Provided that this rule is observed, a direct as well as indirect procedure, perhaps in the sense of the method of conversational therapy, can lead to the goal, at least in relation to the area of thoughts and attitudes. However, when an individual's cognitive systems are still relatively undifferentiated, direct stimuli may achieve more success than indirect or hidden ones. For this reason, it seems that client-centered therapy turns a viewpoint which is certainly correct into an absolute; and, beyond this, overlooks the fact that a moment of influence and behavioral control is always included, even in the indirect procedure of this therapy, which can be dangerous if it is not disclosed and reflected on.

It is not enough, however, to encourage new objectives and thus to set off a laborious and conflict-ridden process of differentiation and new integration. The environment must also be prevented from jeopardizing and destroying this process through inappropriate expectations and unreasonable demands. On the other hand, the client must be provided with additional internal and external aids for the furtherance and control of this developmental process. We know very well that the cognitive system of each individual presents a more or less complex and many-layered organization. Thus, above all, the capacity of the individual to direct his conceptual and active problem-solving processes by means of higher conscious or unconscious conceptions, images, thoughts, and verbalizations must be utilized. This can take place in a variety of ways, for example, through mental training or systematic desensitization. Demonstration and role-play are more apt to fulfill this function on the external behavioral level.

Phenomena and measures which are often designated "extrinsic motivation" also belong in this context where new objectives are being set and the process of change is being advanced through higher mechanisms of control. Extrinsic motivation is always given when relatively "remote" structural systems and the needs expressed in them take over the function of setting new goals and of activating potentials (in Berlyne's sense; cf. Seiler, 1975) on their behalf. The external incentives as such (money, prestige, career, etc.) are not thereby the carriers of this function, but rather the images, concepts, and needs of each particular individual which are applied to them. Therefore, one can also only explain and predict whether and how these external incentives are effective in reference to the representational and activating systems of the individual subject. Because Skinnerian theory rejects this recourse, it must, in my judgment, fail in this fundamental aspect also (cf. the discussion of the "reinforcer" concept on p. 74). From the standpoint of cognitive theory, therefore, it seems legitimate and, above all when dealing with poorly differentiated structural systems to some degree necessary, to look for support in foreign and remote systems of cognitive structure and needs in order to force open relatively undifferentiated and solidly entrenched structures of thought and action. However, it should be ensured step by step that through a gradual "weaning" the newly developed thought and action systems become independent and self-reliant, and develop a certain self-dynamic and self-satisfaction. It is probably the neglect of this last-named condition in many applications of behavior-therapy techniques, for example, token economy, which causes the behavior to collapse again after the reinforcer has been removed.

In addition to and independent of this gradual detachment there is the need to generalize the newly formed integrations, which at the start can only be activated under the specific and concrete conditions of the original situation. This generalization requires a practicing application of newly formed modes of thought and behavior, in gradual and systematically varied situations, and faced with the most varied objects and inquiries for which they are relevant. The structure must be extended step by step to new objects and areas. In this way, it simultaneously acquires more and more consistency, resistance to interference, and mobility. As we have seen, these are the qualities on which the self-dynamic and the motivational potential of a structure are based.

In the principles previously discussed an important factor was omitted, namely, the emotional loading of cognitive structures. This aspect must not be disregarded either during diagnosis or in the therapeutic operation. In other words, it is important for the therapist to bear in mind the emotional composition of the cognitive structures with which he has to deal from the very beginning and throughout the entire course of the therapy. He will not only account continually for the emotional composition of his client's modes of thought and reaction, but will supply him with pleasant experiences, and ground the therapeutic interaction in a positive affective climate. Positive social relationships and the experiences made possible through them are an essential source of positive emotional qualities. Moreover, the therapist will bear in mind that feelings never exist in and of themselves, but are always conveyed by some perceptions and judgments around which they are intertwined. For this reason, also, feelings cannot be changed directly. However, one can possibly try, with the aid of extrinsic structural systems that have a positive emotional quality, to achieve the goal of ensuring that the newly formed structures acquire for the client a pleasant, enjoyable, and satisfying quality. In pedagogic as well as in therapeutic functioning it is unreasonable to expect and demand that behavioral reactions, conceptual tendencies to social interactions, and problem solutions shall almost bring themselves into being, if their affective composition is not positive and attractive. The demand often raised for purely intrinsic motivation also fails, in my opinion, to appreciate the emotional side of human thought and action. Of course, the changing of structures which have negative emotional emphasis represents one of the most important and most difficult tasks of pedagogic and therapeutic assistance. Some possibilities will be pointed out when we come to discuss systematic desensitization in the following section.

4. Cognitive-Theory Interpretations of Behavior Therapy Techniques

I should like to conclude my discussions with a short comparison between the two theoretical approaches, the cognitional and the behavioral, and their respective therapeutic methods. For this a few general preliminary remarks seem appropriate.

1. Since identical theses and operationalizations can often be derived from different theories, it is all the more valid with regard to practical measures and techniques of therapeutic or pedagogic influence that they can be based on different theoretical systems. In other words, many techniques are, in relation to the context of both discovery and of explanation, independent of the theory by which they are explained. This seems to me to hold true for the methods of both depth-psychology and behavior-therapy. Although most methods of treatment have emerged from a foundation in some particular method of thought, it can nevertheless be shown in many cases that their connection with the theory on which one believes them to be founded is at best very loose. In particular, the way a method works can be explained by linguistic conventions which are extremely different from one another theoretically. No one will deny that close relationships are often brought to bear between techniques of behavior therapy and particular theses from the tradition of behaviorist learning theory. Nevertheless, one often overlooks that, in the first place, most of these techniques were already in existence earlier and, in the second place, that they can be settled on different theoretical terrains.

2. In view of the multiplicity of different theoretical approaches and practical methods, a certain eclecticism is understandable, which orients itself intuitively to the conditions and needs of practice. Against the background of the first remark, an eclectisism of methods might be more easily justified than the simultaneous recourse to various theoretical models of explanation and their blendings.

3. In continuation of the remarks made in the introduction, one could speak of a cognitive revolution in modern psychology. This cognitive revolution, however, as stated there, is not in general connected with the development of an explicit cognitive theory; rather, individual cognitive aspects and conditions (i.e., images, ideas, expectations, etc.) are taken into explanations, based until now purely on behavioral theory, when certain findings and phenomena can no longer be described and explained otherwise. In this way, systematic desensitization, for example, when working explicitly with the client's perceptions, builds on assumptions which, at least in this form, have been explicitly justified in very few learning theories, perhaps excepting Tolman and Berlyne. A detailed comparison of cognitive and behavioral modes of explanation cannot be made here. It is also in no way to be disputed, that behavioristically oriented learning research has contributed enormously to the progress of psychological knowledge in questions concerning both basic principles and application. In this connection I would, nevertheless, advocate the thesis as I might have shown with regard to the techniques, that many of its findings and laws can be integrated into a theory of cognition and can be interpreted from that standpoint. A reduction in their meaning and im-

portance goes along with this; that is, their validity is made to depend on particular conditions and situations; their practical relevance, however, could at the same time be increased by this rather than diminished. Most learning interpretations, which are approximations of more comprehensive and general cognitive theses, are limited to special situations and conditions. This explains both their limited validity or specificity and their quality of being more susceptible of empirical verification. At the same time, however, it is to be emphasized that, from my own epistemological standpoint, the quality of being more susceptible to empirical verification does not represent an argument in favor of a theory.

4. I support a classification and explanation of the measures of behavior therapy based on a theory of cognition not only because it seems to me to do greater justice to human behavior, and because I believe it explains the effect of these procedures with better arguments, but also very simply because this explanation seems to be better in accord with the measures and their intentions, the linguistic conventions, and the conditions that must be taken into account. This was already indicated above in the case of systematic desensitization. These general assertions will now be supported by the examples of a few concepts and techniques in behavior therapy.

"Reinforcement" is a concept common to all discussions and measures in behavior therapy. The heritage of learning theory stands out clearly here. We know that in modern learning theory the central role is no longer ascribed to the concept of reinforcement (cf. Saltz, 1971) although formerly it was sometimes considered to have, and today still has in some popular-science descriptions of behavior-therapy techniques. The concept of reinforcement, if understood as a direct effect of a constellation of external stimuli on the consolidation of the behavior preceding it, is incompatible with a cognitive-theory interpretation. Neither constellations of external stimuli nor consequences in external behavior lead to a further differentiation and new integration of existing conceptual or behavioral structures. This occurs only through their own internal dynamic whereby the various structures reciprocally regulate and control one another. The numerous and undoubtedly correct observations concerning the effect of "reinforcement" in experimental and therapeutic situations are therefore, in my opinion, to be explained otherwise; not through the effect of external stimulus variables as such, but rather through the complex interplay of internal factors which can be considered as partial representations of the external variables. We pointed out above, using the examples of extrinsic motivation and "token economy," a few of the complex processes of mediation and representation which can occur here. The concept of reinforcement seems to be a quite inadequate abbreviation for a complex interaction and mutual influencing of cognitive need structures which do selectively represent external events and situations, but the effect of these structures does not depend on those external events and situations. It is an abbreviation that possesses little explanatory value and a very limited, because merely statistical, predictive value under the assumption of comparable conditions.

The technique of systematic desensitization contains numerous practical components and conceptual aspects, for example, the factors of relaxation and of graduated confrontation with the anxiety-producing stimuli based on the concept of counterconditioning, and in addition the alternative method using stimuli which are either factually given or only imagined. The explicitly subjective and cognitive component in the latter case has already received sufficient mention. Concerning this variant, however, it also seems worth mentioning that it implicitly postulates a close nexus between the conceptual aspects and the components of feeling and acting, without more closely specifying or accounting for this relationship. In more recent explanations the necessity for relaxation and the concept of counterconditioning have been called into question. Irrespective of this discussion, it seems meaningful to explain the often-observed effect of relaxation as follows: In a state of relaxation, a large number of irrelevant and interfering conceptual and behavioral systems are excluded, making more room available for structural systems activated intentionally. At the same time, we assume that the pleasant affective mood connected with the experience of relaxation, as it is gradually transferred to the cognitive structures activated in this situation, eventually weakens and represses negative emotional experiences connected with them. What seems more essential, however, is that in such a calm, safe activation of the anxiety-laden structures, taking place under limited pressure of excitation, these structures are more likely to be in a position to evoke additional higher and adjacent experiences, arguments, and interpretations, which then become gradually embedded in the anxiety-laden system and transform it completely from within, at the same time giving a smaller relative share or weight to the anxiety-laden elements. It is also possible to achieve the same effect by exposing anxiety-laden cognitive systems to concrete situations where they prove themselves to be unfounded and are thereby refuted. According to our theoretical principles, this case is possible only when the relevant structures are still sufficiently flexible and ready for expansion that they can open themselves to the refuting situation. Intense rigidification of a structure through overly great anxiety and excitation is not only to be considered and explained from an emotional standpoint; such a situation is to be analyzed structurally as well. Just as each cognitive structure is associated with a feeling quality, which definitely can be changed and influenced, so other concepts and representations often correspond to different emotional levels of intensity.

Therefore, it seems definitely possible to explain the power of be-havior-therapy techniques in terms of cognitive theory. Beyond this, how-ever, the developmental theory of cognition advocated here has the great advantage of requiring, on principle, a systematic analysis of the individual systems of action and concept which underlie any pedagogic or thera-peutic process. Fortunately, cognitive theory has a long tradition in the analysis of such systems, and can point to remarkable progress in a great variety of areas. Here I am thinking principally of the information-theory models of processing and action, which have been made in recent years in the area of the development of conceptual systems for operations. Beyond the analysis of the conceptual and structural components, how-ever, which have been primarily investigated up to now, their motivational and emotional aspects and components require attention and ought to be investigated.

References

Beck, A. T. *Cognitive therapy and the emotional disorders*. New York: International Uni-versities Press, 1976.

Goldberg, R. A., Schwartz, S., & Stewart, M. Individual differences in cognitive processes. *Journal of Educational Psychology*, 1977, *69*, 9–14.

Hunt, E., Frost, N., & Lunneborg, C. Individual differences in cognition: A new approach to intelligence. In G. Bower (Ed.), *The Psychology of learning and motivation* (Vol. 7). New York: Academic, 1973.

Hunt, E., Lunneborg, C., & Lewis, J. What does it mean to be high verbal? *Cognitive Psychology*, 1975, *7*, 194–227.

Kelly, G. A. *The psychology of personal constructs*. New York: Norton, 1955.

McFall, R. M. Behavioral training: A skill-acquisition approach to clinical problems. In J. T. Spence, R. C. Carson, & J. W. Thibaut (Eds.), *Behavioral approaches to therapy*. Morristown, N. J.: General Learning Press, 1976.

Meichenbaum, D. Cognitive behavior modification. In J. T. Spence, R. C. Carson, & J. W. Thibaut (Eds.), *Behavioral approaches to therapy*. Morristown, N. J.: General Learning Press, 1976. (a)

Meichenbaum, D. Toward a cognitive theory of self-control. In G. E. Schwartz & D. Shapiro (Eds.), *Consciousness and self-regulation: Advances in research* (Vol. I). New York: Plenum, 1976. (b)

Miller, G. A., Galanter, E., & Pribram, K. H. *Plans and the structure of behavior*. New York: Henry Holt, 1960.

Nisbett, R. E., & Wilson, T. D. Telling more than we can know: Verbal reports on mental processes. *Psychological Review*, 1977, *84*, 231–259.

Powers, W. T. *Behavior: The control of perception*. Chicago: Aldine, 1973.

Saltz, E. *The cognitive bases of human learning*. Homewood, Ill.: Dorsey Press, 1971.

Scheele, B., & Groeben, N. *Voraussetzungs- und zielspezifische Anwendung von Kondi-tionierungs-VS. Kognitiven Lerntheorien in der klinischen Praxis*. Bericht aus dem Psychologischen Institut der Universität Heidelberg, 1976.

Seiler, T. B. Die Bereichsspezifität formaler Denkstrukturen: Konsequenzen für den päd-agogischen Proze. In K. Frey & M. Lang (Eds.), *Kognitionspsychologie und natur-wissenschaftlicher Unterricht*. Bern: Huber, 1973. (a)

Seiler, T. B. (Ed.). *Kognitive Strukturiertheit, Theorien, Analyse, Befund.* Stuttgart: Kohlhammer, 1973. (b)

Seiler, T. B. *Die Rolle des Konflikts in der kognitiven Entwicklung und im Informationsverarbeitungsprozess:* Eine Theorie und ihre Grenzen. Institut für Psychologie der Freien Univ. Berlin, 1975.

Seiler, T. B. Entwicklungssequenzen: Metatheoretische Betrachtungen zum Konzept der Entwicklungssequenz und zur genetischen Erklärungsweise. In S. Hoppe, C. Schmid-Schönbein, & T. B. Seiler (Eds.), *Entwicklungssequenzen: Theoretische, empirische und methodische Untersuchungen, Implikationen für die Praxis.* Bern: Huber, 1977.

Seiler, T. B. Grundlegende Entwicklungstätigkeiten und ihre regulative systemergeugende Interaktion. In *Die Psychologie des 20. Jahrhunderts* (Band 7). Zürich/München: Kindler-Verlag, 1978.

Seligman, M. E. P. *Helplessness: On depression, development and death.* San Francisco: W. H. Freeman, 1975.

Valins, S., & Nisbett, R. E. Attribution processes in the development and treatment of emotional disorders. In J. T. Spence, R. C. Carson, & J. W. Thibaut (Eds.), *Behavioral approaches to therapy.* Morristown, N. J.: General Learning Press, 1976.

3

Attitude Change and Cognitive Therapy

NICOLAS HOFFMANN

1. Introduction

In recent years the significance of attitude change in the broadest sense of the term has been increasingly referred to in the psychotherapeutic literature as an important component of every psychotherapeutic process.

Some authors, for instance Murray and Jacobson (1971), indeed define psychotherapy as "a set of social-influence techniques in which the individual's beliefs about himself and others are modified, resulting in behavioral and emotional changes" (p. 741). Similarly, Frank (1974) writes, "Psychotherapy tries to relieve a person's distress and improve his functioning by helping him to correct errors and resolve conflicts in his attitudes about himself and others" (p. 44).

This more intensive consideration of conscious streams of thought and value conceptions in psychological therapy was called by Allport (1968) a "significant revolution." He speaks of an "attitude-centered therapy," and sees within it the possibility of a convergence of various approaches.

In fact, the current emphasis on such factors as important determining aspects of human behavior represents a considerable turning point in the development of psychotherapy. It signifies a departure from the central psychoanalytic thesis that the decisive determinants of behavior are unconscious (Rapoport, 1960), and at the same time corresponds to a tendency within behavior modification, in which the one-sided emphasis on environmental aspects implemented by behaviorist ideology is relativized

NICOLAS HOFFMANN • Institut für Psychologie, Freie Universität Berlin, D-1 Berlin 41, Bundesrepublik Deutschland.

by a growing recognition of the role of internal "behavioral determinants" (Kanfer, 1976).

Even if, in this sense, the assertion made by Johnson and Matross (1975, p. 52) seems convincing, that no psychological problem can be solved and no helping process be carried out without the attempt to change "attitudes," the concept of "attitude" is used in a very undifferentiated way in much of the psychotherapeutic literature, and the assumptions about its function in determining behavior are relatively diffuse (cf. Frank, 1974; Johnson & Matross, 1975).

In this paper the attempt is made to discuss some important results of experimental investigations about attitude change as a possible basis for cognitive therapy. Here a few preliminary remarks are necessary concerning the concept of "attitude" and its relationships to behavior, particularly pathological behavior.

2. Attitude and Behavior

2.1. The Concept of Attitude

In spite of the high prestige which the concept of "attitude" still enjoys in psychology (in this connection Allport spoke of attitude as "probably the most distinctive and indispensable concept in contemporary American social psychology") there has been no agreement on an even partially binding definition even after a century of involvement with the subject.[1]

Whereas previously much effort was expended in attempting to unify diverse suggestions for definitions (Allport, 1935; Nelson, 1939), today, as Greenwald (1968) observes, "One seems to accept this diversity of definitions of attitudes and the impossibility of establishing a consensus about generally accepting any one of them" (p. 361).

One point, which at least the most important authors agree, is this: rather than seeing in them a particular class of behaviors (for example, opinions on a questionnaire), they consider attitudes to be intervening variables, which at least partially regulate behavior. This hypothetically inferable behavioral determinant is, as Fishbein and Ajzen (1975) state, "a learned predisposition to respond in a consistently favorable or unfavorable manner with respect to a given object" (p. 6).

Yet this description is not very precise. Also, from Roth's (1967)

---

[1]Allport's (1935) compilation of sixteen different definitions is well-known. In the meantime, far more than 500 operations for measuring attitudes have been reported (Fishbein & Ajzen, 1972), and approximately forty theoretical models for changing attitudes (Oštrom, 1968).

attempt to differentiate the concept of attitude from related concepts, such as what one acquiesces in, one's state of consciousness, disposition, determining tendency, set, belief, stereotype, prejudice, or value, the impression is conveyed that because of its globality and diffuseness attitude is a "concept which can scarcely be dealt with empirically" (Fietkau, 1977, p. 26).

Thus it is not surprising that ideas about the significance of attitudes in regulating behavior differ greatly, and that the relevant empirical results are partly contradictory. In the following pages the most important elements of this discussion are presented, as well as the conclusions which result from them for making the concept of attitude more precise.

2.2. Attitudes and Behavior: Empirical Evidence

From a naive point of view, a rather close connection is generally presumed to exist between attitudes and behavior. The concept of attitude was explicitly introduced into social psychology as an attempt to explain the emergence of a particular behavior. The aggregate "attitude" is frequently subdivided into an emotional, a cognitive, and a behavioral aspect, and one implicitly presupposes a consistency among the three aspects.

If one describes attitudes, as is usually the case, as predispositions to respond to an object in a consistent way, then the close connection between attitude and behavior is already implied.

Attitudes are often even inferred directly from observed behavior, with the effect that the problem of the connection between attitudes and behavior is reduced to a pseudoproblem.

Thus, Campbell (1963) has stated that a social attitude is verified by the consistency of the response toward social objects. Green (1954) believes that the concept of attitude implies the consistency or predictability of responses, and that its contents are determined by the responses composing it.

Generally, attempts to furnish evidence for the dependence of behavior on attitudes, assumed from the start, were undertaken in a simplistic way. The attempt was made to prove the usefulness of the concept of attitude by pointing out that persons who behave differently also hold different attitudes. Thus, for example, it was discovered that persons belonging to a pacifist organization displayed a more negative attitude toward war than other people did, etc.

However, Fishbein and Ajzen (1975) point out that these studies, which have often served to validate attitude scales, used instruments to measure attitudes which were constructed in such a way that differences between the comparison groups inevitably had to result. Moreover, the "behavioral criterion" that was generally used consisted of a "behavioral syndrome" rather than a specific response to a stimulus.

Designed in such a way, these investigations are scarcely in a position to furnish conclusive evidence for a close connection between attitude and behavior. However, they are repeatedly brought up under this assumption.

On the other hand, serious doubts about a close connection between attitude and behavior have resulted from a series of other works.

Thus, Wicker (1969) considers numerous experimental studies in which "at least one attitudinal measure and one overt behavioral measure toward the same object were obtained for each subject" (p. 48). He comes to the conclusion that "it is considerably more likely that attitudes will be unrelated or only slightly related to overt behaviors than that attitudes will be closely related to actions" (p. 65).

In the comprehensive presentations by Benninghaus (1973) and Six (1974) regarding the correspondence between attitude and behavior it was also brought out that most attempts to prove a close relationship are methodologically and theoretically insufficient.

Benninghaus writes, "Practically all the attempts to identify a close relationship between attitude and behavior can be considered as failures. . . . the failure of these attempts apparently has made little impression on most of the researchers and theoreticians of attitudes" (p. 697).

The adherence to the old interpretation, which Kiesler (1971) assumes is so persistent not least because it lends the laboratory experiments on attitudes a flair of practical relevance, is still documented in credos such as the following: "Man's social actions—whether involving religious behavior, occupation, practical activity, or buying and selling goods—are directed by his attitudes" (Krech, Crutchfield, & Bellachey, 1962, p. 139).

Also, in view of the disappointingly small support which this position has received lately, it is not surprising that other authors had fundamentally challenged the concept of attitude all along, and denied its usefulness.

This position has been supported with most consequence by the behaviorist learning psychologists, who (at least on the programmatic level) reject every recourse to the "inner man," as Skinner disparagingly dismisses cognitive attempts at explanation, and frequently defend this interpretation with the obstinacy of self-appointed guardians of scientific orthodoxy (for a critique of this position, see Breger, 1969; Koch, 1964; Seiler, 1973).

Nevertheless, a more evenly balanced way of proceeding seems to lie in subjecting to a more precise analysis those factors which determine whether the connection between attitude and behavior is strict or loose. In this way it becomes possible—under consideration of the results which speak in favor of behavior as being in part regulated by attitudes—to arrive at more differentiated models of explanation and at established predictions.

2.3. The Connection between Attitudes and Behavior

The inconsistency of the empirical results and the low correlations between attitude and behavior found in many investigations have stimulated a more intensive attempt, in recent literature, to clarify the relationship between the two variables. Some important considerations concerning this question will be dealt with briefly.

2.3.1. Problems of Measurement

Many contradictions which have arisen among diverse investigations of the connection between attitudes and behavior may be explained by the different procedures of measurement used.

In many studies, the attitude is raised to a very global and comprehensive object, after which behavior is recorded in a very specific stimulus situation.

Thus, in numerous experiments the general attitude, for instance, toward ethnic minorities was recorded, and was then compared to a concret behavior toward a particular representative of this minority (for example, it was investigated whether the subjects were willing to sit down to eat with a particular black person). In view of the low correlations often resulting between attitude and behavior in such cases, Herkner (1975) states that "the correspondence between attitude and behavior will be greater, the more similar the object of the attitude measurement is to the object of the behaviorally relevant attitude" (p. 177).

Thus, inaccuracy in prediction can arise merely due to attitudes being raised to the level of concepts rather than to the level of particular behaviors. It has been variously pointed out (Campbell, 1963; Doob, 1947; Thurstone, 1939; Tittle & Hill, 1967) that the measurement of attitudes to a concept is connected with the person's *pattern* of behavior rather than with his specific response towards the object.

As Fishbein (1973) points out in this connection, if the attitude to a concept is assumed as the predictor for behavior, it is not inconsequential whether a behavior is recorded only once and used as a criterion (single-act criterion), whether the behavioral measurement is repeated (for instance, at various points in time), or whether different behaviors toward the same object are recorded (multiple-act criterion). The predictive value of the attitude in question can vary according to the kind of behavioral measurement. (For a detailed discussion of the problem, see Fishbein & Ajzen, 1975.)

2.3.2. "Other Variables" Approach

A further attempt to explain the inconsistency between attitude and behavior is based on the finding that attitudes represent only *one* determinant of behavior, and that their effect is impaired by other factors. Freedman, Carlsmith, and Sears (1970) present this position as follows:

> Attitudes always produce pressure to behave consistently with them, but external pressures and extraneous considerations can cause people to behave inconsistently with their attitudes. Every attitude and change in attitude tends to produce behavior that corresponds with it. However, this correspondence often is not apparent, because of other factors involved in the situation (pp. 385–386).

Herkner (1975) also holds the view that attitudes determine behavior as long as no other factors are involved. He sees the cause in processes of self-reinforcement for attitudinally consistent behavior and of self-punishment for attitudinally discrepant behavior; whereby he considers the various intensities of these processes to depend on the conditions of socialization which affect the development of conscience.

Other frequently cited factors which can appear as concurrent determinants of behavior are contrary motives, verbal, intellectual, and social skills, normative prescriptions toward one's own behavior, the expected or actually emerging consequences of the behaviors, and unforeseen external events (Fishbein & Ajzen, 1975).

According to this interpretation, attitudes represent neither necessary nor sufficient conditions for behavior; rather, as Triandis (1971) writes, they have a determining and canalizing function, and their predictive value for behavior is all the greater the more other important behavioral determinants, such as norms, habit, expectations of reinforcement, etc., are in conformity with them, and the more intensely the situational variables promote the expressions of the corresponding behavior.

As Wicker (1969) notes, the assumption of additional factors, through which one explains the discrepancy between attitudes and behavior actually taking place, has often the character of a *post hoc* explanation, and there have been few investigations which have been able to clarify the relative significance of these factors as behavioral determinants compared with attitudes.

2.3.3. Beliefs, Attitudes, Intentions, and Behavior

Fishbein and Ajzen (1975) provide a differentiated attempt toward a conceptual framework for the theoretical analysis of the phenomena which are usually summarized under the global concept "attitude."

With reference to the interpretation advocated by many authors (e.g., Rosenberg & Hovland, 1966) that a cognitive, an affective, and a behavioral component can be differentiated in attitudes, they distinguish between beliefs, attitudes, intentions, and actual behavior. In what follows the most important elements of their paradigm will be briefly presented.

2.3.3a. Beliefs. The central element in the conception of Fishbein and Ajzen is the notion of belief. They define a belief as "the subjective probability of a relation between the object of the belief and some other object, value, concept, or attribute" (1975, p. 131).

Thus, beliefs represent subjective connections between two different aspects of the individual's world. Owing to the fact that in belief a particular attribute is ascribed to a particular object with a certain probability, beliefs form the informational basis for attitudes.

Beliefs about an object can originate in various ways. Thus, a relationship between two objects can be traced to direct observation. On the basis of the information supplied to a person by his sensory organs, he may perceive that a particular object manifests a particular attribute. On the basis of this experience he forms beliefs about the perceived object which Fishbein and Ajzen call "descriptive beliefs." If the person has sufficient time available to assimilate this information, these beliefs are, as a rule, correct, that is, they reflect well the actual relationships which are given in the observational situation. As Fishbein and Ajzen (1975) emphasize, there are practically no indications that already existing beliefs, attitudes, or personal characteristics exert any kind of systematic influence on the formation of descriptive beliefs based on direct observation.

The relationships are different with beliefs based on processes of inference. It is typical for processes of inference that the individual, in addition to the stimulus factors of the actual situation, uses residues of earlier experiences in order to formulate a current judgment.

Although the formal processes of thought applied here do not correspond to the principles of logic in every case—Abelson and Rosenberg (1958) speak of "psycho-logic" in this connection—the attempt has been made in a series of investigations to find out what principles they follow (Abelson & Kanouse, 1966; Chapman & Chapman, 1959; DeSoto & Albrecht, 1968; Wason, 1964).

In the formation of these beliefs, motivational, emotional, and personality factors apparently play a greater part than in the origin of descriptive beliefs, although presently not much can be said about the systematic effects of these factors (cf. Fishbein & Ajzen, 1975; Herkner, 1975).

Finally, a third kind of belief originates neither through direct observation nor through processes of inference, but rather from the fact that information about an object is adopted from external sources (through conversations with others, media, etc.). We shall go into further detail later about the formation of these beliefs based on external information coming from third persons.

2.3.3b. Attitudes. In the belief-forming process, an object is linked with particular attributes. According to Fishbein and Ajzen the "attitude" toward the object is a function of the subjective valuation of these attributes. The subject's attitude toward an object thus localizes the object on a hypothetical scale representing a continuum from an extreme positive to an extreme negative valuation. To the extent that a person forms beliefs about an object, attitudes are simultaneously being formed, because the attributes connected with the object are located on this affective scale of valuation.

A person's attitude about an object can be estimated in that the valuation of the attributes connected with the object is multiplied by the subjective probability with which the person assumes that the object possesses this attribute; then the products for all the relevant beliefs are summed up. Likewise, the person's attitude about a behavior can be estimated in that the valuation of each of the behavioral consequences is multiplied by the subjective probability with which the person assumes that the behavior will lead to this consequence; the products for all the relevant beliefs being again summed up.

As a rule, an individual forms a great number of beliefs about an object or a behavior through observation, by inference, or by adopting the beliefs of others. Some of these beliefs prove to be very stable and lasting; others fade or are replaced by new ones. At any particular time, all these beliefs are not equally important in terms of forming attitudes about the object. It is the most significant ones that determine this attitude. Fishbein (1967) and Kaplan and Fishbein (1969) advocate the interpretation that, as a rule, the first five to nine beliefs occurring to an individual about a particular object are the ones most likely to be responsible for the formation of the attitude.

2.3.3c. Intentions. Fishbein and Ajzen (1975) understand by an intention the subjective probability with which a person assumes that he will perform a particular behavior. In the literature, intentions are interpreted by many authors as the conative or behavioral aspect of attitudes, with the assumption that this intentional aspect is very closely connected with the cognitive and affective aspects. Empirical results do not support the global claims of this interpretation.

An evaluation of pertinent works (cf. Fishbein & Ajzen, 1975) reveals that, although attitudes may correlate well with indices representing a wide variety of intentions, the relationship between attitudes and a very specific intention is often not very close.

In order to clarify the relationship, it is essential to analyze the elements which make up intentions. Four aspects can be identified, namely, the behavior which is to be performed; the goal toward which it is directed; the situation in which the behavior is to take place; and the time of performance.

Each of these four elements can be more or less specific on the level of intention. An example is adduced by Fishbein and Ajzen (1975, p. 292) to illustrate what differences intentions can display in relation to specificity. Someone might plan to drink a glass of grog with George in the harbor bar at five o'clock in the afternoon; whereas someone else might intend to socialize more widely.

Even if a relatively heterogeneous spectrum of intentions still correlates with a very global attitude to make positive or negative responses toward the object, the relationship to the attitude becomes the weaker the more specific the determination of the intention is. This makes it necessary to investigate more closely the other conditions of intentions in addition to attitudes.

Fishbein (1967) proposed the following model for doing this. The intention to perform a particular behavior in a particular situation depends mainly on two factors: an "attitude factor," which, as described above, is a function of the assumed consequences of the behavior and their valuation, and a "social" or "normative" factor, which reflects the influence of the social surroundings on the respective behavior. This subjective norm is determined by the assumptions which the person makes about the judgment of the behavior by his important social partners, and his readiness to conform to this judgment.

These two factors determining the intention—attitude and subjective norm—are differently weighted according to the respective behavior. For certain behaviors, normative considerations (the expectations of others) are preeminent; for others, attitude factors (the expected consequences for the individual) take precedence. Moreover, the relative weighting of the two factors can be influenced by situational variables such as the visibility of the behaviors, and by personality characteristics.

This model, which can describe the determinants of intentions on various levels of specificity, permits an analysis of the relationship between attitudes and behavior which is more precise than those undertaken in many other approaches.

2.3.3d. Behavior. In the analysis by Fishbein (1967) and Fishbein and Ajzen (1975), a high correlation is assumed between a person's intention to perform a specific behavior and the actual expression of this behavior. There are three factors essentially determining the probability that the intention will be followed by the corresponding behavior.

First, it can be assumed that the intention is an even better predictor of a behavior, the more intention and behavior coincide on the level of specificity. Another series of conditions concerns the stability of the intention over time. If there is a longer span of time between the declaration of intention and the performance of the behavior, a number of events can alter the intention or can interfere with the performance. Thus, expressing the behavior can depend on behaviors which were to be carried out previously, and whose realization can be only imprecisely estimated at the time of measuring the intention. Moreover, an additional uncertainty relating to performing the behavior can arise owing to the fact that particular behaviors of others or particular events are preconditions for it. Finally, factors such as strongly established habits leading to an alternative behavior, as well as a lack of mastery of the behavior which is to be performed, can impair its expression.

The model outlined briefly here seems to permit a substantially differentiated access to the problem of the modification of attitudinal factors determining behavior. However, before dealing with this question, some remarks concerning the problem of the pathogenic function of attitudes are presented.

2.4. Attitudes and Problem Behavior

The view that problem behavior is to a considerable extent traceable to the effects of past and present environmental influences dominates thinking in the area of psychological therapy today to an almost unlimited extent. The emphasis on the significance of a learning history for the acquisition and maintenance of abnormal behavior takes on its major importance only if one assumes that besides "overt" behaviors, cognitive and affective response patterns form an important part of the results of previous learning. This view, familiar to more psychodynamically oriented systems all along, is also showing up more frequently in the behavior-theory perspective. In connection with empirical studies such as those of Seligman (1975) and Beck (1976) and with critical objections to the models of psychological disorders based on S–R theories (Breger & McGaugh, 1965), theories guaranteeing a greater inclusion of cognitive-symbolic and affective factors are also favored by this viewpoint.

In this sense, Mahoney (1974) writes, "The human organism responds to a 'constructed' reality, and the nature of that 'construction' seems to dramatically moderate performance variance (p. 227). Various orientations have undertaken the task of investigating the particular forms of the construction of reality reflected in pathological or problem behavior. In so doing, each orientation has remained largely dependent on its own terminology, often created *ad hoc*.

A few attempts make explicit reference to the concept of "attitude." Thus, Frank (1974) speaks of the part that mistakes in the attitudinal systems toward oneself and others play in psychological problems, and Böttcher and Kässner-Reitler (1971) emphasize the central importance of "faulty attitudes." They define them as "structured, relatively stable, dynamically-regulating reaction tendencies which, although they arise particularly from social experiences, adequately reflect not the social realities and their relationships but, at best, particular aspects of these realities. These aspects are characterized by the fact that they originate from highly affect-laden experiences which lend themselves quite easily to overgeneralization" (p. 136). As a result, these faulty attitudes prevent the full receptive attention to new things; they are connected with unrealistic or exaggerated expectations, and people with faulty attitudes of this kind are particularly indecisive regarding action, and are, therefore, incapable of independent and active confrontation with reality.

Ellis (1962) also identified a number of "beliefs" according to him are frequently found in clients with behavior disorders. Since these beliefs involve interpreting many social situations in a particular way, they have almost taken on the character of an irrational philosophy of life, which again and again generates the same pathological reactions, mostly of an affective kind, in the individual. Johnson and Matross (1975) consider psychological health to be determined by interpersonal effectiveness, that is, by the ability to achieve intended effects through behavior, and the ability to enter into genuine and humane relationships to others. They believe that four attitudes are of particular significance here: first, the attitude that one can trust others and rely on their help; next, trust in one's own behavior and the possibility of effecting changes in the environment; then the belief that one's own life is meaningful; and finally, the conviction that one possesses a coherent and integrated personal identity.

It would not be very productive to continue enumerating the attitudes which, in the opinion of many authors, lead either to "psychological health" or to disorders. The use of the concept "attitude" is in most cases extremely imprecise, and the contents are kept so general that they scarcely allow more precise behavioral predictions (on this, Section 2.3.).

Moreover, the attempts made on such a general level to identify the faulty attitudes responsible for certain types of disorders or for disorders in general seem very questionable. Here, too, an analysis of the respective individual problems will be necessary, in order to isolate—on the level of the pathogenic attitudinal factors—those elements which are behaviorally relevant, and in order to avoid inadmissible generalizations which stem from some particular ideology.

3. Attitude Change and Cognitive Therapy

In social psychology the belief has always been held that by changing an individual's attitudes it is possible to influence his behavior in decisive life situations. Thus, most of the experimental works are less concerned with the origin of attitudes, their behaviorally regulative function, and their interaction with other determinants of behavior than with the attempt to effect certain changes in attitudes or attitudinal systems; and thus the changes resulting on the behavioral level were often simply postulated, without the effort having been made to prove them or to analyze more closely the conditions of their emergence. Also the best elaborated theories in this field relate to the processes for changing attitudes.

Recently, however, social psychology has commented rather cautiously about the significance and the relevance of most of these investigations. Thus, Lackenmeyer (1970), for example, claims that many social psychologists investigate relatively insignificant and irrelevant problems, and Katz (1972) states, "Of the thousands of experimental studies published in social psychology in the past twenty years, surprisingly few supply new information to a cumulative body of knowledge" (p. 577).

In view of the numerous skeptical judgments of the previous accomplishments of social psychology within the areas of its own problems, it is not surprising that the possibility of transferring these results to the clinical sphere has been assessed even more cautiously.

Indeed, Mahoney (1974) writes, "The experimental analysis of belief could hardly be overemphasized in terms of its relevance for and potential impact upon future cognitive-clinical developments" (p. 227). However, in relation to the effectiveness of strategies of change in the therapeutic situation, we are dependent on speculations and extrapolations from other fields, as he concedes. In fact, with very few exceptions, there have been almost no investigations into the optimal strategies for changing faulty attitudes under the conditions of psychological therapy. In what follows, a few comments will be discussed which are suggested by the literature of social psychology on this subject.

3.1. Strategies for Changing Beliefs, Attitudes, and Intentions

Mahoney (1974) designates as sterile the controversy concerning whether psychotherapy's "actual" attempt to influence is directed at changing attitudes or at changing behaviors, and (p. 238) correctly states that it has already used up more energy and professional talent than can be justified.

In the complex interpersonal situation represented by a therapeutic process, it becomes—according to the aspect of the problem situation at the forefront—at times more necessary to convince the client of the uselessness or harmfulness of some of his beliefs and attitudes, in order to introduce new response patterns in critical situations. Occasionally it will be most exigent to arrange a setting for processes of learning and practice in order to establish desired behaviors, whose performance including their consequences in turn have repercussions on the cognitive and affective systems. In practice, these attempts at change are usually so closely connected that a strict separation scarcely seems possible.

In this section, however, some principles are discussed resulting from research in social psychology for the therapeutic change of beliefs, attitudes, and intentions, that is, the cognitive and affective determinants of behavior.

As Fishbein and Ajzen (1975) emphasize, every attempt to make such a change implies providing the individual with new information about an object, a behavior, or an event, and the resulting changes in beliefs form the necessary basis for the effectiveness of the attempt.

A direct change in beliefs can occur in two ways. On the one hand, the individual who is to be influenced, can be told that an object is connected with a particular attribute. On the other hand, this person can be put into a situation where he is in the position of observing the corresponding relationship himself. The two basic strategies for change, namely, verbal communication and active participation, correspond to these two possibilities.

3.2. Changes through Verbal Communication

An important part of the actions initiated by therapists with the goal of changing their clients lies in attempts to influence them verbally. This is certainly true for all forms of psychotherapy, without regard to whether the therapist's attempts at persuasion are openly admitted and directly presented, as in Ellis's rational-emotive therapy, or whether they are more covert, as in the diverse forms of psychoanalytic treatment and in client-centered therapy.

In behavior therapy, which London (1964) has called "action therapy" in contrast to more verbally-oriented approaches, the therapist's power of persuasion also plays a significant part, as is increasingly recognized (see, e.g., Lazarus, 1971; Locke, 1971).

The principles which would allow for the most effective persuasion possible through communication were investigated in detail by Hovland

and his colleagues in the Yale research project (Hovland, 1957; Hovland & Janis, 1959; Hovland, Janis, & Kelley, 1953). They define communication as the process through which an individual (the source) transmits stimuli (mostly of a verbal kind) in order to modify the behavior of the other persons (the receivers).

3.2.1. Mechanism of Persuasion Based on Verbal Communication

According to the Yale school, the effectiveness of communication depends on the extent to which the messages are perceived, understood, and accepted. In this process

> Attention and comprehension determine what the recipient will *learn* concerning the content of the communicator's message; other processes, involving changes in motivation, are assumed to determine whether or not he will accept or adopt what he learns. (Hovland & Janis, 1959, p. 5)

McGuire (1968, 1969) extended this approach to a two-factor theory of persuasion, in which he combines attention and comprehension forming a process of receiving, followed by a second stage of conforming to the contents which were received, in the sense that the receiver accepts the message, retains it in his memory, and adjusts his behavior accordingly. McGuire (1969) states, "The receiver must go through each of these steps if communication is to have an ultimate persuasive impact, and each depends on the occurrence of the preceding step" (p. 173).

With their theory of social judgment, Sherif and Hovland (1961) have provided a more exact designation of the parts of the persuasive process. According to this theory, the position held by an individual as well as related points of view form the "area of acceptance" on an arbitrary continuum of judgment; points of view to which he has strong objections, and similar positions, form his "area of rejection"; whereas all remaining points of view belong to his "area of indifference."

According to this theory, every attempt at persuasion exerts pressure on the individual to change his belief, and does so all the more strongly the more distant is the viewpoint communicated in the message from that of the individual.

If the new point of view is located within the areas of acceptance or indifference, then it is predicted that the change in attitude increases with the perceived discrepancy. If it belongs to the area of rejection, however, one expects the change in position to decrease in proportion to the perceived discrepancy. The viewpoint taken by the individual thus serves as an "anchor" or point of reference. Those positions represented by others, which have been set within the area of acceptance, are adapted to the individual's point of view through an effect of cognitive distortion; whereas those belonging to the area of rejection are experienced as being more discrepant than they actually are. In addition, the degree of ego-participation plays an important part in this matter: the stronger it is, the more pronounced, among other things, is the area of rejection.

3.2.2. Changes through Therapeutic Communication

There has been little investigation of the effectiveness of attitudinal changes brought about through direct communication between therapist and client. It is only in the area of manipulating expectations of success in systematic desensitization that a number of experiments have been performed, but their predictive power often proves limited, owing to methodological defects and to the fact that analogous patients were used (for a summary and critique, see Borkovec, 1973). A very few other investigations deal with the effectiveness of Ellis's rational-emotive therapy (for a summary, see Ellis, 1962; Mahoney, 1974).

There is also an absence in the literature of suggestions for plans of intervention, which—after investigating the pertinent literature and taking into consideration the most important results of the experimental research on attitudes—would allow access to the problem of changing attitudes, in the broadest sense, through therapeutic communication.

Some references toward this goal which are emerging on the basis of Fishbein and Ajzen's (1975) differentiation between beliefs, attitudes, and intentions will be mentioned briefly in what follows:

1. Since intentions represent the best predictors for the behaviors that are to be established, according to the model of Fishbein and Ajzen (1975), the goal of the process of cognitive change lies in attempting to promote intentions which coincide on the level of specificity with the behaviors which are to be performed. This means that, while intentions are undergoing formation, the behavior to be performed, the intended goal, the situation in which it is to take place, and the time when it is to be performed are to be made explicit if at all possible. One can scarcely expect a realization of the corresponding behaviors from intentions which are too general.

2. Supplementing the establishment of an intention, an analysis should follow of the conditions which can complicate or prevent the expression of the behavior. This applies above all to the questions whether the individual masters performance of the behavior under similar conditions, whether the opportunity for performance prepared by the discriminating stimuli can be produced, and whether any predictable events up to the time of performance can lead to a change in the intention.

3. At the moment when the client has established a particular intention, not only do the concrete modalities of the performance have to be

dealt with, but in addition, measures for stabilizing the intention must follow. An important measure in this regard lies in attaining a higher degree of "committment" to the intention, for instance, through the client's communications to important social partners. In addition, the performance of preparatory behaviors can be encouraged in order to create conditions which facilitate the performance of the behavior or establish facts which are difficult to undo.

4. To make possible the formation of the desired intention, normative conditions must be considered along with the attitudinal factors. The establishment of an intention can fail not only because the attitude change necessary for it does not occur, but also because negative responses to the performance of the behavior are anticipated from the social environment. Therefore, one must examine to what extent the person has really experienced negative sanctions in analogous situations in the past, or to what extent the expectations are founded on unjustified inferential processes based on insufficient or wrongly interpreted information. In the first case, it would be necessary to correct the degree of the client's adjustment to the expectations of others—a correction which Lazarus (1971) labeled the "undoing of social overadaptation," and which Ellis also strongly encouraged. In the second case, one should strive for an examination of the inferential processes on which the client's normative expectations are based.

5. For the actual process of changing attitudes, it is necessary to clarify which beliefs, that is, which object–attribute connections and subjective valuations of these attributes constitute the immediate attitudinal state in the relevant area. Subsequently, one can attempt through communication to change the probability with which the individual links certain attributes to the respective object, or to establish linkages to new attributes, which change the valuation of the object and lead to new inferential processes. The precondition for the success of attitude change is, of course, that the beliefs expressed by the therapist do not fall within the client's area of rejection, that is, that new information, in light of the existing attitude structure, is still considered acceptable. A brusk confrontation with strongly discrepant interpretations is to be avoided for this reason. Investigations concerning the so-called "Socrates-effect" (McGuire, 1968; Rosen & Wyer, 1972) also speak against a rash expression of beliefs, interposed in an excessively authoritarian manner, which diverge strongly from those of the client. Accordingly, cognitive changes are especially evident and enduring if the client himself is induced, through a kind of Socratic inquiry, to examine the congruence and rationality of his own belief systems.

The numerous investigations performed in the wake of experiments by Janis and Feshbach (1953, 1954) concerning the problem of anxiety evocation and attitude change speak in favor of proceeding cautiously.

Although the relationships do not seem to have been totally clarified as yet, there is much to support the statement that anxiety arising from verbal messages, when it goes beyond a certain point, stands in the way of an attitude change.

6. McGuire (1968, 1969) pointed out that a sufficient reception of messages (for which attention and comprehension are preconditions) is highly significant for the process of attitude change. For this reason, it is necessary to communicate in a well-structured and verbally clear manner, and to a certain extent to strengthen these messages through repetition.

7. An important measure aimed at stabilizing changed attitudes lies in making them more resistant to "counter-propaganda." Lumsdale and Janis (1973) demonstrated that "two-sided" communications, that is, those containing arguments not only for the point of view to which one is trying to persuade the client, but also for other points of view, make the change more stable. In addition to this "inoculation" against possible counter-arguments, Tannenbaum (1967) described three further safeguards which can be used to stabilize newly acquired attitudes. These are support of the attitude toward the object by positive arguments, attempts to deny discrepant statements, and discrediting persons who advocate contradictory communications. However, the refutation of such arguments beforehand seems to represent the most effective countermeasure.

8. Finally, the profusion of investigations relating to the receiver's valuation of the author of the communication and its effect in promoting change also has great relevance for the therapeutic situation. In many studies it has been possible to prove that a positively valuated source achieved greater success in changing attitudes with the same communication than one who was negatively or neutrally valuated. Optimizing the therapist–client relationship by building trust and communicating interest, involvement, and understanding, but also by expertise, will favorably shape the conditions for an attempt at change (for a comprehensive presentation, see Johnson and Matross, 1975).

In contrast to the relatively well-standardized techniques of behavior therapy, the methods with which the therapist can systematically and reliably influence the client's attitudinal systems by communicating with him are quite vague, and contain a degree of uncertainty which can be only imperfectly made up for through "therapeutic experience" and "tact." This is certainly due to the temporary shortcomings in basic research, and also to the long period of latency needed to convert this area of psychology into applicable form regarding its therapeutic implications.

3.3. Changes Based on Active Participation

The second basic strategy for changing beliefs, attitudes, and intentions is instruction relating to active participation in selected situations.

This strategy is meant to provide the participant with new opportunities for receiving information through his direct observation of certain objects, people, or events. In contrast to the attempts at persuasion through communication, the individual can directly form new descriptive beliefs about relevant subjects and can initiate inferential processes based on them without being dependent on others as sources of information. In this way many therapeutic techniques, especially those of behavior therapy, attempt not only to establish certain behaviors in critical situations, but also to produce changes of attitude.

Thus, changes can be promoted in the desired direction by arranging a series of situations in which the client performs a behavior which accords with the target belief but contradicts his current belief (so-called counterattitudinal behaviors). On the other hand, inadaptive beliefs and attitudes can be corrected if the client is exposed to experiences which contradict his viewpoints, expectations, and valuations. It is sometimes maintained that this procedure is more effective and economical than that which aims at changing attitudes directly; in this general form, however, the assertion is not tenable (Fishbein & Ajzen, 1975).

In the method of active participation, something often neglected is to specify precisely which beliefs are targeted for change in the client. Another considerable difficulty can arise from the therapist's limited control over the situation in which the learning processes are supposed to take place; this means there is no guarantee that the client will be confronted with the relevant information, or that he will take correct notice of it and retain it. Indeed, many discrepant results can be explained by the fact that information is taken in which produces an opposite effect. Moreover, as has been emphasized several times and also applies here, even if changes in beliefs and attitudes do take place, they do not unconditionally lead to changed intentions or to changes in future behavior. In this case the precautions mentioned under point 3.2.2. must be taken.

In spite of numerous unsolved problems regarding the exploration of human attitudes, this part of psychology is also beginning to provide important incentives for therapeutic tasks. However, we are still far removed from a technology for changing attitudes which might be learned with relative ease and practical application.

As Mahoney (1974) writes,

> We have devoted invaluable human skills and material resources in efforts to change beliefs about the relative merits of deodorants and political candidates. Meanwhile, our clinics, hospitals and homes are inhabited by individuals whose existence and daily well-being are painfully jeopardized by dysfunctional beliefs. (p. 238)

One can only agree with him in stating that a reorientation of the research in this area would be of great benefit.

Perhaps our contribution will lead to something more than simply further disputes as to whether it is an attitudinal change or a behavioral change that is required for this purpose.

References

Abelson, R. P., & Kanouse, D. E. Subjective acceptance of verbal generalization. In S. Feldman (Ed.), *Cognitive consistency*. New York: Academic, 1966.

Abelson, R. P., & Rosenberg, M. J. Symbolic psycho-logic: A model of attitudinal cognitions. *Behavioral Science*, 1958, *3*, 1–13.

Allport, G. W. Attitudes. In G. Murchison (Ed.), *Handbook of social psychology*. Worcester, Mass.: Clark University Press, 1935.

Allport, G. W. The historical background of modern social psychology. In C. Lindzey & E. Aronson (Eds.), *Handbook of social psychology* (Vol. 1, 2nd ed.). Reading, Mass.: Addison-Wesley, 1968.

Beck, A. T. *Cognitive therapy and the emotional disorders*. New York: International Universities Press, 1976.

Benninghaus, H. Soziale Einstellungen und soziales Verhalten. In G. Albrecht, H. Daheim, & F. Sack (Eds.), *Soziologie*. Opladen, 1973, 671–707.

Borkovec, T. D. The role of expectancy and physiological feedback in fear research: A review with special reference to subject characteristics. *Behavior Therapy*, 1973, *4*, 491–505.

Böttcher, H. F., & Kässner-Reitler, R. Einige Bemerkungen zum Begriff der Fehleinstellung. In M. Vorwerg (Ed.), *Psychologische Probleme der Einstellungs- und Verhaltensänderung*. Berlin: Deutscher Verlag der Wissenschaften, 1971.

Breger, L. The ideology of behaviorism. In L. Breger (Ed.), *Clinical-cognitive psychology*. Englewood Cliffs, N. J.: Prentice-Hall, 1969.

Breger, L., & McGaugh, J. L. Critique and reformulation of "learning-theory" approaches to psychotherapy and neurosis. *Psychological Bulletin*, 1965, *63*, 338–358.

Campbell, D. T. Social attitudes and other organized behavioral dispositions. In S. Koch (Ed.), *Psychology: A study of a science* (Vol. 6). New York: McGraw-Hill, 1963.

Chapman, L. J., & Chapman, J. P. Atmosphere effect reexamined. *Journal of Experimental Psychology*, 1959, *58*, 220–226.

DeSoto, C. B., & Albrecht, F. Cognition and social orderings. In R. P. Abelson, E. Aronson, W. J. McGuire, T. M. Newcomb, M. J. Rosenberg, & P. H. Tannenbaum (Eds.), *Theories of cognitive consistency: A sourcebook*. Chicago: Rand McNally, 1968.

Doob, L. W. The behavior of attitudes. *Psychological Review*, 1947, *54*, 135–156.

Ellis, A. *Reason and emotion in psychotherapy*. New York: Lyle Stuart, 1962.

Fietkau, H.-J. *Die Einstellung in der Psychotherapie*. Salzburg: Müller, 1977.

Fishbein, M. A behavior theory approach to the relations between beliefs about an object and the attitude toward the object. In M. Fishbein (Ed.), *Readings in attitude theory and measurement*. New York: Wiley, 1967.

Fishbein, M. The prediction of behavior from attitudinal variables. In C. D. Mortensen, & K. K. Sereno (Eds.), *Advances in communication research*. New York: Harper & Row, 1973.

Fishbein, M., & Ajzen, I. Attitudes and opinions. *Annual Review of Psychology*, 1972, *23*, 487–544.

Fishbein, M., & Ajzen, I. *Belief, attitude, attention and behavior*. Reading, Mass.: Addison-Wesley, 1975.

Frank, J. D. *Persuasion and healing*. New York: The Johns Hopkins University Press, 1974.

Freedman, J. L., Carlsmith, J. M., & Sears, D. O. *Social psychology*. Englewood Cliffs, N. J.: Prentice-Hall, 1970.

Green, B. F. Attitude measurement. In G. Lindzey (Ed.), *Handbook of social psychology, Vol. 1: Theory and method*. Reading, Mass.: Addison-Wesley, 1954.

Greenwald, A. L. (Ed.). *Psychological foundations of attitudes*. New York: Academic, 1968.

Herkner, W. *Einführung in die Sozialpsychologie*. Bern: Huber, 1975.

Hovland, C. I. (Ed.). *The order of presentation in persuasion*. New Haven: Yale University Press, 1957.

Hovland, C. I., & Janis, I. L. (Eds.). *Personality and persuasibility*. New Haven: Yale University Press, 1959.

Hovland, C. I., Janis, I. L., & Kelley, H. H. *Communication and persuasion*. New Haven: Yale University Press, 1953.

Janis, I. L., & Feshbach, S. Effects of fear-arousing communications. *Journal of Abnormal and Social Psychology*, 1953, *48*, 78–92.

Janis, I. L., & Feshbach, S. Personality differences associated with responsiveness to fear-arousing communication. *Journal of Personality*, 1954, *23*, 154–166.

Johnson, D. W., & Matross, R. P. Attitude modification methods. In F. H. Kanfer & A. P. Goldstein (Eds.), *Helping people change*. New York: Pergamon, 1975.

Kanfer, F. H. *The many faces of self-control, or, behavior modification changes its focus*. Paper presented at the Eighth International Banff Conference, Banff, Scotland, 1976.

Kaplan, K. J., & Fishbein, M. The source of beliefs, their saliency, and prediction of attitude. *Journal of Social Psychology*, 1969, *38*, 63–74.

Katz, D. Some final considerations about experimentation in social psychology. In G. L. McClintock (Ed.), *Experimental social psychology*. New York: Holt, 1972.

Kiesler, C. A. *The psychology of commitment*. New York: Academic, 1971.

Koch, S. Psychology and emerging conceptions of knowledge as unitary. In C. W. Wann (Ed.), *Behaviorism and phenomenology*. Chicago: University of Chicago Press, 1964.

Krech, D., Crutchfield, R. S., & Bellachey, E. L. *Individual in society*. New York: McGraw-Hill, 1962.

Lackenmeyer, G. W. Experimentation: Mis-understood methodology in psychological and social-psychological research. *American Psychologist*, 1970, *25*, 617–624.

Lazarus, A. A. *Behavior therapy and beyond*. New York: McGraw-Hill, 1971.

Locke, E. A. Is "behavior therapy" behavioristic? *Psychological Bulletin*, 1971, *76*, 318–327.

London, P. *The modes and morals of psychotherapy*. New York: Holt, Rinehart & Winston, 1964.

Lumsdale, A. A., & Janis, I. L. Resistance to a "counter-propaganda" produced by one-sided and two-sided "propaganda" presentation. *Public Opinion Quarterly*, 1973, *17*, 311–318.

Mahoney, M. J. *Cognition and behavior modification*. Cambridge, Mass.: Ballinger, 1974.

McGuire, W. J. Personality and susceptibility to social influence. In E. F. Bagotta & W. W. Lambert (Eds.), *Handbook of personality theory and research*. Chicago: Rand McNally, 1968.

McGuire, W. J. The nature of attitudes and attitude change. In B. Lindzey & E. Aronson (Eds.), 1969.

Murray, E. J., & Jacobson, L. I. The nature of learning in traditional and behavioral psychotherapy. In A. E. Bergin & S. L. Garfield (Eds.), *Handbook of psychotherapy and behavior change*. New York: Wiley, 1971.

Nelson, E. Attitudes. *Journal of General Psychology*, 1939, *21*, 367–436.

Ostrom, T. M. The emergence of attitude theory: 1930–1950. In A. E. Greenwald et al. (Eds.), Psychological foundations of attitudes. New York: Academic, 1968.

Rapoport, D. The structure of psychoanalytical theory: A systematic attempt. New York: International Universities Press, 1960.

Rosen, M. A., & Wyer, R. S. Some further evidence for the "Socrates effect" using a subjective probability model of cognitive organization. Journal of Social Psychology, 1972, 24, 490–494.

Rosenberg, M. J., & Hovland, C. I. Cognitive, affective and behavioral components of attitudes. In C. I. Hovland & M. J. Rosenberg (Eds.), Attitude organization and change. New Haven: Yale University Press, 1966.

Roth, E. Einstellung als Determinanten individuellen Verhaltens. Die Analyse eines Begriffes und seiner Bedeutung für die Persönlichkeits-psychologie. Göttingen: Hogrefe, 1967.

Seiler, T. B. Kognitive Strukturen und kognitive Persönlichkeitstheorien. In T. B. Seiler (Ed.), Kognitive Strukturiertheit. Stuttgart: Kohlhammer, 1973.

Seligman, M. E. P. Helplessness. San Francisco: W. H. Freeman, 1975.

Sherif, M., & Hovland, C. I. Social judgment: Assimilation and contrast effects in communication and attitude change. New Haven: Yale University Press, 1961.

Six, B. Norm und Verhalten. In R. Bergler (Ed.), Sauberkeit, Norm-Verhalten Persönlichkeit. Stuttgart: Klett, 1974.

Tannenbaum, P. H. The congruity principle revisited: Studies in the reduction, induction and generalization of persuasion. In L. Berkowitz (Ed.), Advances in experimental social psychology. New York: Academic Press, 1967.

Thurstone, L. L. The measurement of attitudes. Journal of Abnormal and Social Psychology, 1939, 26, 249–269.

Tittle, C. R., & Hill, R. J. Attitude measurement and prediction of behavior: An evaluation of conditions and measurement techniques. Sociometry, 1967, 30, 199–213.

Triandis, H. G. Attitude and attitude change. New York: Wiley, 1971.

Wason, P. C. The effect of self-contradiction on fallacious reasoning. Quarterly Journal of Experimental Psychology, 1964, 16, 30–34.

Wicker, A. W. Attitudes as actions: The relationship of verbal and overt behavioral responses to attitude objects. Journal of Social Issues, 1969, 25, 41–78.

4

The Problem of Attribution and Cognitive Therapy

JÜRGEN OTTO

1. Introduction

The following chapter, which presents an introduction to the research on attribution and its clinical relevance, is divided into three main sections. In the first part, the classical theories of attribution by Heider (1958)— to whom the theory of attribution is often attributed—Jones and Davis (1965), and Kelley (1967) will be presented with regard to its sphere of application in therapy. In the second part, those aspects of the classical theories will be described towards which the interest of recent research has been directed, whereby those aspects in particular which seem relevant for a therapeutic process will be emphasized, such as certain forms of cognitive processes of judgment, aspects of verbal usage, and emotional disorders. In the third and final section, investigations which have become part of the clinical experimental literature under the heading "attribution therapy," will be specifically presented in detail.

2. Classical Theories of Attribution: General Introduction and Comparison of the Theories

The theory of attribution developed out of a branch of social psychology, the perception of persons, which adopted Brunswik's "lens model" (1934) and investigated phenomena such as the "primacy effect" (Asch,

JÜRGEN OTTO • Institut für Psychologie, Freie Universität Berlin, D-1 Berlin 41, Bundesrepublik Deutschland.

1946) and "self-presentation" (Goffman, 1959) in interaction. Two research traditions were of particular significance. These dealt, on the one hand, with the characteristics of persons who had good critical judgment (symbolic interactionism, Mead, 1934; components of overall judgmental accuracy, Cronbach, 1955; REP-test, Kelly, 1955) and, on the other, who were interested in the influence of needs upon perception ("subception," Lazarus, 1954). It was also found possible to develop an alternative presentation, for which the therapeutically relevant topic of emotion is central, out of the later theory on the self-attribution of arousal states (Schachter, Bem; cf. Hastorf, Schneider, & Polefka, 1970). Here one might recall the classical theories of emotion (Wundt; James and Lange, Cannon, Lindsley) as well as the critique of Schachter's "two-factor theory" (which will be mentioned briefly in the third section) and its continuation of Lazarus's "cognitive-emotive theory." In an essay on self-regulation, Lazarus (1954) suggests combining his "coping model" with the attribution theory of Weiner.

Like other cognitive processes of selective attention or stimulus categorization, a process of attribution reduces the amount of information for the individual and, in a "naive" way, allows him to explain and predict behavior. As Jones (1979) points out, the differences between the theory of attribution, which claims to explain reality, and the theory of consistency, which claims to attain a consistent impression of reality, are perhaps trivial. Kelley stresses that attribution encompasses only a limited area of social perception, and is distinct from evaluations and interactions. Causal interpretations, attributed characteristics and intentions, and perceived trustworthiness are all part of estimations of value, and of evaluational, supervisory, and punitive behaviors. Causal inference ("whyness") and descriptive and explicative constructs ("whatness") of behavior are at issue here.

In general, three stages can be differentiated (Shaver, 1975): the observation of behavior (also as self-observation), the evaluation of intention, and, finally, the process of dispositional attribution.

All classical theories must proceed under the following assumptions; a minimal determinism of behavior, and a need to explain and predict the behavior or the environment in a systematic way. As motivational factors, one could cite Festinger's processes of social comparison or Schachter's (1959) experiments concerning affiliation. For the systematic character of explanation or prediction, one could cite the structure of the theory of Heider, Jones and Davis, Bem, and Schachter and Singer. An additional assumption is the validity of attribution relative to the causes of behavior, that is, that an attribution has important consequences. The later articles on therapy (e.g., Storms & Nisbett, 1970) refer to the consequences of the choice of causes.

Attribution is applied knowledge for the person. According to Kelley (1971), attributions are neither more nor less rational—rather, on closer analysis, even irrational attributions prove to be meaningful. In this matter a characteristic bias toward controlling the environment is the basis of the causal need. Thus, for example, in evaluating the behavior of other persons, too little attention is paid to external causes (contextual factors) (Jones & Nisbett, 1971). Actions are too strongly related to the self (Kelley, 1971). Negative information is weighted more heavily, as in general in forming impressions (Kanouse & Hanson, 1971).

The questions which the individual theories attempt to answer are different. The "philosopher" in Heider's theory asks himself, "What must a perceiver consider, before attributing a given action to an underlying personal disposition?" The "information processor" of Jones and Davis asks himself, "What are the basic steps in the process of dispositional attribution?" And Kelley's "social scientist" asks himself, "How can an attribution to a personal disposition be distinguished from some other attribution?" Proceeding from the common assumption that behavior is a consequence of personal and environmental factors (determinism), the individual theories make different statements about the stages of the attribution process. For the observational phase, both the personality factors and the environmental factors are defined differently. The personality factors are, according to Heider, intention, exertion, and skill; according to Jones and Davis, intention, knowledge about behavioral effects, and practicability; Kelley formulates no elements apart from intention. The environmental factors are, according to Heider, difficulty of the task, chance, compulsion, and opportunity; according to Jones and Davis, difficulty of the task, chance, compulsion, and situational and role demands; according to Kelley, entities (difficulty, chance), situation (opportunity), and other persons (role pressures).

As the second phase, Heider names three factors for the evaluation of intention: equifinality, local causation, and exertion; whereas Jones and Davis assume that the actor expresses his existent intentions and knows of their consequences. Kelley emphasizes the predictability of the consequences. Three distinct meanings can be differentiated for the dispositional attribution of the third phase. These are, according to Jones and Davis, descriptive; according to Kelley, predictive; and, according to Heider, causal. In this last case and relative to this psychological process, it is a matter of an interesting philosophical "mistake of categories" (Ryle, 1949)—personality dispositions are constructs and not "persons" as actual causes.

The historical background, the purpose, the requirements, and the stages of attribution having been presented, and the theories introduced by way of comparison, these are now to be briefly and individually described.

2.1. Heider's Naive Phenomenology (1958)

Proceeding from Brunswik's probabilistic functionalism, Heider developed his "naive" behavioral analysis pursuant to his experiments on phenomenological causality (Heider & Simmel, 1944). The role of the dimension of causality is central in his approach. Piaget (1975) describes how the concept of causality developed.

Heider's analysis conceives the effect of an action as the additive function of forces in the environment and forces in the person, which are themselves the combined multiple of competence and exertion:

Effect = f(environmental force + personal force [competence × exertion])

The environmental force is expressed particularly in the difficulty of a task, and, in combination with the assessment of capability, it forms the possible "can"-components of an action (whether it is at all possible); whereas exertion, in the direct sense as intention and in the qualitative sense as effort, forms the "attempt"-components (how it is carried out), as a more extensive approach used in the "naive" analysis.

However, one of the most important decisions for the observer remains the choice between causation through the environment or the person.

As part of intentional causality (components of exertion), personal causality is viewed as intended and as different from interpersonal causality, which refers not only to external but also to unintended effects, and enters into the evaluation process as an interference factor.

This is not a systematic theory which permits predictions. An elaboration of the theory and the limitations connected with it in this respect has been carried out by Jones and Davis (1965).

2.2. Jones and Davis: Correspondence Theory (1965)

This theory likewise proceeds by tracing behavioral effects to their causes; it limits itself, however, to the attribution to the person, that is, to the area of internal causality.

"Correspondence" describes the extent to which (1), an intention can describe the behavior, (2), a disposition is responsible for the intention, and (3), a disposition can through implication describe the behavior. It is postulated that the correspondence varies directly with the hedonistic relevance and with the personal relationship to the observer, and inversely with the social desirability and extraordinary effects of the behavior of the person observed ("choice circles"). Thus, the respective informational value lies in the following points: The hedonistic relevance means that the actions of a person can be rewarding or "dear" to the observer;

they appeal to him directly, and thus call forth more extensive attention, which consequently also reduces the number of unusual effects. The personal relationship means that the presence of the observer has an effect on the actor which leads him to act in certain ways. This is a special case of hedonistic relevance, and, at the same time, represents a bias arising through the motives of the observer. Social desirability signifies that "normal" behavioral patterns express little about persons. "To act out of character" has high information value. Noncommon effects mean that, on the basis that the person performing the action freely chooses his behavior, the results unique to a particular action pattern represent valuable information.

In this original version, the theory refers only to one unit of information, one act. In 1971 Jones and Goethals (1971) put forth a more refined theory regarding the explanation of primacy effects and recency effects and the sequence of information in the process of attribution. They postulated processes of attention, distraction, and assimilation, on the one hand, and of readiness of recall and effects of contrast, contents, and context, on the other.

2.3. Kelley: Attribution Theory (1967, 1973)

The principle of covariation between possible causes and effects, which originates historically in J. S. Mill's method of difference (according to Heider), is the central theme of this theory, which attempts to explain the attribution of the behavioral patterns of others as well as of one's own feeling states.

Covariation is viewed in this, as a "naive" analysis of variance relative to three factors: person (who attributes), time and modality of the attribution, and entity (object of the attribution), and thereby is distinct from Heider's person–environment differentiation. An effect is attributed to the dimension which varies with the effect. Several observations on a *first level of evaluation* are required. The "object" is seen as a cause if the effect appears only in it, is the same for various persons, and is consistent for each person, through time as well as for different kinds of interaction with the "object." An effect is attributed to a person, if it occurs in this person only, if it takes place in the interaction of this person with various things, and if it is consistent.

Adults have a repertoire of abstract ideas about the interaction of causal factors—a causal schema, in the sense of Piaget, which helps to structure minimal information—wherein it is a matter of operational schemata on a *second level of evaluation*. A causal schema is a general concept which the person has regarding ways in which different causes call forth a particular effect. According to Singer (1968), it is a matter of existing assumptions about how the world is probably organized.

A frequently adopted schema, "multiple sufficient causes," refers to the experiencing of multiple causes leading to the same effect, and another schema, "multiple necessary causes," refers to the case of multiple causes which must come together in order to produce an effect.

If it is a matter of an intense effect which is to be evaluated, the person involved in the process of making attributions will probably adopt the schema "multiple necessary causes." However, if the causes are intense, the "multiple sufficient causes" schema is applied; if they are weak, then the "multiple necessary causes" schema is applied.

The contribution of a cause to an effect is devalued by the discounting principle, if other plausible causes exist. If, however, an effect occurs in the presence of a possibly obstructing condition, then the opposite, the augmentation principle, is applied; the promoting cause is rated more highly.

If the person making the attribution is able to include in his evaluation process the boundary between the emergence and the absence of the effect, and can weigh the causes against each other, then he can use the "compensatory causes" schema. If, in addition, he can gradually modulate the effect, then he probably assumes that the effect becomes more distinct with the cumulative intensity of relevant causes. According to this "graded additive effects" schema, a person's competence is typically derived from his maximal achievement. On a third evaluative level, not only are the emergence or nonemergence and the degree of emergence of the causal factors taken into consideration, but sets of causal factors which are qualitatively different are compared. A frequent explanation of this is that some part of the person and some part of the stimulus explain the effect of "sufficient causes." If precise knowledge about the circumstances of the effect is available, then the "person–entity pairing" schema can be completed, as long as the effect is to be based on the unique concurrence of person and object. More imprecise generalizations are possible here, pointing in the direction of the effect being somewhat more uniform for different persons than it is for different things. This is the case, for instance, when effects which are dependent on verbal usage relate to all persons but only to a certain number of things, that is, "person–entity" schema for the generalization "person–verb entities." If the object is, likewise, another person, then the judgments become somewhat more complex; it is a matter of social schemata (according to DeSoto).

Within the meaning of a causal schema, a person can produce an effect either as a person or as an entity (reflexivity), or if A as person and B as entity cause an effect, then this leads to the conclusion in the causal schema that A as entity and B as person can also produce the effect (symmetry).

When A as person and B as entity produce the effect, and, further, when B as person and C as entity give rise to the same effect, then it follows within the causal schema of the naive analysis, that A as person and C as entity can also trigger the effect (transitivity). The symmetrical attribution schema is thus broken up into subgroups, whose boundaries can be specified by further conclusions.

There are only a few possibilities of interpreting the world in a meaningful way, and the methods of the lay person and of the scientist lie on a continuum of preciseness. The analysis of variance is an ideal model. The lay person is often underestimated on two points: that he sees the causes as independent, and that he does not deal with any gradations of causes and effects.

In this, he is at the mercy of the bias of colloquial speech, which in its verbs attributes actions to persons and feelings to entities. This "bias" in the verbs and similar central factors are to be discussed in the sections that follow.

3. Aspects of the More Recent Attribution Research Relevant to Clinical Practice

The influence of different perspectives and of linguistic usage on attribution will be described first; this will be followed by self-attribution and, especially, attributions which promote different methods of treatment.

Whereas the first two points are relevant for therapy in general (information about social interaction, therapy as a primarily verbal occurrence), the last two points are already especially directed toward therapeutic procedure, as is to be explained and criticized in the third section.

Naturally, the formulation of achievement motivation in terms of attribution theory by Weiner (1972) is also relevant for therapy as achievement-oriented behavior. His model summarizes the historical theory of attribution to the effect that it differentiates between an internal/external causal dimension, which determines the affect, and a stable/unstable causal dimension, which determines the expectation. It also seems interesting that Miller, Galanter, & Pribram (1960) differentiate between value, which they ascribe to the image, and intention, which they ascribe to the plan, in their problem-solving model relating to motivation.

Jones and Nisbett (1971) were able to point out the cognitive factors responsible for the tendency of the actor to emphasize situational factors and of the observer to emphasize personality dispositions in attribution. They distinguish between two kinds of data in the process of attribution: (1) data about effects, which relate to the kind of action itself, its results in the environment, and the experiences of the actor in the situation, and (2) data about causes, which relate to the cause in the environment (stimuli, task difficulty) and the intentions.

In comparison with the observer, the actor has more information relating to his experiences, his intentions, and his history. For this reason, the behavior is evaluated on a different scale of comparison for actor and for observer.

The action—its topography, rhythm, style, and content—is more striking for the observer than for the actor. From the observer's point of view, the environment is stable and contextual, but the action is figural. The actor, however, no longer needs to observe his behavior, and pays more attention to the surroundings in which he is acting. If the observer is, moreover, still active during his observation, then his cognitive capacity for processing is further impaired, and he comes to even cruder simplifications. In many cases the observer still tends toward an attribution to personality dispositions, even though this violates the rules of phenomenological causality of Jones and Davis and of Kelley.

The observer acts like a bad theorist of personality characteristics (according to Mischel, 1968), who bases himself not only on mistakes of information processing and lack of information, but also on the factors of distorted random sample, influence of his own behavior on the observed behavior, striving for consistency, verbal biases, implicit theories of personality (Cronbach, 1955), and evasion of possible refutations of his views.

The actor, on the contrary, behaves approximately as does Mischel (1968); he categorizes his behavior into triggering and sustaining conditions.

In making his attributions, the individual, as observer or as actor, is an enhancer of his own value, a retainer of equilibrium, a reducer of dissonance, and a liberator from reactance, besides being a seeker of truth; all of which, according to Beck and Ellis, are "incorrect" cognitions which can become relevant in therapy.

Attributions are forthcoming even after only a very few observations. Referring to the discussions of Kelley, when information is lacking about the generality of a relationship of persons or objects, individuals make normative assumptions of a psychological kind about the generality, which allow them to form attributions (Kanouse, 1971).

In recent years the "point-of-view effect" has become a major topic of research. Storms (1973) showed in an ingenious test that under conditions of reorientation, when subjects saw a new point of view on videotape, the differences of attribution between actors and observers were exactly reversed.

Taylor and Fiske (1975) proved that point of view or attention determines what information is salient and that perceptually salient information is then overrepresented in subsequent causal explanations. Taylor and Fiske (1978), in summarizing the research on this phenomenon, concluded that information about salient stimuli is more available and that availability mediates the attention–causality relationship. Or, in other words, "I realize I have called one error as an explanation for another, but the anchor-adjustment heuristic appears to be a more basic cognitive phenomenon than the fundamental attribution error itself, and it ties the latter into a broad literature on conservatism in judgment and decision making" (Jones, 1979, p. 115).

Through his research on evaluation, Abelson (Abelson & Kanouse, 1966) was able to show that inductive conclusions occur more rapidly for objects than for subjects of sentences, and deductive conclusions more rapidly for subjects than for objects. This demonstrates a bias for attributions of persons, as opposed to attributions of entities. General attributions are forthcoming when the action is first generalized to a larger class of objects and then explained through intention, etc., as if it were explained first and then generalized.

Before an attribution is made, the process involved is very susceptible to the influence of chance events, such as choice of words and situational aspects. Once an attribution has been made, however, new information is scarcely taken into account.

The language, particularly the verbs, can have a general influence, in that its description of events and actions contains implicit attributions (for example, I "have" a body, or I "am" a body).

Verbs differ in their implicit quantifiers, which influence the processing of what they assert when a generalization is made; thus, for example, "to avoid" refers to everything, and "to buy" refers only to some things. These different implicit quantifiers have an influence on the suitability of the verb for inductive or deductive conclusions.

Moreover, through its level of description, the language determines the level of generality of the processing, which is also correspondingly retained in the explanation of the action. The interest in those words that are used to describe affects (lists of characteristics) which discriminate between attributions, moved to the center of Weiner's research on attribution (Workshop, Technical University of Berlin, 1976).

Particularly relevant for therapy is the case in which one's own behavior is to be attributed (Nisbett & Valins, 1971). Just as we draw conclusions about attitudes and dispositions in others through observing their behavior, we also get to know our own attitudes (ourselves) through observing ourselves (Bem).

We have no a priori independent intuitive knowledge about our attitudes and feelings, not even directly about the causes of our behavior. Many aspects of our self-image have often been learned incorrectly. We acquire knowledge only when our behavior is stimulated through our own motives ("tact"), and does not appear to be triggered by situational pressure ("mand").

This distinction between causal factors which are intrinsically connected with the stimulus (one's own motives) and those which are extrinsic (circumstantial) is quite essential to the perception of the self (and to therapy), and must not be confused with the differentiations made by Kelley (external-internal) or Jones and Nisbett (situational-dispositional). With these, it is a matter of the separation between environmental and personality factors; whereas in stimulus-related versus extrinsic (circumstantial) factors, the accentuation of different aspects of the environment is involved.

Here emotions are often significantly determined by the attribution of the autonomous behavioral components (Nisbett & Schachter, 1966; Schachter & Singer, 1962; Storms & Nisbett, 1970; Valins 1966; Valins & Ray, 1967). This has an influence even when its share of information (as cause and degree of arousal) is given only verbally and is even incorrect, as will be shown. Here the emotion is to be seen as the most striking event of a longer behavioral sequence, that of mastery (coping). However, this process is not to be conceived of as passive, but as an active testing of hypotheses (problem solving; Dörner, 1976). Behavior is often an attempt at validation, and not a reflection of an attitude. It seems to be valid that knowledge or belief about one element of the problem situation—behavior, causes, consequences, emotions about the object of the goal—distorts the perception of all the others. Up to now, the cause has more often been investigated as the independent variable and the emotions as the dependent variable. In general, a higher explanatory value is ascribed to the approach of attribution theory, against the background of Bem's theory of self-perception, than is ascribed to the explanation according to dissonance theory as defined by Festinger.

Processes of attribution are involved in the origin of emotional disorders, and must be taken into consideration in therapy and be meaningfully employed (Valins & Nisbett, 1971). In doing this, the attribution of the client has to be called into question as a first step. Very often the behavioral disorder is erroneously ascribed to some dispositional attribution, rather than to reversible learning processes. Certainly a correct logical attribution is often forthcoming (R. D. Laing proved that the attributive systems of schizophrenics have an explanatory purpose), but a social comparison of the explanations does not ensue. Schachter (1959) characteristically started from investigations on affiliation. Suffering often results from an incorrect attribution—a well-known example is the attributive mistakes in the classroom in educational psychology: Pygmalion effect, late bloomer, (cf. Weiner, 1972)—particularly in the aftermath of burdensome explanations of unscientific therapies, which work with pompous, eschatological concepts (guilt, Oedipus complex, etc.) and can give rise to the symptoms they allege to explain. Here one should recall the words of Karl Kraus, "Psychoanalysis is the sickness which it purports to cure."

As a second step, the dispositional attributions must be converted into situational attributions, and these then lead to an improvement in the symptom. The current diagnosis of personality traits does not appear to be particularly inviting in this framework.

According to Nisbett and Valins's (1971) subcategories of situational causes "intrinsic" and "extrinsic" (see above), it is advisable in the therapeutic process first to attribute undesirable symptoms to an extrinsic cause—that this is not a matter of mere suggestions will be shown below—, for instance, when at the dentist Bertrand Russell reattributed his symptoms, which certainly stem from fear, to the injection of procaine in a solution with epinephrine, the classical Schachter stimulus, and was thus able to endure more pain. Accordingly, the arousal of acrophobics might be explained to them as the natural result of the optical perception of converging lines. Second, it is advisable to attribute desirable symptoms to an intrinsic cause. According to the reverse logic of the positive and negative placebo effect, the persons must be convinced that their achievement rests on a newly developed behavior and not on the circumstances of treatment (medication). The conversion must be made from an attribution to the stimulus to an attribution to the person. In order to facilitate this transition, drugs, from the start, should not be portrayed as having too strong an effect. Typical inferences of self-attribution are, entirely within the sense of Ellis's cognitive therapy, that the world is not so terrible (as a new evaluation of the stimulus situation), and that one was successful and is competent and can also behave better in the future (cf. Davison & Valins, 1969).

In general, the patient is offered solutions which correspond more to the "truths" as the therapist and scientist see them than to his own, his "naive" behavioral theory, according to Laucken (1974).

Actually we already have here the essence of attribution therapy. For a historical understanding, however, it is necessary briefly to present Schachter's "two-factor theory" of emotion.

4. Attribution Therapy

The theme of self-attribution is inseparably connected with the two-factor theory of emotion (Schachter & Singer, 1962), which forms the theoretical framework for models describing the effect of causal attributions on emotional reactions. For this reason, self-attribution will be briefly described, together with a critique, before the resulting investigations are detailed. It was thanks to these investigations, which became well known under the name of "false feedback" that the self-attribution approach came to develop a new interpretation of systematic desensitization. This led in turn to attribution therapy.

In his noted, classic experiment (Schachter & Singer, 1962)—together with Lazarus's coping model in Spielberger (1966)—based on activation theory in the psychology of emotions, only the situational knowledge of the subjects was very generally manipulated in an experiment with artificially induced arousal (epinephrine injection) through supernumerary behavior. The subjects reported correspondingly about anger or joy ("emotional plasticity").

Because of possible interfering factors, subsequent investigations were found necessary. Schachter and Wheeler (1962) were able to eliminate the interference factor of self-arousal by using a psychopharmacological "blocker." Singer (1963) and Latané and Schachter (1962) did the same for the interference factor of self-informing by the use of nonattributing rats. Weiner (1972), however, assumes that rudimentary attributive processes exist even in this species.

The criticism of Schachter (Wengle, 1975; Lang, 1973; Plutchik & Ay, 1967; Lazarus, 1968) served to clarify the following aspects: Some results (Valins & Ray, 1967) could not be replicated; Schachter's cognitive-evaluative system is too slow for rapid changes in emotions; the experimental procedure (design, measurement, injection) leaves something to be desired; a one-dimensional arousal was assumed, the actual physiological pattern was not recorded, and the labeling aspect rather than the controlling aspect of the cognitive activity was emphasized—that is, the cart was put before the horse (according to Lazarus). The subjects were made insecure, were aroused and made suggestible (Zillmann, 1978). Their attention was manipulated or they were brought to a state of heightened readiness for imitation. Mandler (1975, pp. 92–93, 105), for instance, weakened the critiques of Plutchik and Ax (1967), Ax (1971), and Lazarus (1968). In the course of discussion very little attention has been paid to the interaction between real and feigned arousal (cf. Harris & Katkin 1975, Liebhart, 1978).

The subsequent experiments on false feedback investigated the influence of different attributive sets on the emotional experience (cognitions which applied to the source of arousal were introduced as the matters to be explained). Nisbett and Schachter (1966) dispensed with the trick of injection and allowed the possibility of attributing the arousal of fear to drugs or to the expectation of electroshock. The dependent variable was the verbal report (self-report) concerning fear. And in fact the subjects in one experimental group allowed themselves to be convinced that their natural arousal through the expectation of shock had an external cause (drug).

In their early article "Toward an Attribution Therapy," Ross, Rodin, and Zimbardo (1969) manipulated the possibilities of attributing the arousal of fear to shock expectation or noise (instead of the placebo condition of the above experiment), and set up the behavioral indicator "occupation with a puzzle" as the dependent variable; with respect to this variable, through which the shock could be avoided, obvious differences between the experimental groups became apparent. Besides Schachter's two components "arousal" and "cognition," the authors considered their "naive" causal link to be essential, designating it as the third component of emotions. They therefore paid careful attention in their investigation to the temporal relationship (contiguity as "causality") of physiological arousal and cognitions. They intended their experiment (misattribution model) to be understood as a therapeutic model or experimental analogy for the reduction of fear through the manipulation of attribution. Besides irrelevant cognitions, a concealment of the link between arousal and cognition contributed to the reduction of fear. The authors recommended the following therapeutic procedures: (1) to attribute the state of the body in critical situations to alternative aspects of the external situation (in acrophobics, to the converging lines; see above), and (2) artificially to introduce into the situation a new cause to which the client should attribute his arousal, such as placebos, whose effect can then be taken as the cause for the fear and, in addition, are still under the patient's control.

Subsequent to this experiment, Davison and Valins (1969) proceeded in their experiment on the presumption of identical attribution systems (sets), and on the presumption of refined replication relative to necessary concealments of the design of the experiment.

In an early investigation concerning shock expectation (Nisbett & Schachter, 1966) the authors emphasized the active search for information during a self-attributed visceral reaction. Proceeding from the problem of the transition from drug-induced changes to a state without medication, the authors developed the hypothesis, in accordance with attribution theory, that persons after being told that a supposed drug which had caused the behavioral changes in them had been only a placebo, would retain these behavioral changes for a longer period of time than persons who continued to believe in the effect of the drug. In an analogous experiment, these hypotheses were tested and confirmed by measuring the tolerance of pain for electroshocks, providing a placebo which was supposed to be a medication, and artificially lowering the shock intensity during a second phase of testing the tolerance for pain, in order to make it appear the effect of the supposed drug. Among the tests were further included communicating to half the subjects in the experiment that they had really only received a placebo, and in a third procedure, measurement of the reactions for the threshold of pain without further drugs. It was supposed that subjects in the experiment who had to attribute their behavioral change during the second threshold measurement to themselves rather than to the drug ("disabused," in the sense of Nisbett & Valins, 1971), would subsequently raise their threshold for pain, the other subjects would not do this; and so it proved.

The investigators supposed three intermediary processes, which begin when the person determines that the behavioral change was caused by himself: first, reevaluation, that the shocks were not so painful as was first thought; second, change of expectation and of aspiration that future behavior will be similar to that at threshold II and that one is motivated to endure stronger shocks; and third, emergence of positive affects, pride in one's own achievement.

Referring to the similarity of their data to that on attitudinal changes (Bem), the authors discuss the use of drugs in psychotherapy and their implications for attribution theory, to the effect that drugs, rather than the individual's own behavior, are considered a cause for his improvement in psychotherapy. With discontinuation, they note, a corresponding relapse ensues. They also critically consider the situationally oriented behavior therapy and its difficulties with the continuance of treatment effects, which could be, in part, contingent on neglect of the implications for attribution theory of the subjective perception that the causes for change are "private stimuli."

The interest of attribution theory was also directed to systematic desensitization and, commensurate with this technique, information relating to the degree of arousal was affected.

Valins (1966) used manipulated heart palpitations as internal stimuli as a source of nonveridical cognitive information for the rating of *Playboy* pictures. The "Valins effect"—namely, the phenomenon, that information, independent of reality, about unexpected physiological reactions generates the same effects as do procedures which produce real physiological changes—was to be made effective by replacing the muscular relaxation training in systematic desensitization (SD) in accordance with Wolpe (1958) through manipulating the cognitive representations within the framework of cognitive desensitization (and to explain the original SD).

Valins and Ray (1967) were able to manipulate the feedback (cognition) about slides of increasingly more threatening snakes and mounting shock intensity to such an extent (with the slides of snakes, the feedback remained constant) that snake phobias could be extinguished. The individual believes in his objective or nonobjective cognitions, which form the core of the behavioral change, and on which Valins places the major emphasis in his theory. In a subsequent informal inquiry, not one subject in the experiment expressed a conflict between incorrect and yet possibly correct information about his own arousal, which indicates the slight extent to which, on the average, emotional events are verbalized.

In the theoretical part of their recent investigation, Cohen, Meyer-Osterkamp, & Grusche (1974) engage in an emphatic criticism of this influential Valins–Ray study. They particularly emphasize the role played by discrepancies among the individual indicators of behavior (cognitive, psychological, behavioral) in the unsuccessful replication studies (Kent, Wilson, & Nelson, 1972; Rosen, Rosen, & Reid, 1972; Sushinsky & Bootzin, 1970), and report a reinterpretation of the theory on "cognitive" desensitization, as follows: The slides with the word "shock" are conditioned stimuli (CS) for electric shocks; the alternately presented pictures of snakes are, on the other hand, the signal for safety from these shocks, and thereby for a feeling which can reduce the originally released anxiety in the sense of reciprocal inhibition. They also see no new attribution therapy arising in connection with this.

The authors attempt to predict the effects of the manipulated feedback in their experiment (female subjects only!) on the basis of both contrast effects (firm establishment of the evaluation) and the effect of positive or negative evidence, within a theory about the level of adaptation (thereby actually leaving the framework of this work), rather than by means of an attribution theory. The experimental design used by Valins and Ray suggests contrastive processes (shock and slides); the design used by Cohen *et al.* suggests processes of assimilation (rest or shock). This also may be part of the cause for the unsuccessful replication.

A reduction of the phobia was expected in the experimental group who saw their anxiety in contrast to electric shocks (and not rest) and received evidence that the original anxiety reactions disappear in the course of the experiment (and do not remain unchanged). The results showed, however, that nine out of ten subjects from the group entitled "established stimulus 'rest,' evidence 'positive'" had the impression that their anxiety had been reduced in the course of the experiment. A uniform interpretation of the findings is very difficult.

The authors emphasize the role of discrepancies in the reaction pattern "anxiety," which also appears in their results, and deplore the absence of a theory about the interaction of the subsystems of "anxiety." This looks comforting in view of Lazarus's coping model (cf. Weinstein, Averill, Opton, & Lazarus, 1968).

Strong (1970) points out the contribution which the old classical attribution theories (Heider 1958, Jones & Davis 1965, Kelley 1967) make to counseling, in the behaviorist sense.

Self-knowledge as an important condition for behavior is understood to be verbal behavior, which describes other behavior. The self-concept consists of observations of one's own behavior (Bem). Attributions of intentions and dispositions as components of self-knowledge are interfered with by mistakes from three sources: (1) egocentrism, as an overestimation of the effects of the environment; (2) minimal data for the conclusions; and (3) hedonistic relevance (see above). The goal of counseling is to (1) increase the stability and subjective validity of the attributions, and (2) reduce the phenomenological guilt and anxiety. For example, the evaluative determinants of a new reference group can be analyzed by means of social-comparison processes.

Strong comes to the conclusion that counseling is restricted to the extent that it is able to influence behavior only when the capacities for observing and describing the behavior are not already severely disturbed.

Storms and Nisbett (1970) investigated the reattribution of the perceived source of arousal in insomnia. For one condition of arousal, in which the subjects were led to believe that a medication (in reality a placebo) triggers off arousal, it was predicted and confirmed that this group of insomniacs fell asleep faster than otherwise. This was the case because since they attributed their arousal to the medication rather than to their emotions, they were therefore less emotional, and fell asleep. The opposite hypothesis was formulated and confirmed for a corresponding condition of sedation.

Alternative explanations such as relief, disappointment, distraction of attention, bedtime behavior, as well as decrease in worry about insomnia, are not to be excluded. It seems essential, however, that the symptoms be externalized, or not interpreted pathologically: thus the vicious circle of symptoms, worry about the symptoms and, through this, intensification of the symptoms, is broken.

The individual often makes mistakes in ascribing causes, and then becomes the victim of these mistakes (cf. Kelley, 1967).

The paradoxical result, also found in other studies (Davison & Valins, 1969; Nisbett & Schachter, 1966; Valins & Ray, 1967; Zimbardo, Cohen, Weisenberg, Dworhin, & Firestone, 1966), concerning the cognitive manipulation of emotions also appeared here. The differences in the manipulated emotions, which were weaker in the self-report than they were on either the physiological or the behavioral level, cannot be explained.

Here it is already critically anticipated that precisely these discrepancies in an elaborate basic model of emotions (Lazarus) will make possible substantial access to an understanding of the emotional pattern (cf. Weinstein et al., 1968).

Without allowing this to further dampen their enthusiasm for reattribution therapy, and based on the fact that there was only a mild disorder, and a single therapeutic effort with but one technique and lacking a follow-up, Storms and Nisbett make the following therapeutic recommendations. First, offer nonemotional attributions for natural states of arousal, such as drawing the attention of the insomniacs to their higher baseline (according to Monroe, 1967). Second, convince the client in the first place that "just" one reattribution had caused his improvement, by the revealing of and subsequent self-attribution of placebo effects, similar to Davison and Valins (1969). Third, pay attention to possible consequences of suggestion within the framework of therapy as a process of persuasion. In reattribution, the placebo effects showed up in the opposite direction from that shown in suggestion. This might be owing to the fact that the subjects were not only exposed to the information (suggestion) by the conductor of the experiment but, in addition, had reliable experiences with their insomnia, and knew about their typical level of symptoms, which led to changed perceptions about them. Accordingly, Rickels, Lipman, and Raab (1966) found no placebo effects or effects of suggestion with patients who were experienced with their illness or with medications, but rather found only detrimental effects very much like the "paradoxical" results of reattribution.

Davison, Tsujimoto, & Glaros (1973), carried out their investigation in the area of attributional flexibility, relating it more specifically to the maintenance of behavioral change, and dealing only with the single aspect, from out of the heterogeneous phenomena of insomnia, of falling asleep.

As an enlargement upon the Davison–Valins design (1969, see above), an exercise in relaxation and a schedule for going to bed were inserted as a promoting factor additional to the treatment effect. These were supposed to serve as attribution anchors for behavioral change in the phase after treatment, once the true "medication effect" had been revealed.

After a treatment phase, the true "medication effect" was presented as (1) optimal for sleeping disorders, or (2) only minimal for the elimination of sleeping disorders. The maintenance of the behavioral change was supposed to be better for group (2), who could not attribute the effects to the drug (belief in inefficient medication and subsequent self-attribution), which proved to be the case.

The advantages of this field study, as opposed to the laboratory experiment by Davison and Valins (1969), lie in the fact that it took into account a genuine psychoactive drug in a minimal and an optimal dosage, a genuine change in behavior (instead of external manipulation of the shock intensity), and relevant behavior (falling asleep instead of tolerance for shock). Also, they worked in an ethically demanding way, and with only minimal deception regarding the experimental design.

Davison et al. (1973) clearly emphasize that their investigation is to be classed within the "attribution therapy style." But, on the one hand, the question of the clinical utility of attribution research (or systematic desensitization, see above) has not been clarified, and, on the other, the difference between statistical and clinical significance underscores the problematic nature of the concept of normality.

One should not design a treatment program according to these methods, but should be conscious of the fact that, for both client and therapist, explanation of the causes of therapeutic improvement is one of many factors involved in maintaining the behavioral change.

Liebhart (1976) well understands attribution to be the stabilization program for therapy and not a necessary condition for its effects. The range of the cognitive control of neurotic reactions has been overestimated. The influencing of attributions (technique of internalization) has only a subsidiary function. A function in the framework of attention processes and of the search for information is ascribed to attribution; the reproduction of learned responses depends upon similar mediating contextual stimuli, which can also be of a "private" nature and thus have transsituational presence. Stabilization can, therefore, be expected from the internal attributions of the effect of treatment (internalization).

In 1974 Liebhart (1974) was able to improve the discomforts of heart neurosis slightly by producing an external attribution (to a placebo) for a number of the symptoms. The present stabilization program (Liebhart, 1976), by means of internalization (internal attribution), is supposed to strengthen the improvement beyond the end of the manipulation which had been effected through externalization—that is, beyond the removal of the placebo. In addition to the well-known internal/external factor and the effects of feedback, Liebhart includes factors from attribution research (also, stable/instable) and the control/noncontrol dimension. The improvement is (not) maintained if the patient ascribes it causally to controllable (uncontrollable) factors.

The very accessible attributive manipulation arrived through the mail. In the old investigations, the manipulation of the instable/stable dimension is confounded with the manipulation of the controllable/uncontrollable dimension. Internal factors are usually perceived as controllable. Liebhart (1976), by assuming that the manipulations on the instable/stable dimension can be explained by control effects, can then make his results consistent with the older ones. "In a certain sense, therefore, one can also speak of an internalization effect in the present experiment" (p. 300).

Liebhart also assumes that the special active mechanism (see above), or process of mediation, between internal attribution and alteration of the symptoms, is a lessening of the unrest.

> Therefore, the manipulation of internalization in the present experiment (attribution of desired behavioral changes to controllable factors) presumably operates in a manner similar to the manipulation of externalization (attribution

of undesired automatic reactions to nonemotional causes), namely, through the distraction of aversive stimuli and the reduction of their intensity. (Liebhart, 1976, p. 302; cf. Mischel, Ebbesen, & Zeiss, 1973; Weiner & Sierad, 1975)

5. Summary and Critique

The general suggestions made by Strong (1970) regarding counseling based only on the old attribution theories (Heider, Jones & Davis, Kelley) to, first, improve the subjective validity of attribution and thus, second, reduce guilt and anxiety, were made more specific by Ross, Rodin, and Zimbardo (1969) in the misattribution model in "Toward an Attribution Therapy." They specified, first, that the arousal in critical situations should be attributed to alternative situational factors, and, second, that if possible a new cause should be artificially introduced into the situation.

These tips are supplemented in the reattribution model for insomnia (Storms and Nisbett, 1970) as follows: first, nonemotional attributions are to be found for natural states of arousal; second, one can lead into the dynamics of a disorder through the divulgence, and subsequent self-attribution, of placebo effects; and, third, paradoxical suggestions (see above) can be instituted in the course of therapy.

The tips by Valins and Nisbett (1971) were thus summarized subsequent to the refinement made by Nisbett and Valins (1971): first, destroy the "naive" attributions of the client, and, second, attribute undesired symptoms to external, and desired symptoms to internal, causes.

Recent investigations are more sceptical. Davison et al. (1973) do not recommend developing a treatment program in this direction. However, they consider the subjective causal attribution of therapeutic changes by client and therapist to be a variable in the maintenance of behavioral change. Liebhart (1976) limits himself only to this subsidary function. He tries to understand the externalization and internalization of symptoms in a more refined way through the attribution dimension of controllability; however, he estimates the range of cognitive control to be slight. In their investigation of manipulated feedback, Cohen et al. (1974) prefer to make reference to the theory concerning adaptation level (anchor effects of evaluation, positive and negative evidence) rather than to the attribution theory.

In general, an explicit model of thought, rather than the simple dichotomy of "internalization" and "externalization" and the mediating process of "worries," seems to be needed in attribution therapy; for instance, within the meaning of König (1976), Dörner (1976: problem analysis, barrier, area of reality, operators, heuristics, training procedure), or Fischhoff (1976). These areas of cognitive control may also become therapeutically useful through the sequence cognitive, emotional, motivational, and behavioral behavior change.

Similar to other topics in attribution research, such as "point-of-view-effect" or "false-consensus-effect" for the topic of affect, additional processes of intuitive judgment, popular induction, or lay epistemology have to be considered in order to account for the observed phenomena of attention and suggestion. At first sight the man on the street does not believe in these processes, "Subjects . . . made little pretense of believing that any subject could have gone through such processes" (Nisbett & Wilson, 1977, p. 258).

As a second point of criticism, however, a concept of emotion more extensive than Schachter's is necessary in such sequential approach. The "links" of Ross, Rodin, and Zimbardo (1969), for instance, can scarcely be interpreted as a further theoretical development. Attribution therapy is helpless in view of this phenomenon of discrepancy (Storms & Nisbett, 1970, p. 324; *there*: Davison & Valins 1969, Nisbett & Schachter 1966, Valins & Ray 1967, Zimbardo *et al.*, 1966, or Cohen *et al.*, 1974, pp. 144, 163, & 164; *there*: Sushinsky & Bootzin, 1970; Kent *et al.*, 1972, Rosen *et al.*, 1972) and even allows its therapeutic optimism to be dampened by it; whereas Weinstein *et al.* (1968) intentionally start out at this point and see a vital point of access toward understanding the reaction pattern of an emotion within the framework of Lazarus' model.

In its present form, attribution therapy is condemned to "fall asleep." It represents only an accumulation of "tips," as again became clear above. It could come out of its "subsidiary" corner (Liebhart, 1976) through the extension of cognitive control by means of a problem-solving model which would adequately formulate the more recent attribution research in its operator approach, or it could do this through the integration of judgment research (Fischhoff, 1976).

References

Abelson, R. P., & Kanouse, D. E. Subjective acceptance of verbal generalization. In S. Feldman (Ed.), *Cognitive consistency*. New York: Academic, 1966.

Asch, S. Forming impressions of personality. *Journal of Abnormal and Social Psychology*, 1946, *41*, 258–290.

Ax, A. F. Review of Neurophysiology Discovers the Mind. *Contemporary Psychology*, 1971, *16*, 365–367.

Brunswik, E. *Wahrnehmung und Gegenstandswelt*. Wien: Deuticke, 1934.

Cohen, R., Meyer-Osterkamp, S., Grusche, A. Eine Untersuchung zum Einflumanipulierter Rückmeldung auf Angst-Reaktionen. *Zeitschrift für Klinische Psychologie*, 1974, *3*, 143–169.

Cronbach, L. J. Processes affecting scores on "understanding of others" and "assumed similarity." *Psychological Bulletin*, 1955, 177–193.

Davison, G. C., & Valins, S. Maintenance of self-attributed and drug-attributed behavior change. *Journal of Personality and Social Psychology*, 1969, *11*, 25–33.

Davison, G. C., Tsujimoto, R. N., & Glaros, A. G. Attribution and the maintenance of behavior change in falling asleep. *Journal of Abnormal Psychology*, 1973, *82*, 124–133.

Dörner, D. *Problemlösen als Informationsverarbeitung*. Stuttgart: Kohlhammer, 1976.

Fischhoff, B. Attribution theory and judgment under uncertainty. In J. H. Harvey, W. J. Ickes, & R. F. Kidd (Eds.), *New directions in attribution research* (Vol. I). New York: Halsted, 1976.

Goffman, E. *The presentation of self in every day life*. Garden City, N. Y.: Doubleday, 1959.

Harris, V. A., & Katkin, E. S. Primary and secondary emotional behavior. *Psychological Bulletin*, 1975, *82*, 904–916.

Hastorf, A. H., Schneider, D. J., & Polefka, J. *Person perception*. Menlo Park, Cal.: Addison-Wesley, 1970.

Heider, F. *The psychology of interpersonal relations*. New York: Wiley, 1958.

Heider, F., & Simmel, M. An experimental study of apparent behavior. *American Journal of Psychology*, 1944, *57*, 243–259.

Jones, E. E. The rocky road from acts to dispositions. *American Psychologist*, 1979, *34*, 107–117.

Jones, E. E., & Davis, K. E. From acts to dispositions: The attribution process in person perception. In L. Berkowitz (Ed.), *Advances in experimental social psychology* (Vol. 2). New York: Academic, 1965.

Jones, E. E., & Goethals, G. R. Order effects in impression information: Attribution context and the nature of the entity. In E. E. Jones, D. E. Kanouse, H. H. Kelley, R. E. Nisbett, S. Valins, & B. Weiner, *Attribution: Perceiving the causes of behavior*. Morristown, N. J.: General Learning Press, 1971.

Jones, E. E., & Nisbett, R. E. The actor and the observer: Divergent perceptions of the causes of behavior. In E. E. Jones, D. E. Kanouse, H. H. Kelley, R. E. Nisbett, S. Valins, & B. Weiner (Eds.), *Attribution: Perceiving the causes of behavior*. Morristown, N. J.: General Learning Press, 1971.

Kanouse, D. E. Language, labeling, and attribution. In E. E. Jones, D. E. Kanouse, H. H. Kelley, R. E. Nisbett, S. Valins, & B. Weiner (Eds.), *Attribution: Perceiving the causes of behavior*. Morristown, N. J.: General Learning Press, 1971.

Kanouse, D. E., & Hanson, L. R., Jr. Negativity in evaluations. In E. E. Jones, D. E. Kanouse, H. H. Kelley, R. E. Nisbett, S. Valins, & B. Weiner (Eds.), *Attribution: Perceiving the causes of behavior*. Morristown, N. J.: General Learning Press, 1971.

Kelley, H. H. Attribution theory in social psychology. In D. Levine (Ed.), *Nebraska symposium on motivation* (Vol. 15). Lincoln: University of Nebraska Press, 1967.

Kelley, H. H. Attribution in social interaction. In E. E. Jones, D. E. Kanouse, H. H. Kelley, R. E. Nisbett, S. Valins, & B. Weiner (Eds.), *Attribution: Perceiving the causes of behavior*. Morristown, N. J.: General Learning Press, 1971.

Kelley, H. H. The processes of causal attribution. *American Psychologist*, 1973, *28*, 107–128.

Kelly, G. A. *The psychology of personal constructs* (Vols. 1 & 2). New York: Norton, 1955.

Kent, R. N., Wilson, G. T., & Nelson, R. Effects of false heart rate feedback on avoidance behavior: An investigation of "Cognitive Desensitization." *Behavior Therapy*, 1972, *3*, 1–6.

König, F. Die Verbesserung der Problemlösefähigkeit durch gesprächspsychotherapeutische Reduktion internal motivierter Konflikte. In *Klientenzentrierte Psychotherapie heute:*

Bericht über den 1. Europäischen Kongre für Gesprächstherapie, Würzburg 1974. Göttingen: Hogrefe, 1976.

Lang, P. J. Die Anwendung psychophysiologischer Methoden. In N. Birbaumer (Ed.), *Neuropsychologie der Angst.* München: Urban & Schwarzenberg, 1973.

Latané, B., & Schachter, S. Adrenalin and avoidance learning. *Journal of Comparative and Physiological Psychology,* 1962, *55,* 369–372.

Laucken, U. *Naive Verhaltenstheorie.* Stuttgart: Klett, 1974.

Lazarus, R. S. Is there a mechanism of perceptual defense? A reply to Postman, Bronson and Grapper. *Journal of Abnormal and Social Psychology,* 1954, *49,* 396–398.

Lazarus, R. S. Emotions and adaptation: Conceptual and empirical relations. In W. J. Arnold (Ed.), *Nebraska symposium on motivation.* Lincoln: University of Nebraska Press, 1968.

Liebhart, E. H. Attributionstherapie: Beinflussung herzneurotischer Beschwerden durch Externalisierung kausaler Zuschreibungen. *Zeitschrift für Klinische Psychologie,* 1974, *3,* 71–94.

Liebhart, E. H. Attributionstherapie: Stabilisierung der Besserung herzneurotischer Beschwerden durch Internalisierung kausaler Zuschreibungen. *Zeitschrift für Klinische Psychologie,* 1976, *5,* 287–306.

Liebhart, E. Wahrgenommene autonome Veränderungen als Determinanten emotionalen Verhaltens. In D. Gorlitz, W.-U. Meyer, & B. Weiner (Eds.), *Attribution.* Stuttgart: Klett, 1978.

Mandler, G. *Mind and emotion.* New York: Wiley, 1975.

Mead, G. H. *Mind, self and society.* Chicago: University of Chicago Press, 1934.

Miller, G. A., Galanter, E., & Pribram, K. H. *Plans and the structure of behavior.* New York: Holt, 1960.

Mischel, W. *Personality and assessment.* New York: Wiley, 1968.

Mischel, W., Ebbesen, E. B., & Zeiss, A. R. Selective attention to the self: Situational and dispositional determinants. *Journal of Personality and Social Psychology,* 1973, *27,* 129–142.

Monroe, L. J. Psychological and physiological differences between good and poor sleepers. *Journal of Abnormal Psychology,* 1967, *72,* 255–264.

Nisbett, R. E., & Schachter, S. Cognitive manipulation of pain. *Journal of Experimental Social Psychology,* 1966, *2,* 227–236.

Nisbett, R. E., & Valins, S. Perceiving the causes of one's own behavior. In E. E. Jones, D. E. Kanouse, H. H. Kelley, R. E. Nisbett, S. Valins, & B. Weiner (Eds.), *Attribution: Perceiving the causes of behavior.* Morristown, N. J.: General Learning Press, 1971.

Nisbett, R. E., & Wilson, T. D. Telling more than we can know. *Psychological Review,* 1977, *84,* 231–257.

Piaget, J. *Die Entwicklung des Erkennens* II. Stuttgart: Klett, 1975.

Plutchik, R., & Ax, A. F. A critique of determinants of emotional state by Schachter and Singer (1962). *Psychophysiology,* 1967, *4,* 79–82.

Rickels, K., Lipman, R., & Raab, E. Previous medication duration of illness and placebo response. *Journal of Nervous and Mental Disease,* 1966, *142,* 548–554.

Rosen, G. M., Rosen, E., & Reid, J. B. Cognitive desensitization and avoidance behavior: A re-evaluation. *Journal of Abnormal Psychology,* 1972, *80,* 176–182.

Ross, L., Rodin, J., & Zimbardo, P. G. Toward an attribution therapy. *Journal of Personality and Social Psychology,* 1969, *12,* 279–288.

Ryle, G. *The concept of mind.* London: Hutchinson, 1949.

Schachter, S. *The psychology of affiliation.* Stanford: Stanford University Press, 1959.

Schachter, S., & Singer, J. E. Cognitive, social and physiological determinants of emotional state. *Psychological Review,* 1962, *69,* 379–399.

Schachter, S., & Wheeler, L. Epinephrine, chlorpromazine, and amusement. *Journal of Abnormal and Social Psychology*, 1962, *65*, 121–128.

Shaver, K. G. *An introduction to attribution processes.* Cambridge, Mass.: Winthrop, 1975.

Singer, J. E. Sympathetic activation, drugs, and fright. *Journal of Comparative and Physiological Psychology*, 1963, *56*, 612–615.

Singer, J. E. Consistency as a Stimulus processing mechanism. In R. P. Abelson, E. Aronson, W. J. McGuire, T. M. Newcomb, M. J. Rosenberg, & P. H. Tannenbaum (Eds.), *Theories of cognitive consistency: A sourcebook.* Chicago: Rand McNally, 1968.

Spielberger, C. D. (Ed.). *Anxiety and behavior.* New York: Academic, 1966.

Storms, M. D. Videotape and the attribution process: Reversing actors and observers' points of view. *Journal of Personality and Social Psychology*, 1973, *27*, 165–175.

Storms, M., & Nisbett, R. E. Insomnia and the attribution process. *Journal of Personality and Social Psychology*, 1970, *16*, 319–328.

Strong, S. R. Causal attribution in counseling and psychotherapy. *Journal of Counseling Psychology*, 1970, *17*, 388–399.

Sushinsky, L. W., & Bootzin, R. R. Cognitive desensitization as a model of systematic desensitization. *Behavior Research and Therapy*, 1970, *8*, 29–33.

Taylor, S. E., & Fiske, S. T. Point of view and perceptions of causality. *Journal of Personality and Social Psychology*, 1975, *32*, 439–445.

Taylor, S. E., & Fiske, S. T. Salience, attention, and attribution: Top of the head phenomena. In L. Berkowitz (Ed.), *Advances in experimental social psychology* (Vol. 11). New York: Academic, 1978.

Valins, S. Cognitive effects of false heart rate feedback. *Journal of Personality and Social Psychology*, 1966, *4*, 400–408.

Valins, S., & Nisbett, R. E. Attribution processes in the development and treatment of emotional disorder. In E. E. Jones, D. E. Kanouse, H. H. Kelley, R. E. Nisbett, S. Valins, & B. Weiner (Eds.), *Attribution: Perceiving the causes of behavior.* Morristown, N. J.: General Learning Press, 1971.

Valins, S., & Ray, A. A. Effects of cognitive desensitization on avoidance behavior. *Journal of Personality and Social Psychology*, 1967, *4*, 400–408.

Weiner, B. *Theories of motivation.* Chicago: Rand McNally, 1972.

Weiner, B., & Sierad, J. Misattribution for failure and the enhancement of achievement rings. *Journal of Personality and Social Psychology*, 1975, *31*, 415–421.

Weiner, B., Frieze, J., Kukla, A., Reed, L., Rest, S., & Rosenbaum, R. M. Perceiving the causes of success and failure. In E. E. Jones, D. E. Kanouse, H. H. Kelley, R. E. Nesbitt, S. Valins, & B. Weiner, *Attribution: Perceiving the causes of behavior.* Morristown, N. J.: General Learning Press, 1971.

Weinstein, J., Averill, J. R., Opton, E. M., & Lazarus, R. S. Defensive style and discrepancy between self-report and physiological indices of stress. *Journal of Personality and Social Psychology*, 1968, *10*, 406–413.

Wengle, M. E. Die systematische Desensibilisierung. In C. Kraiker (Ed.), *Handbuch der Verhaltenstherapie.* München: Kindler, 1975.

Wolpe, J. *Psychotherapy by reciprocal inhibition.* Stanford: Stanford University Press, 1958.

Zillmann, D. Attribution and misattribution of excitatory reactions. In J. H. Harvey, W. Ickes, & R. F. Kidd (Eds.), *New directions in attribution research* (Vol. 2). New York: Wiley, 1978.

Zimbardo, P. G., Cohen, A. R., Weisenberg, M., Dworhin, L., & Firestone, J. Control of pain motivation by cognitive dissonance. *Science*, 1966, *151*, 217–219.

5

Implications of Action Theory for Cognitive Therapy

NORBERT SEMMER AND MICHAEL FRESE

1. Introduction

When Breger and McGaugh (1965) reproached behavioral therapy for supporting the "foundations of its learning theory" mainly on analogies in linguistic usage, and pleaded that central mediators (as opposed to peripheral processes) and action strategies (as opposed to single behavioral actions) be granted more significance, it was still possible to dismiss them with an arrogant reply (Rachman & Eysenck, 1966).

In the meantime quite a few of their assertions have been commonly accepted into psychology, as for example the lack of foundation for behavioral therapy in learning theory (Westmeyer, 1977), but above all the role of cognition (cf. Mahoney, 1974), and of general strategies (cf. e.g., Meichenbaum, 1974). Even Eysenck (1976), in referring to the necessity for greater consideration of Pavlov's "second signalling system," thereby acknowledges the significance of central cognitive processes.

Two developments in the area of psychotherapy which parallel this development can both be seen as reactions to the narrow perspective of classical behavioral therapy. The *cognitive* counterreaction is apparent in the increasing importance being given to the cognitivist forms of therapy, preeminent among which must be cited the "rational-emotive therapy" of Albert Ellis (1962) and the cognitive approach of Beck (e.g., 1976). A counterreaction aimed more at the emotional aspect appears in

NORBERT SEMMER • Büllowstrasse 90, D-1 Berlin 30, Bundesrepublik Deutschland. MICHAEL FRESE • Technische Universität Berlin, Gesellschaftswissenschaften, D-1 Berlin 10, Bundesrepublik Deutschland.

forms of therapy and training which are based on humanistic, more holistic view, as for example in the so-called client-centered therapy of Rogers, and the encounter groups which have arisen in part from it, as well as in other group-dynamic methods which partly emphasize emotional and partly physical experiences (Gestalt therapy, bioenergetics, etc.). Various mixed forms, derived to some extent eclectically and to some extent from a learning-theory heuristic (e.g., Lazarus, 1976) are everywhere available and very well received under the label of "seeing the total person."

In the course of this counterreaction, however, a more exact analysis of the role of cognitive, emotional, and behavioral processes *in their relationship to each other* is often neglected. Thus, Beck (1976), for instance, in emphasizing the decisive role played by cognitive patterns of interpretation and automatic thoughts, globally contrasts this approach with the behavioral one. Although Beck definitely takes behavior-therapy *techniques* into account, he makes no attempt to *integrate* the behavioral approach. Ellis is more concerned to "sell" his approach as a cure than to attempt a comprehensive analysis. Comparative and integrating approaches of this kind are introduced above all by Mahoney (1974) and Meichenbaum (1974, 1977).

Now, one cannot really blame the protagonists of new approaches for not immediately presenting their ideas in a form integrated with everything that came before, and leaving this further comparative and integrative development to others. There is another shortcoming, however, which seems to us more serious. The role of cognitions themselves, their precise significance in the course of regulating actions, is for the most part not sufficiently worked out; it has often seemed enough to point out their dominant significance without more precisely analyzing this significance with respect to various kinds of cognitions. Findings from social-psychology research on attitudes, for instance, that cognition and behavior show very little correlation (Fishbein, 1967), are completely overlooked.

In our opinion, psychological *action-theory*, as brought to its most highly articulated state thus far, in relation to the precise processes of the cognitive control of action, by the Dresden industrial psychologist Hacker (1973, 1976) (basing himself on Miller, Galanter, & Pribram [1960] as well as on Soviet psychology), supplies several points of departure for determining more precisely the role of cognition in the control of actions, and for deriving conclusions for therapy from this determination (as is to be made clear in sections 5. and 6.).

The relationship between cognition and behavior is, therefore, in the foreground of this chapter. In order to elucidate the general approach which forms the background to these thoughts, we should like briefly to go into the problems both of cognition and motivation, and of cognition and emotion, following this with a short presentation of the action-theory approach and the consequences which can be drawn for diagnosis and therapy.

2. Cognition versus Reinforcement: Is There a Noncognitive Therapy?

Findings and arguments are accumulating which make it increasingly less tenable to interpret the successes of behavior therapy on the basis of a pure conditioning paradigm—that is to say, as an automatic connection, with the emphasis on peripheral processes.

A typical example of this is provided by the explanation for systematic desensitization. Originally this was seen as a mechanistic conditioning process in which both the hierarchy of items and (peripheral) relaxation play an important part. It has since been shown that neither the hierarchy of items nor muscular relaxation is a necessary condition (cf. Jacobs & Wolpin, 1971). The now-famous experiments concerning avoidance learning under the impact of curare (thus eliminating peripheral feedback processes—Solomon & Turner, 1962) conclusively allow only an explanation relating to central mediation. Expectation evidently plays a decisive role, as the following study by Jaffe (1968) shows. He worked with four groups, varying, on the one hand, the forms of therapy (treatment, placebo, no treatment) and, on the other, the induced expectation of success. Group one was treated, and the treatment was presented to them as effective (treatment + expectation of success). The second group received the same treatment, but were led to believe that they were in a control group (treatment without expectation of success). The third, the placebo group, were shown tachistoscopic representations of travel scenes, and were given simple mathematical assignments. They were told, however, that they were seeing subliminal anxiety stimuli, and that working at the assignments would reciprocally inhibit the unconsciously produced anxiety reactions. The fourth group was a control group without treatment.

Group one (treatment and expectation of success) displayed the greatest progress. The placebo group, for whom improvements could occur only by means of the expectation of success, exhibited the same improvements—and on a subjective scale even greater—than Group 2, which had received therapy without the expectation of success.

A cognitive interpretation of the effects of behavioral therapy is also further supported by a comparison of covert negative reinforcement and *backward* covert sensitization (Mahoney, 1974, p. 120). Both contain the same course, namely, the cognitive imagery of an aversive situation, followed by the performance of a particular action. In one case, however, the aversive action is to become less aversive, while in the other, the same activity is to become more aversive—and both were successfully employed! Much the same considerations about systematic desensitization and covert sensitization are presented by Murray and Jacobson (1971).

Apparently expectation as to the effect also plays an important part in determining the effect.

The conclusion can thus be maintained, regarding therapeutic techniques constructed according to the paradigm of classical conditioning that "The critical change required appears to be that the person comes to believe that he can cope with the situation" (Murray & Jacobson, 1971, p. 725). The crucial mechanism in the therapy seems to be that it supplies "nonconfirming experiences."

Regarding not only the area of respondent, but also that of operant behavior, the extensive investigations of Bandura and his colleagues, above all others, have supplied more than sufficient evidence that the learning process itself needs no reinforcement (cf. Bandura, 1969, 1971, 1973, 1976). This work has become so well known that it is not necessary here to go into further detail. In so far as reinforcement influences the learning process itself, it does so indirectly, by way of drawing attention, practice, etc. Otherwise, it plays a part above all in decisions as to when a particular behavior is appropriate. A large part of the therapeutic process lies, then, in learning under which circumstances which consequences are to be expected from which behavior!

An additional phenomenon, scarcely to be interpreted through traditional reinforcement approaches, concerns the effects of control (cf. Frese, 1977; Seligman, 1975). Here the experiments of Glass & Singer (1972) have become especially well known. Equal situations of stress (noise or shock) produced more limited tolerance of frustration, more mistakes at cognitive tasks, and more intense physiological reactions, when they were unforeseeable or uncontrollable.

Quite a lot of additional evidence could be quoted, but the central statement seems clear: in the therapeutic process, particular modes of behavior are not simply connected to reinforcing or punishing stimuli. The change comes about—to the extent that the behavioral repertoire itself is not expanded (cf. here 4.)—rather in the *expectation* that particular positive or negative consequences will follow certain environmental events or one's own actions, or in the appraisal of one's own influence on the consequences (control).

This is not, of course, to deny that reinforcement plays a role in action. It applies merely to the significance of reinforcement in the learning process.[1] To the extent that therapy is characterized by such a learning process, the conclusion seems to be justified that there is no such thing as a noncognitive therapy.

3. Cognition and Emotion

Emotional factors are frequently regarded as motives for actions, in particular for avoidance behavior. There is an intensive debate in progress about the question of the reciprocal influence of cognitive and emotional processes.

In our opinion, the investigations made by R. S. Lazarus (1966) and the work of Schachter (1964) have supplied particularly important indications about the nature of emotional processes.

In one now-famous experiment (Lazarus, 1966), a film, showing a cruel tribal ritual, had different soundtracks, either emphasizing or playing down the painfulness of the operation. These situational *appraisals* had an obvious influence on the emotional reactions of the spectators.

Such investigations and ones like them support the *cognitive model of emotions* of Lazarus and others (Lazarus, Averill, & Opton; 1970), according to which emotional experience is connected with specific situational appraisals, which differ for different emotions. According to this view, if one is successful in altering the interpretation of the situation, then the emotion will change.

Now this was also precisely the result of the discussion about systematic desensitization: anxiety is removed by changing the expectation.

Basing himself on a similar approach, Beck (1976) attempted to classify different emotions according to their cognitive content. Thus, sadness is characterized by the thought of loss, anxiety by the thought of threat, anger by the thought of infringement on standards (similarly Lazarus, 1976). To be sure, Beck's procedure in this is mainly clinical-intuitive; the experiments mentioned above however, speak for the correctness, in principle, of his approach. A series of his own investigations also supports his procedure. Thus, Beck & Rush (1975) could effectively separate phobics from patients with anxiety neuroses, according to the cognitive contents reported by the patients. Phobics had clearer and more specific

---

[1]It is also not to be denied on principle that there can be automatic processes of conditioning. The studies reported here and, moreover, those which are stated in great number in the literature, offer, nevertheless, strong evidence for the thesis that if they exist at all these are borderline cases, and that, in general, a decisive importance is to be attributed to cognitive variables.

triggering-stimuli of a chiefly external character, whereas anxiety-neurotics were more apt to report unspecific and often internal stimuli as triggering-agents for anxiety. Unfortunately this study does not carry very much weight, since all statistical information is lacking. Nevertheless, the theme of danger, which Beck considered typical for anxiety, showed up in *all* patients.[2]

An important problem, which will be gone into more precisely later, lies in the fact that different, even contradictory, cognitions about the same circumstances can exist at different periods of time (Beck speaks of a "dual belief system"). Every therapist knows that phobic clients are, as a rule, definitely aware that they at least overestimate the real danger. Beck (1976) even defines a phobia on this basis as, "fear of the situation that, by social consensus and the person's own intellectual appraisal *when away from the situation,* is disproportionate to the probability and degree of harm inherent in that situation" (p. 159; italics by authors). One case reported by him illustrates this. He had clients who were afraid of flying estimate the probability of a crash at different points in time. The estimations varied from 1:100,000 in situations when no flight was planned in the foreseeable future, to 50:50 at departure, and 100:1 during a rough flight!

Certainly Beck's material is more illustrative than conclusive. Seen in connection with the overall evidence, however, it nevertheless represents a convincing interpretation.

The investigations of Schachter (Schachter, 1964; Schachter & Singer, 1962) are likewise often quoted as evidence that emotions are under cognitive control. In this general formulation, the interpretation is correct, to be sure, though Schachter's experimental paradigm illuminates a different aspect of the phenomenon. Whereas here it has been a matter of seeing the emotional reaction (whether measured verbally, physiologically, or behaviorally) as a result of an appraisal of the situation, in Schachter's work it is a matter of tagging an already existent physiological reaction with a label; thus, for example, interpreting one's own arousal as "anger" or "joy." This says nothing about how the arousal itself comes about under "normal" circumstances (namely, as a result of the situational appraisal) (cf. Bem, 1974). In so far as Schachter's position supports a general cognitive view, it is also, accordingly, relevant here. In so far

---

[2]A further basic methodological objection to this kind of investigation might be seen in the fact that the presence of corresponding cognitions in phobics does not allow the reverse conclusion, that such cognitions are the factors which trigger anxiety (problem of the actuarial conclusion—Wiggins, 1973). On the other hand, such results suggest that the corresponding conditions are at least a *necessary* if not a sufficient condition.

however, as Schachter does not explain how arousal comes about, but presupposes it in his experiments, these experiments cannot be interpreted as confirmation of a cognitive view of emotions.

Altogether, however, there seems to be sufficient material at hand telling in favor of the cognitive mediation of emotional states. Beyond this, we have shown by illustration that goal expectations play a part both in classical and in instrumental conditioning.

4. Cognition and Behavior I: Cognitive Factors in the Regulation of Behavior

The previous presentation has been an attempt to show that cognitive appraisals of situations and actions, and their possible consequences, are decisive for the choice of behavioral strategies as well as for emotional reactions. Here we wish to discuss the question whether cognitions also play a part in the actual execution of (motor) actions; whether cognitive strategies, therefore, have an influence in the expansion of action-repertoires as well.

The work of Bandura is extremely relevant for this area too. In his theory of model learning, cognitive (imaginal or verbal) representations of what is learned take on the function of directing the corresponding behavior in a later situation. This thesis can be substantiated when one varies the quality of these internal representations and predicts a corresponding variation in the quality of the behavior. Gerst (1971), for example, was able to show that movements from the sign-language of deaf-mutes can be executed better if they are acquired through a meaningful "summary label" than when the cognitive rehearsal ensues imaginally or through a concrete description of the individual sequences. A study by Bandura and Jeffrey (1973)[3] presented analogous results.

The effectiveness of so-called "mental training" (cf. Däumling, Engler, Smieskol, Tiegel, Triebe, Ulich, & Wilke, 1973; Ulich, 1964) provides

---

[3]The conclusion which Bandura draws from experiments of this kind, at least in his earlier articles and books (1969, 1974)—that central processes are exclusively responsible for the learning process, and that peripheral feedback plays no part, as a rule, in the regulation of action—is, however, not justified. Bandura has, however, of late moved slightly away from this position and its consequence, that active practice-processes are considered irrelevant. This is indicated in his introducing phases of active practice under the (in our opinion, not very adequate) concept of "participant modeling" (for example, Bandura, 1976). On this in more detail cf. Semmer & Pfäfflin (1978a,b).

further indication for the role of cognitive factors. Used up until now primarily in sports and in the training of sensorimotor tasks (Rohmert, Rutenfranz, & Ulich, 1971), this form of training consists of imagining a movement (or sequence of movements) precisely, or of precisely thinking it through. This procedure has clear effects, which, for example, (employed at times in isolation) are superior to training through observation. In this connection the so-called ideomotoric phenomenon is interesting (also known as the Carpenter effect): when a subject precisely imagines a movement, action potentials can be detected in the muscular areas which would participate in the execution of this movement.

The success of Meichenbaum and his colleagues (Meichenbaum, Turk, & Burstein, 1975) in influencing the behavior of clients (among others schizophrenics as well as impulsive children) by means of self-verbalizations (cf. Meichenbaum, 1975a,b) are also clear evidence for the role of cognitions in the regulation of behavior.

The procedure based on the work of Luria—from instructions given by the experimenter switching over first to audible self-verbalizations and finally to silent internal speech—was used by Elssner (1972) in connection with the relearning of an already highly automatic movement. The new movement (one conducive to avoiding health-damage) was first described in detail. In addition to the internalization, the description was abbreviated as progress increased in practice, that is, increasingly shorter summary expressions were applied in place of the detailed description.

From the area of industrial psychology, Hacker (1973) supplies a great deal of evidence for the significance of cognitive representations. Thus, for example, effective and less effective workers differ in their "signal inventory": those who were more effective had more precise knowledge about the signals in the work process which indicate the necessity of an intervention. Another study revealed that effective workers could specify more precisely the probability of breakdowns. The adequacy and differentiation of such internal images makes possible the transition from a "momentary" to a "planning" strategy: the latter strategy implies that, for example, sufficient supplies are made available when starting to work that in case of breakdowns the machine whose damage can be quickly repaired is repaired first, that actions particularly important for the further course of the process are performed with extreme care, etc.[4]

Finally, indications for the role of cognition also come from experiments dealing with anxiety. An assumption which is in the meantime widely accepted and well corroborated postulates that, in a state of anx-

---

[4]In what appears to be a paradox, they are therefore also performed more slowly than by less efficient workers.

iety, cognitions irrelevant to the task are produced which interfere with the courses of action (Hamilton, 1975; Sarason, 1975).

Thus we have altogether more than enough indications and evidence available to substantiate the role of cognition in the regulation of action. Can one conclude from this that the so-called cognitive therapies are the most adequate ones?

Such a line of reasoning can definitely be found among representatives of cognitive therapy (e.g., Beck, 1976). However, the question "cognition or conditioning" is too global, and thereby in the last analysis incorrect:

1. If therapeutic successes presuppose cognitive changes, it does not unconditionally follow that the attempt to modify these cognitions directly and immediately is the most adequate one. Indeed, the cognitive interpretation of behavior-therapy successes demonstrates that indirect approaches are also possible—that is, ways of behaving rebound to the central cognitions. And it is definitely conceivable that in many a case they are the most effective!

2. In demonstrating that behavioral and emotional changes presuppose cognitive changes, it is in no way asserted that every cognitive change also brings in its wake corresponding changes. On the contrary, there is a series of findings according to which this is not the case. A particularly good example of this is provided by social psychology research on attitudes, which regularly finds that attitude and behavior correlate only very slightly with one another (cf., e.g., Fishbein, 1967). The modification of fundamental attitudes toward life, as it characterizes, for instance, Ellis's (1962) approach, does not therefore automatically promise improvement. The previously stated phenomenon of the dual belief system (Beck), that is, the conviction of safety which the phobic expresses when he is a safe distance away from the feared situation, and the reversal of this conviction to its opposite the closer he gets to this situation, illustrates this fact.

Apparently, therefore, cognitions are not always effective in regulating action. If, however, (a) cognitive changes represent only necessary but not sufficient conditions for behavioral changes and if (b) these cognitive changes can also be achieved by indirect approaches, then the previous analysis does not contribute much to a further development of therapeutic interventions. We merely know that the effect of everything previously done was mediated cognitively.

Thus, the question cannot be: cognitive therapy or not? On the contrary, one must ask *under what circumstances cognitions* have a regulative effect on actions. (The adequate therapy might in that respect indeed consist of making already existing cognitions into the regulator of behavior!) For this, it is necessary to investigate regulation more precisely. This mechanism has in no way been clarified yet. In our opinion, the psychological action-theory can provide an important contribution to this clarification.

5. Cognition and Behavior II: Mechanisms of Cognitive Action Regulation

An exact analysis of the cognitive mechanisms which regulate action can scarcely be found in traditional learning-theory approaches. Bandura (e.g., 1971) goes the furthest in this direction. He postulates that through cognitive learning processes internal models for an action are constructed which then regulate the execution of the action. He refines his view, however, only insofar as he (1) makes a distinction between an imaginal and a verbal coding, an (2) postulates a hierarchical organization of the internal models emerging from this.

Other approaches refer only to particular aspects or action patterns, which they analyze more closely. Recently, the investigation of specific mental instructions or interferences has thereby moved into the foreground. Analyses of processes of self-control (cf. Hartig, 1975), automatic thoughts (Beck, Ellis), distracting anxiety cognitions (Sarason, 1975), or specific self-instructions (Meichenbaum) all refer to the role of specific effects of situational cognitions, not, however, to a general model of cognitive action regulation.

One exception to this, however, is to be found in the area of *sensorimotor learning*. Here work has been done in greater detail and more comprehensively with models of action regulation (Schmidt, 1976; cf. Volpert, 1973). Semmer & Pfäfflin (1978a) advocate the view that the conceptions developed there are also to the higher degree relevant for social learning. This refers to single aspects of experiments, for instance the analysis of the informatory aspect of feedback—which is relatively detailed in comparison to the usual learning-theory investigations—as well as to comprehensive explanatory approaches.[5]

In our opinion, the psychological action-theory represents the most productive approach in this area to date. It was introduced in its basic concept principally by Miller, Galanter, & Pribram (1960), and encountered great interest mainly in the socialist countries, where the point of

[5]To be sure, the action-theory approach, to be dealt with in what follows, does not originate in the sensorimotor realm; Miller, Galanter, & Pribram (1960), whose book is fundamental for this approach, refer very strongly to cybernetic approaches and to stimulations of problem-solving processes. It is not, however, a coincidence that their book—at least in the West—remained long unnoticed by learning theorists, and became known in German-speaking countries above all through Hacker's (1973) action-theory approach, which did originate in the sensorimotor realm.

departure had all along been the cognitive reproduction of external reality as a regulative function, and where forerunners of the model of Miller, Galanter, & Pribram already existed (cf. Stadler, Seeger, & Raeithel, 1975). Hacker (above all, 1973) enlarged, extended, and differentiated it into a general model of the psychic regulation of work activities. Its central theme is the hierarchical and sequential regulation of actions by means of internal images on the basis of (self-generated or externally given) goals. These images include the relevant environmental conditions and the course of action and its possible variants, as well as the expected results. From this, it is immediately understandable that the quality of the action is decisively dependent on the quality of these images. The regulative function of the images is to be differentiated in a sequential and hierarchical respect.

5.1. The Sequential Organization of Action

If internal images direct actions, then these images themselves must contain the course of the action. The cognitions must to a certain degree run ahead of the action itself, planning the steps which are to follow ("preliminary run"). And a constant comparison must take place between the current action and the internal model, if a flexible pattern of action is to develop that adapts optimally to the respective environmental conditions. The cybernetic model of the feedback cycle proves fruitful here.

Thus the concept of feedback moves to the center of the analysis. It also plays a large part in the conventional learning theories, and in the forms of therapy based upon them. However, there it is seen primarily with regard to *motivational* aspects: feedback is either reinforcement or punishment. Thus, it provides information only as to whether the respective action is approved or disapproved by those present; it typically occurs subsequent to the action, and refers to the action as a whole; and its effect is considered to lie in lowering or raising the probability of occurrence of the action. The *mastery* of the action itself is secondary in this.

According to the viewpoint of action theory, on the other hand, the *informative* aspect of feedback moves into the forefront. Feedback gives information regarding the extent to which the action meets a particular standard (desired value), it takes place continuously, therefore also *during the course of the action* (and not only afterwards), and it thus makes correction of the action possible, and promotes mastery of it.

The feedback cycle ("Test-Operate-Test-Exit" unit—TOTE unit in Miller, Galanter, & Pribram; Comparison-Change-Feedback unit, abbreviated as CCF in Hacker) is thus the functional unit of action regulation.

Hacker characterizes the internal model as a "system of operative images," that is to say, it must contain the essential components for the action: important environmental conditions, regularities, courses of action. Hacker labels the part of the total system of operative images (SOI) which represents the course of action as "action program" (Miller, Galanter, & Pribram speak of plans). On the basis of the SOI, corresponding CCF-units are then formed for each respective action. These units possess a certain "preliminary run" and react to feedback. Efferent impulse, reafferent feedback, and renewed efferent corrective impulse must blend temporally into one another in order to guarantee a fluid action.

5.2. The Hierarchical Organization of Action

If actions are regulated by internal models in this way, then the question arises whether or not an individual action program must be stored for each action. This would raise insoluble problems, because it would require an extremely high storage capacity of the human memory.

The solution lies in a hierarchical model, according to which the individual CCF-units are hierarchically interlocked with one another and become more and more general the higher one moves. The specific details are respectively generated when they are needed, whereby their formation is regulated in turn by superior CCF-units. In this way, the next steps are respectively generated during the action, and require a certain preliminary run to have the respective action program available; which, however, when it has to be used, must not be so large that feedback from the current action can no longer be incorporated.

Thus, the regulation is a matter of a system of hierarchically interlocked units, in which the ones which are higher up and more general have regulative, controlling, and monitoring functions with regard to those beneath them. This principle of the condensation of many small units into comprehensive ones which can be split up again if necessary has been known for a long time in the perceptual area as the principle of "supercoding" (Frank, 1964; cf. also "chunking" in Miller, 1956). Analogous to this, Volpert (1973) speaks about supercodes for motor-behavior or action, respectively, in so far as a signal of higher level can set off the generation of the corresponding CCF-units of lower rank.

Of course, a certain concept may exist that is not combined with the corresponding actions or operations; the concept leads, so to speak, into a void. Volpert calls this a nonsupercoded concept—to distinguish it from the supercode—a "global code." The goal of therapy can, accordingly, be to replace global codes with supercodes, that is, to connect a general cognition with the action in such a way that a single summons regulates the complete action.

So the essential aspect of our discussions about action theory may be stated thus: global insights, images, intentions, etc. are frequently not relevant to action, because no action plan is so closely connected with them that the corresponding action can be generated with relatively little effort. Disturbing influences then develop their full disruptive impact.

The levels of the postulated hierarchy can be differentiated according to their generality ("above") or specificity ("below"), and according to their consciousness. Actions which are regulated by higher levels require conscious attention, with which plans are developed, decisions made, and feedback processed. Actions which are controlled by lower regulatory levels are in comparison relatively automatic; the higher levels are restricted to occasional control.

Thereby, a differentiating aspect is added to the problem mentioned above, that a cognition may not be relevant to action. Highly automatic actions can often be consciously regulated only within limits. The processing of feedback certainly insures adaptation to environmental conditions, insofar as the action—unchanged in structure—flexibly adapts itself in details. Greater modifications are, on the other hand, often not possible; conscious regulations cannot modify the action; if anything, they can stop it. Thus, actions possibly assert themselves contrary to insight on grounds of too great a routine (which in turn can have an influence on insight, in the sense of a dissonance reduction); that is, even the insight that a particular behavior should be performed in another way often cannot any longer influence an automatic behavioral act.

Hacker attempted to name different levels of action regulation which are characterized by various degrees of conscious attention.

5.3. The Levels of Regulation

In the discussion of the study group in Dresden, first of all two levels of regulation were roughly differentiated: a sensorimotor level, which regulates highly routine, stereotyped movements with minimal participation of consciousness, and an intellectual level, which is responsible for conscious processes of judgment and planning. Quaas (1969) later suggested that a third level be postulated between the first two, which is based on the conscious processing of signals, but which leads not to complex planning processes, but to the actualization of already well-formed patterns of action. Hacker included this third level in his system as the "perceptive-conceptual level."

These three levels are now to be briefly characterized here.

1. The sensorimotor level of regulation. Here we are concerned with the "lowest" level of cognitive regulation. It is responsible for relatively constant, stereotypical sequences of movements, which are highly automatic and run their course without the participation of consciousness.

The operative image contains information about distances and directions. In the action program plans for movement are correspondingly accumulated which represent the dependent components of actions; the control which ensues is predominantly kinesthetic.

An experienced driver, for example, reaching for the gearshift lever (triggered off at higher levels by the impulse "shift"), can perform without visual control, and the act requires little cognitive capacity (the driver can converse uninterruptedly in so doing)—of course, only in the "normal case," that is, when no disturbance arises.

2. The perceptive-conceptual level of regulation. On this level, general "basic action patterns" are controlled. These are relatively constant in their structure and can be flexibly employed according to the situation. The term "perceptive-conceptual" results from the fact that the necessity of its use is mediated by signals, for whose recognizability and integration the conversion into language plays a large part.[6]

Going back to the example of driving a car, in a curve a particular basic action pattern is changed, to the extent that one adapts to the respective sharpness of the curve (steering radius, gearshift operation, etc.). Thus, a particular action pattern is flexibly adapted to the existing experimental conditions.

3. The intellectual level of regulation. This level includes the complex analysis of situations, general principles, etc. The analysis of unexpected or unfamiliar interferences (problem solving) is controlled at this level, and new action plans, not yet available in a supercoded form, can be developed in accordance with heuristic rules. (Here it becomes obvious that the same action can be regulated on respectively different levels in different individuals, or in the same individual at different times of acquisition or of mastery. Thus, for instance, for the beginner, shifting gears is by all means regulated intellectually. Single operations, which at later points in time represent automatic operations dependent on higher levels, are at the beginning still independent actions demanding the highest concentration.)

Hacker's conception relates explicitly to work activities which are directly connected with the production process. Correspondingly, he emphasizes that the processes of thought and decision represent processes of "graphic thinking" on the intellectual level, which are closely involved with the feedback of the work process. (Skell, 1972) points out that the

---

[6]Frese (1978) objects to this label on the ground that perceptive and linguistic processes are in fact generally relevant, and that signals also have the effect of triggering off action on all levels. For this reason, he suggested speaking of a "level of flexible action-patterns." In order to keep the nomenclature consistent within the action theory, we shall continue in what follows to speak of the perceptive-conceptual level, even if the term "level of flexible action-patterns" would be more correct.

possibility of graphically supporting the thought process considerably simplifies the development of plans.)

4. Not included in this conception, however, are activities which take place at a distance from the direct course; thus, for instance, planning activities (as understood in colloquial speech, for example, the plan of a work process made by the designing engineer, the planning of a building complex by the architect) or activities of scientific work (the writing of an article, planning a research project). In our opinion, one ought to postulate an additional level which includes these processes, if one intends to extend Hacker's model to take in activities of a general kind. Therefore, we should like to suggest the additional inclusion of such a level in the action-theory system. We want tentatively to call this the level of *abstract thinking.* In addition to the planning activities mentioned above, thought processes of a general and abstract kind are also to be covered by this level; as, for instance, the testing of statements for logical contradictions, the independent discovery of general regularities, the generating of heuristic rules on the basis of processes which follow a line of abstract reasoning, etc. In our opinion, this level plays an important part for the analysis of forms of cognitive therapy.

Certainly such a classification of levels represents a tentative schema, within which the boundaries are often difficult to specify in detail. Nor is this surprising, since we are dealing not with a typology, but with divisions along one dimension. Nevertheless, an abundance of evidence can be found favoring this classification, which indicates that Hacker's approach can easily be reconciled with the findings of general and of applied psychology. We are of the opinion that such a classification is, in any case, heuristically productive; which is to be shown in what follows.

5.4. Criteria of Effective Action

Irrespective of whether the classification can be retained in this specific form or not, the basic assertion of the model is in any case correct: effective action depends to a decisive degree on how well, how differentiated, and how closely related to reality the internal model of the action and of the factors which influence it becomes. At the same time, however, it is also valid that possession of the *knowledge* alone does not guarantee its conversion into action. For this, it is necessary to learn to process feedback arising during the action, to learn to convert the (abstractly recognized) meaning of signals into actions, etc. However, what characterizes effective action in detail? Volpert (1974) has developed a typology which seems to us very meaningful, and which will be briefly outlined here.

Volpert (1974) assumes two aspects of effectiveness, namely, a factual and a temporal one. He further differentiates, thereby, between an abnormal development of testing and planning processes, on the one hand, and their underdevelopment, on the other. They are abnormally developed, "if they isolate themselves from the concrete steps to action, and thereby from reality; underdeveloped, if they lose their directive function with regard to the performance units (subordinate CCF-units) and thus leave these unguided" (p. 42).

Effective action as realistic. Whereas realistic plans make the attainment of goals possible in a factual and temporal respect, two types of unrealistic plans may be differentiated according to the viewpoints mentioned above. Abnormally developed, isolated plans are illusory; they contain unrealistic parts, or a completely unrealistic time perspective. Underdeveloped plans are not connected with actions; they make possible only aimless groping. Here Volpert speaks of "confused" action.

Effective action as stable-flexible. Here it is a matter of retaining the goal (stability) while at the same time flexibly exchanging subprograms as the situation requires. Abnormal development here means the absence of feedback processing, and thus rigid action. Underdevelopment leads exactly to the opposite: any small disturbance is sufficient to interrupt the flow of action.

Effective action as organized. This criterion refers to the adequate delegational relationship between the regulatory levels. What can be meaningfully delegated to lower levels is delegated, so that the higher levels are free for anticipatory, preparatory tasks.

Here the abnormal development of planning processes leads to the problem that intermediate stages of an action are not sufficiently anticipated; that, in a precipitate goal orientation, action variants are chosen without sufficiently comparing them to possibly better alternatives. Underdevelopment means, on the other hand, that the delegational principle is not sufficiently realized. Higher levels attend to processes which actually can be delegated, and thereby give too much attention to small matters, and can no longer retain the general overview.

This classification also has important implications for social action (cf. also Semmer & Pfäfflin, 1978a,b). The *realistic* aspect draws attention to the knowledge of social rules and of one's own possibilities for action; the *stable-flexible* aspect emphasizes the significance of the capacity—normally, to be acquired in the situation itself—to process feedback adequately. Finally, the *organizational* aspect stresses that this feedback processing should be delegated to as great an extent as possible, in order to achieve the greatest concentration on the essentials.

For therapy, the essential point in the action-theory analysis lies, in our opinion, in the fact that it dismisses the controversy, cognitive or not?, in favor of the question, how are cognitions to be constituted so that they can have a regulatory effect on action? If they do not have this effect, two explanations are possible:

1. The cognition is not sufficiently connected with an action program (plan); the insight which is generally present cannot, therefore, be converted; there are no action supercodes available.

2. The cognitive system is in itself not supercoded. That is, what is generally available as insight (for example, the risk of riding in an elevator is no greater than the risk of many actions which I generally perform without hesitation) is not converted into its logical implications. In the situation itself, "automatic thoughts" specific to the situation speak against this—and they determine the action plan! That is, the inner dialogue of the client with himself also functions according to the same rules as external actions: it can only be stabilized by sufficient supercoding. This problem has been recognized by cognitive therapists, to be sure (cf. the "dual belief system" of Beck), but it has not been further elaborated.

6. Implications of an Action-Theory Approach

In our opinion, many aspects of psychological disorders may be described as ineffective action:[7] unclearly formulated goals, lack of knowledge about general principles of one's own actions and those of others, insufficient strategies, a lack in the ability to convert strategies into actions, automatization of inadequate (at a former time, adequate) actions, insufficient criteria to evaluate or wrong perception of feedback, etc. A diagnosis according to such criteria can, in our opinion, as a supplement to a behavioral analysis, provide a number of indications as to where and with what methods one can start out.

First of all, action theory gives rise to a few general principles for a comprehensive therapeutic (or also preventive) procedure.

6.1. General Therapeutic Rules Derived from Action Theory

1. An adequate supercoding has not only to start out with general cognitions or situational features but also to discuss or practice specific examples (which ought to be as representative as possible for the area in question). Often clients can only begin with the one or the other.

---

[7]This means neither that every ineffective action represents a psychological disorder, nor that psychological disorders can be interpreted in all aspects as ineffective actions. Thus, Gleiss (1978) points out that a suicide, for instance, can be prepared for and carried out with the highest effectiveness. (Of course, here one could ask, from an overlapping standpoint, whether the person in question had not failed to realize other goals.)

Thus, phobics sometimes list an entire series of situations about which they are anxious, without recognizing the connecting principle behind them (cf. Beck, 1976). If this connection is not made, if only separate situations are dealt with in the therapeutic process, then only a slight transference effect can be expected. This is confirmed by Meichenbaum (1975b) among others; systematic desensitization relative to individual situations showed considerably less transference than the mediation of coping thoughts, which can be applied to various situations.

Conversely, some clients have only very general conceptions ("I don't want to be fighting with my wife all the time"), without being able to state the triggering conditions, the specific cognitions, and alternative behavioral modes.

This connection between individual situations and the features they have in common must be achieved in the perceptive area (knowledge of typical situations) as well as the behavioral area (knowledge and mastery of corresponding behavioral styles).

2. With respect to thoughts and actions, a great deal runs its course "automatically." In order to counter this, it is not sufficient to make the respective processes and their possibilities for solution conscious, and to discuss them. Rather, the new behavior must become automatic by means of an (active or cognitive) training process, that is, it must be delegated to lower levels. Meichenbaum's "stress-inoculation training" is a good example of this, because here instructions which give the anxiety a particular interpretation are actively practiced in order to counter the thoughts which usually arise in the stress situation. This interpretation then allows the construction of behavior patterns which overcome the anxiety. By suitably varying the situations the strategic viewpoint is securely established, and thereby the possibility for transference is not lost by becoming rigidly tied to only one or a few situations.

At the beginning of such training, the primary goal is to break up the automatic quality, to interrupt the behavioral chain by a signal. In our opinion, this is the effect that is achieved by thought stop (e.g., Rimm & Masters, 1974): The "stop signal" is connected to a specific thought content and interrupts the continuous chain. Now the client can devote his conscious attention to his thoughts (intellectual regulation), and can consciously and actively employ a counterstrategy. The more often he succeeds in this, the more the cognitive counterstrategy, for its part, becomes routinized and is thereby delegated to lower levels. This constant watchfulness over higher levels still remains necessary for an extraordinary length of time. Research on stress has shown that overlearned behavior patterns, which are executed with a minimum of conscious control and feedback processing, are the most immune to stress (cf. Semmer & Pfäfflin, 1978b). The phenomenon of regression, which can often be observed under stress, is thus the regression to behavior patterns learned at an earlier time and, therefore, more strongly automated. Thus, the old habits tend to appear again under stress. Presumably this can be somewhat alleviated by conscious preparation for stressful situations, but it cannot be completely done away with. It is important, therefore, that the client be prepared for this kind of spontaneous remission, so that it does not become cause for resignation.

3. The *operative representational system* must be developed in such a way that not only positive possibilities, but also frequent mistakes and possibilities for overcoming them, are represented within it. Here a derivative arises for the therapeutic process which is distinctly at variance with classical learning theory. Action theory suggests that incorrect models also be represented (cf. Semmer & Pfäfflin, 1978a), so that the operative representational system will be developed comprehensively (and typical mistakes can, thereby, also be more easily avoided). Moreover, the action theory urges one also to acquire strategies for overcoming the problems arising subsequent to particular behavioral mistakes. This means that in therapy one must be prepared for, among other things, possible sources of danger from new behavioral acts, tendencies toward relapses, possibilities of resignation, and obstructions through the reaction of the environment.[8] Meichenbaum's (1975b) results point in the same direction: training in coping strategies, where one learns, for example, to deal with rising anxiety, show better effects than training in a so-called mastery strategy, where the attempt is made to achieve anxiety-free action.

4. The registration and adequate processing of *feedback* deserves particular attention. One is astonished again and again at how many clients have problems with this. The depressive client who was of the opinion that he had stuttered, when he had in fact formulated his thoughts very well and clearly, though not perhaps quite well enough for publication, is an example of this. Many clients do not notice which of their formulations provoke contradiction or defense, for example, by the marital partner—often even after one has already discussed with them the general features which are responsible for this. Here it is an important task of the therapist, for his part, to give clear feedback, and to do it in such a way that the client becomes independent of it in the course of time. Praise (reinforcement) or rebuke (punishment) or the act of ignoring (extinction) are by themselves of little use here, or represent very complicated and ineffective strategies. Good feedback must, to be sure, take motivational factors into account; it must, however, at the same time have optimal

---

[8]The practitioner will in any case normally be doing this as a matter of routine already. Here is a typical instance where the practice is better than its theory, which in no way suggests this.

informative content. Feedback provides an optimal informative content when the essential aspects are emphasized, without at the same time overwhelming the client with pieces of information which he cannot process. This means that the information has to be adjusted to the respective state of the operative representational system, and must connect with the respective level of information and practice. At the same time, feedback carries an optimal amount of information, when both the correct behaviors and the behavioral mistakes are described.

The demand for concreteness is valid only to the extent that one has to ensure that feedback is concretely interpretable for the client. When, after a series of sessions, a supercode has been developed, often a general comment is sufficient, which the client can then break down for himself and relate to the situation. In our experience, many clients themselves create concepts in the course of time, which aptly characterize a particular situation or strategy (for example, "negative thinking"), and they immediately understand whenever this concept is briefly referred to.

Such supercoding can also be seen as an indication that the client himself is increasingly in a position to make use of the feedback arising from the situation or from his own action. As long as the therapist has to supply very specific commentaries, the client is still quite dependent on him, and thus independent transfer to the daily life situation is still very difficult.

Excessively vague standards of evaluation against which feedback can be interpreted are often cause for the fact that a particular cognitive set is maintained despite apparently clear experience to the contrary. The depressive person, for instance, who resolves to do something "well," immunizes himself. His criterion is so vague that he can always decide after the fact that it is not "good." A clear agreement about an exactly specified standard and the most far-reaching exclusion of subsequent alternative interpretations (for example, attribution to chance of an accomplishment deemed "good" according to the agreement) are extremely important here. (Preparation for sources of danger, discussed above, can have good effect here by providing immunity against subsequent interpretations within the meaning of the depressive set: by predicting a series of such possibilities to the client and, if need be, practicing cognitive counterstrategies with him, the therapist guarantees as far as possible the processing of feedback in accordance with the agreement.)

The point of view introduced here urges one not to be limited to single therapeutic techniques, but to examine a great number of methods and test them for their applicability according to the comprehensive viewpoints discussed.

Indeed, many therapists probably proceed in such a way as to combine a series of techniques. In contrast to this often blind eclecticism, however, the orientation of action theory suggested here has the advantage of supplying a theoretical framework which can be used for heuristic purposes.[9]

6.2. A Taxonomy of Behavioral Disorders in the Context of Action Theory

Up to this point, we have shown that therapies can never proceed in an exclusively noncognitive way, and that the essential question lies in whether the cognitions are also relevant to action. Beyond this, we have presented the criteria for effective and ineffective action as developed by Volpert. Finally, we derived some general rules for therapy from action theory.

In what follows, our concern will be to determine more precisely how behavioral disorders can be interpreted within an action-theory context, and what therapeutic implications follow from such an interpretation. In this necessarily brief presentation, it is not possible to consider all conceivable forms of disorders, even approximately, nor can a complete taxonomy of the disorders be compiled. As a rule, a few examples of the disorders are presented as illustrations. Nevertheless some considerations will be introduced which might within this framework provide useful heuristic methods in the diagnosis and therapy of psychological disorders.

Table I gives a survey of the concepts and ideas which will be used in this discussion. The table serves mainly to clarify the presentation and is not to be considered an exhaustive taxonomy. Besides, the respective positions from which they are viewed differ only in emphasis, so that there is no intention to make rigid assignments to particular spheres. After presenting the contents of this table, we shall illustrate its heuristic value for diagnosis and therapy.

First we proceed to the regulatory levels. These levels are only reltively arbitrary delimitations within one dimension, a dimension ranging from automatic skills to abstract problem-solving processes. This entails certain theoretical consequences; the higher the level (i.e., the more intensely the abstract processes of thought play a part),

- the more conscious are the processes
- the more long-term are the plans
- the longer the time taken for the preliminary run-through of the plans, compared to the actual action

---

[9]In the meantime even Eysenck (1976), who earlier had presumably labeled all this as much too vague, confirms that this should be and can be the function of a theory.

- the more general and thus more adaptable to the respective situations are the plans
- the less situationally specific are the plans.

Conversely, it follows that the lower the regulatory level,

- the more automatic (i.e., to a greater extent unconscious) are the behavioral patterns
- the more short-term are the plans
- the shorter is the time taken for the preliminary run-through of the plan before the action
- the more stereotyped and thereby less adaptable to the situation are the plans
- the more situationally specific are the plans.

The action programs and regulatory basis are distinguished in a somewhat oversimplified fashion in Table I. By regulatory basis we mean the cognitions which serve as a basis for the respective regulation. In comparison with the action program, which is completely oriented toward action, the regulatory basis forms, so to speak, the cognitive background.

Particular disorders exist on each regulatory level:

1. Inadequate regulatory basis. An inadequate regulatory basis can come about because the external and internal conditions of a situation and their connection are incorrectly assessed, or because false or unrealistic goals are set. On the level of abstract thought this means that general rules, those of a social kind above all, are assessed incorrectly, or that incorrect heuristics are applied. Thus, for instance, one reason for marital difficulties can lie in the fact that one of the partners assumes that praise is a sign of weakness, which makes the praised person complacent and lessens his motivation. Therefore, it is also an essential therapeutic step to teach the partners principles of social learning theory, and to refer to the importance of positive feedback (cf. e.g., Azrin Naster, & Jones, 1973).

Another example might be the typical attitude of learned helplessness in the depressive person (Frese & Schöfthaler-Rühl, 1976; Seligman, 1975), which is responsible for the depressive's failure to perceive the effects of his own actions as such, attributing them rather to chance or to other conditions.

On the intellectual level, an incorrect assessment of circumstances is found when the situationally-specific predictions of the actions, for example, of another person, are incorrect. This is the case, for instance, when someone assumes that the other person intends only "evil," and meets every action, even those that are well-intentioned, very aggressively.

On the perceptual-conceptual level, the problem can lie in a misinterpretation of cues specific to the situation. This is the case, for example, when a depressive man connects the negative expression of another person to his not being able to stand him.

Finally, the incorrect assessment of conditions on the sensorimotor level lies in the incorrect assessment of proprioceptive feedback, as, for example, when a person thinks he is stroking tenderly, when in reality he is "grabbing" roughly.

False and unrealistic goals can appear on all levels.

The problem of unrealistic goals in behavioral disorders has been explained in extensive detail by Ellis (1962). The 11 irrational ideas which he considers to be the basis of most psychological disorders center predominantly within the realm of unrealistic goals (and here predominantly on the level of abstract heuristics). Such an unrealistic goal, for example, is the idea that one should be loved and respected by everyone. Unrealistic and false goals can also be found on the tactical and subgoal levels as well.

Often one of the most important therapeutic steps, for example in the depressive patient, is to establish realistic subgoals (cf. for instance Hoffmann, Frese, & Hartmann-Zeilberger, 1976) Unrealistic standards and unclear ideas about goals play a considerable part in the maintenance of negative sets. Whoever does not believe himself capable of anything, and takes it upon himself at some point to do something "well" without specifying this goal any further, will, in all probability, retrospectively make his goal more precise according to how his set defines it, that is, always a bit higher than the achieved result. On the sensorimotor level the criterion for discontinuing an action is especially important. At what point has the standard been achieved, so that the movement can be stopped or changed? Unnatural movements, which signal, for example, affectedness in the social realm, may come about on the basis of inadequate criteria for discontinuing the movement.

2. Lacking a regulatory basis. The consequences of an absence of regulatory basis are similar to those of an inadequate regulatory basis. Particularly confused and unstructured behavior can also emerge, of course, when the conditions have not been assessed, or when no strategical goals exist. Behavior becomes even more disorganized and confused when tactical goals are lacking on the intellectual level, or when situation-specific predictions are not undertaken. In such a case, a person stumbles from problem to problem, which he then must try to overcome through flexible action patterns. Such a problem appears, for example, in alcoholics, who give up long-term goals in favor of short-term goals.

Not rarely encountered is the problem that strategic goals have been drawn up on the level of abstract thought, but without tactical goals or subgoals. As we have already emphasized above, this problem—very

Table I. Assignment of Behavioral Disorders as Specific to the Levels

Regulatory level	Inadequate regulatory basis		Absent regulatory basis	
Level of abstract thought	Incorrect assessment of circumstances General rules, above all social ones, are incorrectly assessed or inadequate heuristics are applied	Incorrect or unrealistic goal setting Unrealistic strategic goals	Lacking assessment of conditions General laws are not known or heuristics for problem solving are not known	Goals not set No strategic goals
Intellectual level	Situation-specific incorrect predictions	Unrealistic tactical, situation-specific goals	No situation-specific prediction, one stumbles from one problem to another	No situationally relevant tactical goals
Perceptive-conceptual level	Misinterpretation of situation-specific cues	Unrealistic subgoals	Nonrecognition of situation-specific cues	No subgoals
Sensorimotor level	Incorrect assessment of distances and circumstances	Incorrect proprioceptive criterion for discontinuance of the movement	Lacking assessment of proprioceptive feedback	No proprioceptive criterion for discontinuance of the movement

Regulatory level	Inadequate program for action		Absent or incomplete mastery of an action program	
Level of abstract thought	Incorrect derivation of programs for action	Inflexible or too-rigid action program	Incomplete mastery of action programs	Lacking program for action
	Incorrect derivation of a strategic plan	Inflexible or too-rigid strategic plan	Incomplete mastery of a strategic plan	Lacking strategic plan
Intellectual level	Incorrect derivation of a tactical plan	Inflexible or too-rigid tactical plan	Incomplete mastery of a tactical plan	Lacking tactical plan
Perceptive-conceptual level	Incorrect derivation of an action pattern	Inflexible or too-rigid action pattern	Incomplete mastery of an action pattern	Lacking action pattern
Sensorimotor level	Inadequate processing of proprioceptive feedback, incorrect distribution of movements	Completely inflexible pattern of movement	Incomplete coordination of movement	Lacking sensorimotor (automatic) skills

common in depressives—can lead to inappropriate standards, and to goals which are set higher in retrospect.

Having concluded this discussion of the regulatory basis, we come next to describe the abnormal developments of action programs, which are even more important for psychological disorders.

3. Inadequate program for action. The action program is the hierarchically structured plan for the execution of actions oriented toward a particular goal.

An inadequacy can be founded, above all, on incorrect inferences from programs for action, or on excessively rigid, inflexible programs for action.

The action program is incorrectly derived from the goal and from the rest of the informational background of the regulatory basis. For example, while general cognitions and insights may be available (for instance, ''I have to be more assertive''), these cognitions are converted into incorrect strategies or tactical plans. The person, who is supposed to be assertive, for example, may always react in an aggressive way, and thereby generally exhibit a behavior negatively sanctioned by society. Incorrect derivation of action programs can occur on each regulatory level—in that incorrect strategical and tactical action programs, incorrect action models, or incorrect sensorimotor skills are all possible. Often such incorrect derivations of action programs are at the root of marital problems, for example, when the immediate response to criticism is massive countercriticism instead of a discussion of the problem itself.

Phobias can also represent incorrect derivations of action programs, for instance, when a person constantly avoids all objects relating to some traumatic experience.

The action program can also be inadequate to the extent that it is rigid and inflexible. This can, but need not, go hand in hand with incorrect derivations of action programs. One can, with Volpert (1974), characterize effective action as stable-flexible, if certain possibilities for correction are utilized and situational changes are adequately met, while the goal is fundamentally adhered to.

The rigidity of action strategies and tactics driven in at some time in the past has been investigated in research on set (Luchins & Luchins, 1959). Rigidity of action in the face of changed environmental conditions apparently underlies most severe behavioral disorders. Thus, in depression research the adherence to the cognition of helplessness is described as a rigid attitude (cf. Frese & Schöfthaler-Rühl, 1976), while avoidance behavior in phobics (Rachman & Bergold, 1976) can likewise be interpreted as rigid adherence to a once-successful (i.e., anxiety-reducing) action strategy.

Reasons for such rigid adherence and inflexible application of action strategies or tactics could lie in the following:

- that an alternative action strategy is lacking and, therefore, the only one available is rigidly and inflexibly maintained,
- that certain strategies become rigidified and fixated under conditions of anxiety and stress (cf. e.g., Maier, 1956),
- and that the actions have become automatic to such a degree (i.e., have been displaced to the sensorimotor level to such an extent) that they can now be stopped only with great difficulty and can no longer be altered on higher levels commensurate with the circumstances.

4. Absent or insufficient mastery of an action program. The incomplete mastery of an action program has been designated by Volpert as a global code. The cognitions are correct, to be sure, and the behavior can also be described by the client, but the cognitions are not connected with the concrete behavior. The cognitions are, therefore, not yet relevant to the action. The global code must, therefore, be replaced by a commensurate supercode through practice. As a rule, this means that the regulatory level is shifted downward. Whereas, in the case of incomplete mastery of an action program, a global code has already been formed, even this is lacking if no action program has yet been drawn up at all. Such a deficit—often described in learning theory as a deficit of the behavioral repertoire—must be broken down by commensurate learning processes.

Typical problems in which a suitable program for action is lacking, or in which the program for action has not been mastered, are work disorders. Here the patient may know that he has to work, but he has not developed suitable strategies, tactics, action patterns, or skills, for converting this "abstract" knowledge.

In this description, developed with the aid of Table I, of an action-theory-oriented taxonomy of behavioral disorders, it has been possible to present the individual levels of scrutiny only briefly, and to illustrate them with just a few examples. This description has, of course, some important therapeutic and diagnostic implications.

The following considerations can be inferred from the hierarchical structure presented in Table I:

1. The higher up the disorder is placed in the regulatory level (i.e., the more conscious the thought processes involved), the more general is the disorder. At the same time, the indication for a program which is cognitive in the narrower sense, in order to bring about change in action, is all the greater the higher up the affected regulatory level lies. This, of

course, remains valid only if the lower levels are not themselves disturbed. If, for example, concrete behavioral patterns capable of being asserted are strategically available to a patient, but are not or are only incorrectly applied because of incorrect assessments of circumstances, then a purely cognitive therapy is sufficient to effect a substantial behavioral change.

One of the most important effects of the so-called nondirective forms of therapy would also have to be placed in this area. These therapies direct the client's attention to which situations he reacts to with which emotions, to what his intention had been, etc. The therapist's repeated inquiries about these aspects, and his compelling the client to deal with these matters, leads to the restructuring of the client's cognitive sphere; it thus becomes more differentiated, evident contradictions are easily recognized, etc. Using a more global manner and without explicitly questioning the client's cognitions, something quite similar happens here to what occurs in the openly directive attempts at cognitive restructuring.

Ellis attempts the latter (cf. also Goldfried, Decenteco, & Weinberg, 1974), in dealing particularly with the direct restructuring of global unrealistic goals. Of course the question arises whether the cognitive structure is in fact so coherent, so differentiated, and so logical, that the implications of changing the strategies on the highest level are actually made as if by themselves, as Ellis sometimes indicates his conception of the matter to be. Alternatively one can postulate the existence of contradictory cognitions (the dual belief system according to Beck), whose range of applicability can vary. Thus, therapy often consists in attempting to narrow or change the range of applicability of certain cognitions, or general programs of action. This occurs, above all, on the intellectual and perceptive-conceptual levels, when, with regard to particular situational factors, the adequacy of particular tactics and goal objectives is supposed to be assessed. Training in the perception of these situations and of its influence on behavior then becomes necessary in this area. Thus, the discussion of the situation and its possibilities for action must here be supplemented by a specific training in perception, in which the client learns to identify those cues which appear sufficiently early in the sequence that the application of an alternative strategy is still possible.

The discussion of models or of role-playing is of service here. The application of self-monitoring, that is, of self-observation and registration of the respective behavior, should follow this, however, so that a connection with the situation is also achieved. Self-monitoring leads to the effect that conscious attention (and thereby the potential capacity for conscious regulation) is achieved in the face of the questionable behavior, and the chain of action is interrupted (Kanfer, 1975). If the disorder can be localized, most especially in the realm of the regulatory basis on the middle levels, even a behavioral analysis alone can contribute to changes of the behaviors in a therapeutically effective way (Zimmer & Fiedler, 1974).

These statements are only valid, however, when the lower action programs are in the client's repertoire, but the action programs of a strategic or tactical kind have been derived incorrectly, or where the regulatory basis is inadequate or absent because of an incorrect assessment of circumstances, and of unrealistic or absent goals.

This general restructuring on the upper regulatory levels must remain limited, of course, unless the implications of the new insight are made clear. After I have realized that I am not a total failure, precisely which of my actions can I have confidence in, and which ones not? Where must I recognize that I do not, in fact, "shine" in this area—without again generalizing from this to overall failure? As already stated, the cognitive structure of the client is not so coherent, differentiated, and logically formed, that he can derive all these implications for himself. It is through pure discussion that the consequences of the new premises can still be most readily achieved.[10]

Under particular circumstances, of course, purely cognitive methods of restructuring and the corresponding learning of insight have their limits, when they are to be converted into action:

—Most actions of daily routine are largely delegated to lower regulatory levels, and are therefore in part automatic. Thus, it will frequently happen that a client notices himself acting contrary to his newly gained insight only after the action has already taken place, or after it has proceeded to such an extent that it can scarcely be stopped any longer, due to the relative independence it has acquired through this delegation. This problem is frequently found, for instance, in marital quarrels. The argumentative ritual is solidly entrenched; minimal triggering stimuli can suffice to introduce it. In therapy one may be successful in convincing the client that the partner is not "guilty" of this with his "stubbornness," "sloppiness," or "coldness"; rather, that it is a matter of a reciprocal process of positive feedback. In the critical moment it frequently happens,

---

[10]The qualification "still most readily" follows, above all, because without confirmatory feedback through reality, even a therapist on whom the client confers adequate authority will achieve an attitudinal change only with difficulty. According to our experience, this breakthrough occurs once the hesitant client has been successfully persuaded to try out a particular action in a particular situation (action and situation must be carefully construed as suitable to one another, and the directions for action suitably precise), and when the predicted result in fact then occurs. This thesis is supported by numerous statements from the field of attitudinal research, which affirms that attitudinal changes are more likely to follow behavioral change than to precede it (Insko & Schopler, 1967), or that both continually influence one another reciprocally: "Attitude and action are linked in continuing reciprocal processes, each generating the other in an endless chain" (Kelman, 1974, p. 316).

however, that this occurs to him only after the sequence has already started, when it can scarcely be corrected any longer.

—Also, difficulties always arise during insightful learning, when the programs for action derivable from the insight do not exist in the person's repertoire, or are insufficiently mastered. Routinized behavior patterns, even if they are faulty, quickly gain the upper hand, particularly where a tricky or stressful situation is concerned (Semmer & Pfäfflin, 1978b).

This means that a therapy oriented in a purely cognitive direction will in many cases probably not lead to success. It must be supplemented by behavioral training, if the absent or inadequacy of programs for action on the lower regulatory levels are implicated in the psychological disorder.

In these cases, learning from models, and practice, must ensue. Learning from models is particularly important when the correct program for action is as yet still only slightly developed. For this, the best way to get the information across is by suitably pointing out positive models (i.e., those worthy of imitation) as well as negative. By the latter, we mean models who make the typical mistakes which are to be avoided (cf. Semmer & Pfäfflin, 1978a).

Through learning from models, of course, the best that can be established is a global code (which is valid, at least when the behavior to be learned is complex). In order to come to a genuine supercoding, however, supplemental practice is needed. This can be done either directly, or through cognitive practice.

Some things have already been said about cognitive practice under the heading of mental training. One can even practice skills of the lowest regulatory level by means of mental training. This has the advantage of enabling one to arrange the situations which are being practiced cognitively in a way that is close to real life. At the same time, the level of complexity can also be changed within the therapeutic process, and can thus be adapted to the skills of the patient. Analogous techniques have become known, in cognitively oriented behavior therapy, for instance, as "idealized self-image" (Susskind, 1970). In a comparison of traditional assertiveness training and the technique of the "idealized self-image," the cognitive-practice method showed a certain superiority (Wohlleben, 1974)—from the viewpoint of action theory this result is not surprising, as one can assume that most social-behavioral patterns are known, at least as global codes.

The concrete practice can take place either in role-play or in everyday reality. This has been described so often that it requires no enlargement here.

From the viewpoint of action theory it is essential that an action be practiced until it becomes sufficiently automatic to remain stable even under the influence of stress. Certain regressions in therapy can often be avoided in this way. Moreover, the action can even be practiced under varying conditions of stress, so as to reinforce its resistance to stress.

The high degree of automatism of new "correct" actions is particularly important when other, conflicting behavioral patterns exist. This will always be the case when a patient is supposed to learn to substitute new action programs for others which are inflexible or too rigid. It follows from action theory that breaking up automatic behavioral patterns is more difficult than learning totally new, alternative behavioral patterns. Thoughts can also appear in automatic form (cf. Beck's concept of "automatic thoughts").

Here it can be postulated that a hierarchy exists in the area of thoughts analogous to that which exists for external action (one can also speak of "internal action"). This means that one can proceed on the assumption that thoughts arise in a more strongly heuristic form, or one more related to the situation, in specific, basic patterns, or even automatic ideas. Automatic thoughts have the fundamental characteristics of automatic behavior patterns, that is, they are very rapid, are associated with particular triggering stimuli, are difficult to break up, and are, in large part, withheld from consciousness. Likewise, automatic behavior patterns have only a small conscious component, that is, they are not consciously directed in their course.

If one intends to break up and change such automatic behavior patterns or thoughts, they must be made accessible to consciousness. Perceiving them can then become the occasion for conscious counterdirecting, and the corresponding adequate behavioral patterns or thoughts must then for their part be made automatic.

This fact has been taken into account in therapeutic research, to the extent that emphasis is often placed on training in alternative behavioral patterns. This happens, for instance, with "habit reversal" in the case of tics, where such muscular regions are trained in a sequence of movements which is most contrary to the tic (Azrin & Nunn, 1973). Rotter (1954) also suggested something similar in his book: the patient is requested to think about alternative strategies for solution again and again, and to practice these whenever he relapses into automatic, inadequate behavioral patterns. Finally, Beck (1972) has suggested that counterthoughts should be employed against automatic thoughts (likewise to the point where they become automatic). Frequently applied methods for breaking up automatic behavioral patterns can also be interpreted as a process of making the action conscious. Beck (1972) has proposed that automatic thoughts are to be "pulled apart," that is, one is supposed to hold for a long time the rapid associations which arise unconsciously in particular situations, and to face them consciously. Something similar can also be done in the area of overt behavioral patterns. One technique of this kind might be what is called negative practice (cf. e.g., Eysenck & Rachman, 1971). In negative practice, the patient is compelled to practice an automatic sequence of movement until all the components of the movement can again be brought into consciousness. After this, a conscious relearning can ensue.

Finally, the technique of "flooding" (cf. e.g., Rimm & Masters, 1974), in which the appearance of an automatic reaction is prevented, might also be interpreted as a process of bringing into consciousness. Through prevention of the avoidance behavior the avoidance impulse is made conscious, and the automatic behavior sequence (of the avoidance behavior) is interrupted. Only then can a new strategy be pursued with respect to the situation which triggers such an avoidance impulse.

Certainly the impression is to be avoided that these techniques are suitable only for the lowest regulatory levels. On the perceptive-conceptual level as well, the analogous action patterns are not necessarily conscious in each case (although they have the capacity of being conscious). Therefore, the comments which have been made are also valid for the new learning of, as well as, the breaking up of flexible action-patterns; only here, the breaking up of such patterns is somewhat simpler. The problem remains, however, that when under stress one falls back upon old, better trained, and thus possibly inadequate behavioral patterns.

2. On the relationship between action program and regulatory basis.

Either the program for action or the regulatory basis can be incorrect or correct. From this results a possible fourfold arrangement.

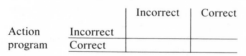

The importance of the cognitive regulatory basis of action is frequently neglected in therapy. Often a particular deficit in knowledge can already lead to disorders. Such deficits in knowledge are especially common in areas which are socially taboo and therefore not easily accessible to the mediation of knowledge, as, for example, in the area of sex, or the intake of drugs and alcohol.

It would be incorrect, however, to separate the regulatory basis and the program for action in such a way as to obscure the interactional effects between these parts of the operative representational system.

Often only the implementation of certain programs of action, that is the actual action and the actual performance of an instruction, can change certain aspects of the regulatory basis.

A person will often alter his opinion on a subject only after having experienced success with certain actions. The necessity for formulating subgoals and adhering to them can frequently be recognized only after he has experienced how the formulation of subgoals leads to an action which achieves better results. This is in accordance with the most important assertion of action theory, which states that the interaction between cognition and action must be taken into account, and that neither side should be made absolute as opposed to the other.

On the other hand, one can recognize from the analysis given here why even therapies which go into relatively little detail about actions (the so-called insight therapies) can achieve success, and within what a limited framework they will be successful (namely, with those persons in whom the regulatory basis is defective or nonexistent, but whose action performances and lower levels of action programs are developed and adequate). This analysis also explains why therapies which scarcely get involved with cognitions (namely, the traditional behavioral therapy of Skinnerian origin, particularly, token-economy programs) can have fruitful consequences. Here, it is left to the patient to find correct generalized action-programs and an adequate regulatory basis. Certain cognitive detours and possible faulty interpretations are thereby tolerated.

It can also happen, however, that the regulatory basis and the analogous global codes have already been adequately developed, and it is then only a matter of practicing the behavior. Here, behavioral therapy in the Skinnerian sense can achieve successes with relative ease.

Proceeding from the action-theory point of view, one can presume that minor disorders of behavior can be changed by almost any form of therapy chosen. If the programs for action are largely adequate and only minor changes have to be undertaken, or if the regulatory basis is for the most part suitable and but slight modifications are sufficient, then almost any kind of therapy—though possibly with a disproportionate expenditure of time and means—can effect behavioral change. The points for initiating new actions are, by virtue of action programs, already partially in existence, sufficiently numerous to, as it were, "radiate outward" by way of both the spontaneous interaction between action and insight, and the spontaneous tendency to form a hierarchy. Only in cases of more severe disorders *must* therapy be applied in a completely goal-oriented way so as to tackle the central points of disorder and explicitly assimilate positive side-effects and transferential possibilities into the program. These considerations can explain the amazing fact that almost every form of therapy has a certain rate of success in its application.

3. Diagnostic impulses stemming from action theory.

The presentation of behavior disorders introduced here implies certain formulations of questions in the diagnostic phase which are rather unusual for therapy:

a. How automatic are the thoughts and behavior patterns of the patient?
b. To what extent is the behavior repertoire dependent on the situation to which it corresponds (that is, which regulatory level is the action program on)?
c. How conscious are the individual steps in the action (i.e., to what extent can strategies for change exist on the higher regulatory levels)?
d. Which problem-solving strategies does the patient adopt, in general, and also in specific situations?
e. To what extent does the basis for the disorder lie in incorrect or unrealistic goals?
f. Does a too-rigid or inflexible—even if in part adequate—action program exist?
g. What alternative programs for action are available to the patient?
h. What knowledge about the regulatory foundations of alternative behavior is available to the patient?

7. Conclusion

In this article our intention was to demonstrate the heuristic fertility of the action-theory approach.

Action theory seems well suited to raise to a higher level, and thus to abolish, the controversy between behaviorists and cognitivists, according to which either the behavior is seen as being directed purely from without, or the cognitions are conceived to be relevant *per se* to action. It has been shown how action-directing cognitions are to be conceived of, and how cognitions can be made into action-directing cognitions. Thus, a cognitively oriented behavior therapy can, to be sure, preserve the heuristic fertility of its behavioral orientation; but it is at the same time removed from the mechanistic conceptions of traditional behavioral therapy and can thereby more adequately comprehend the cognitions and behavior of the patient.

In this way, the various aspects of therapy, practice, feedback, and insight are illuminated anew, and are more adequately understood in their respective significance and integration.

In the action-theory framework, the difference between teaching and therapy naturally becomes blurred. This approach proceeds under the assumption, as does classical behavior modification, that therapy is the acquisition through training of new, more adequate skills (and cognitions). Moving beyond the conception of classical behavior modification, however, action theory can explain why certain propensities remain so amazingly persistent in view of attempts at modification, and how one can break through the automatic quality of behavioral patterns and bring about changes by bringing the components of the action to consciousness.

The considerations presented could be discussed in this short space only in their strategic implications; the tactical level, which is directly relevant to therapy, was addressed only sporadically by means of examples. Only on occasion do new techniques result from action theory. In this presentation, action theory has contributed, above all, to a theoretical summary and integration of techniques of behavioral and cognitive therapy which are already well known. Unlike some authors who advocate a cognitive therapy, we have here introduced, by means of the theoretical integration of different techniques, a noneclectic procedure which views the techniques within a theoretical context and assigns to each of them a particular place and value. In this way, action theory provides a valuable stimulus for the therapist and, beyond this, for therapeutic research as well.

References

Azrin, N. H., & Nunn, R. G. Habit-reversal: A method of eliminating nervous habits and tics. *Behaviour Research and Therapy,* 1973, *11,* 619–628.

Azrin, N. H., Naster, B. J., & Jones R. Reciprocity counseling: A rapid learning based procedure for marital counseling. *Behaviour Research and Therapy,* 1973, *11,* 365–382.

Bandura, A. *Principles of behavior modification.* New York: Holt, Rinehart & Winston, 1969.

Bandura, A. Analysis of modeling processes. In A. Bandura (Ed.), *Psychological modeling: Conflicting theories.* Chicago: Aldine Atherton, 1971.

Bandura, A. Effecting change through participant modeling. In J. D. Krumboltz, & C. E. Thoresen (Eds.), *Counseling methods.* New York: Holt, Rinehart & Winston, 1976.

Bandura, A., & Jeffrey, R. Role of symbolic coding and rehearsal processes in observational learning. *Journal of Personality and Social Psychology,* 1973, *26,* 122–130.

Beck, A. T. *Depression.* Philadelphia: University of Pennsylvania Press, 1972.

Beck, A. T. *Cognitive therapy and the emotional disorders.* New York: International Universities Press, 1976.

Beck, A. T., & Rush, A. J. A cognitive model of anxiety formation and anxiety resolution. In I. G. Sarason & C. D. Spielberger (Eds.), *Stress and anxiety* (Vol. 2). Washington, D. C.: Hemisphere, 1975.

Bem, D. Cognitive alteration of feeling states: A discussion. In N. London & R. E. Nisbett (Eds.), *Thought and feeling.* Chicago: Aldine, 1974.

Breger, L., & McGaugh, J. L. A critique and reformulation of "learning theory" approaches to psychotherapy and neurosis. *Psychological Bulletin,* 1965, *63,* 335–358.

Däumling, M., Engler, J. J., Smieskol, H., Tiegel, G., Triebe, J. K., Ulich, E., & Wilke, K. *Beiträge zum Mentalen Training.* Frankfurt/M.: Limpert, 1973.

Ellis, A. *Reason and emotion in psychotherapy.* Secaucus: Lyle Stuart, 1962.

Elssner, G. Erlernen motorischer Arbeitshandlungen auf der Grundlage von Sprechimpulsen—dargestellt an einer Anlernmethodik für das Aufstecken von Kuosamseide in einem Kunstseidewerk. In W. Skell (Hrsg.), *Psychologische Analysen von Denkleistungen in der Produktion.* Berlin (DDR): Deutscher Verlag der Wissenschaften, 1972.

Eysenck, H.-J. Behaviour therapy: Dogma or applied science? In M. P. Feldman & A. Broadhurst (Eds.), *Theoretical and experimental basis of the behaviour therapies.* London: Wiley, 1976.

Eysenck, H.-J., & Rachmann, S. *Neurosen: Ursachen und Heilmethoden.* Berlin (DDR): VEB Deutscher Verlag der Wissenschaften, 1971.

Fishbein, M. Attitude and the prediction of behaviour. In M. Fishbein (Ed.), *Readings in attitude theory and measurement.* New York: Wiley, 1967.

Frank, H. Was ist Kybernetik? In Ders. (Hrsg.): *Kybernetik—Brücke zwischen den Wissenschaften.* Frankfurt am M.: Umschau, 1964.

Frese, M. *Psychische Störungen bei Arbeitern.* Salzburg: Müller, 1977.

Frese, M. Partialisierte Handlung und Kontrolle: Zwei Themen der industriellen Psychopathologie. In M. Frese, S. Greif, & N. Semmer (Hrsg.), *Industrielle Psychopathologie.* Bern: Huber, 1978.

Frese, M., & Schöfthaler-Rühl, R. Kognitive Ansätze in der Depressionsforschung. In N. Hoffmann (Ed.), *Depressives Verhalten.* Salzburg: Müller, 1976.

Gerst, M. S. Symbolic coding processes in observational learning. *Journal of Personality and Social Psychology,* 1971, *19,* 7–17.

Glass, D. C., & Singer, J. E. *Urban stress.* New York: Academic, 1972.

Gleiss, I. Pathogene Anforderungsstrukturen der Arbeit—aus der Sicht des Tätigkeitsansatzes. In M. Frese, S. Greif, & N. Semmer (Hrsg.), *Industrielle Psychopathologie.* Bern: Huber, 1978.

Goldfried, M. R., Decenteco, E. T., & Weinberg, L. Systematic rational restructuring as a self-control technique. *Behavior Therapy,* 1974, *5,* 247.

Hacker, W. *Allgemeine Arbeits—und Ingenieurpsychologie.* Berlin (DDR): Deutscher Verlag der Wissenschaften, 1973.

Hacker, W. Psychische Regulation von Arbeitstätigkeiten: Innere Modelle, Strategien in Mensch-Maschine-Systemen, Belastungswirkungen. In Ders (Hrsg.), *Psychische Regulation von Arbeitstätigkeiten.* Berlin (DDR): Deutscher Verlag der Wissenschaften, 1976.

Hamilton, V. Socialization anxiety and information processing: A capacity model of anxiety-induced performance. In I. G. Sarason & C. O. Spielberger (Eds.), *Stress and anxiety* (Vol. 2). New York: Wiley, 1975.

Hartig, M. (Ed.). *Selbstkontrolle.* München: Urban & Schwarzenberg, 1975.

Hoffmann, N., Frese, M., & Hartmann-Zeilberger, J. Psychologische Therapie bei Depressionen. In N. Hoffmann (Ed.), *Depressives Verhalten.* Salzburg: Müller, 1976.

Insko, C. A., & Schopler, J. Triadic consistency: A statement of affective-cognitive-conative consistency. *Psychological Review,* 1967, *74,* 361.

Jacobs, A., & Wolpin, M. A second look at systematic desensitization. In A. Jacobs & L. B. Sachs (Eds.), *The psychology of private events.* New York: Academic, 1971.

Jaffe, L. W. *Nonspecific treatment factors and deconditioning in fear reduction.* Unpublished doctoral dissertation, University of Southern California, 1968.

Kanfer, F. H. Self-management methods. In F. N. Kanfer & A. P. Goldstein (Eds.), *Helping people change.* New York: Pergamon, 1975.

Kelman, H. C. Attitudes are alive and well and gainfully employed in the sphere of action. *American Psychologist,* 1974, *29,* 310.

Lazarus, A. A. Multimodal behavior therapy: Treating the Basic ID. In A. A. Lazarus (Ed.), *Multimodal behavior therapy.* New York: Springer, 1976.

Lazarus, R. S. *Psychological stress and the coping process.* New York: McGraw-Hill, 1966.

Lazarus, R. S. *Pattern of adjustment.* New York: McGraw-Hill, 1976.

Lazarus, R. S., Averill, J. R., & Opton, E. M., Jr. Towards a cognitive theory of emotion. In M. Arnold (Ed.), *Feelings and emotions*. New York: Academic, 1970.

Lazarus, R. S., Averill, J. R., & Opton, E. M. Ansatz zu einer kognitiven Gefühlstheorie. In N. Birbaumer (Hrsg.), *Neuropsychologie der Angst*. München: Urban & Schwarzenberg, 1973.

Luchins, A. S., & Luchins, E. H. *Rigidity of behavior*. Eugene: University of Oregon Press, 1959.

Mahoney, M. J. *Cognition and behavior modification*. Cambridge, Mass.: Ballinger, 1974.

Maier, N. R. F. Frustration theory: Restatement and extension. *Psychological Review*, 1956, *63*, 370–388.

Meichenbaum, D. *Cognitive behavior modification*. Morristown, N. J.: General Learning Press, 1974.

Meichenbaum, D. A self-instructional approach to stress management: A proposal for stress inoculation training. In C. D. Spielberger & I. G. Sarason (Eds.), *Stress and anxiety* (Vol. 1). New York: Wiley, 1975.(a)

Meichenbaum, D. Self-instructional methods. In F. H. Kanfer & A. P. Goldstein (Eds.), *Helping people change*. New York: Pergamon, 1975.(b)

Meichenbaum, D. *Cognitive behavior modification: An integrative approach*. New York: Plenum, 1977.

Meichenbaum, D., Turk, D., & Burstein, S. The nature of coping with stress. In I. G. Sarason & C. D. Spielberger (Eds.), *Stress and anxiety* (Vol. 2). New York: Wiley, 1975.

Miller, G. A. The magical number seven, plus or minus two. *Psychological Review*, 1956, *63*, 81–97.

Miller, G. A., Galanter, E., & Pribram, H. *Plans and the structure of behavior*. New York: Holt, Rinehart & Winston, 1960.

Murray, E. I., & Jacobson, L. I. The nature of learning in traditional and behavioral psychotherapy. In A. E. Bergin & S. I. Garfield (Eds.), *Handbook of psychotherapy and behavior change*. New York: Wiley, 1971.

Quaas, W. Zu einigen Aspekten des Wissens und der Rolle von Signalen in der Arbeitstätigkeit. *Probleme und Ergebnisse der Psychologie*, 1969, *28/29*, 11–19.

Rachman, S., & Bergold, J. B. *Verhaltenstherapie bei Phobien*. München: Urban & Schwarzenberg, 1976.

Rachman, S., & Eysenck, H. J. Reply to "a critique and reformulation of behavior therapy." *Psychological Bulletin*, 1966, *65*, 165–169.

Rimm, D. C., & Masters, J. C. *Behavior therapy: Techniques and empirical findings*. New York: Academic, 1974.

Rohmert, W., Rutenfranz, J., & Ulich, E. *Das Anlernen sensomotorischer Fertigkeiten*. Frankfurt a.M.: EVA, 1971.

Rotter, J. B. *Social learning and clinical psychology*. Englewood Cliffs, N. J.: Prentice-Hall, 1954.

Sarason, I. G. Anxiety and self-preoccupation. In I. G. Sarason & C. D. Spielberger (Eds.), *Stress and anxiety* (Vol. 2). New York: Wiley, 1975.

Schachter, S. The interaction of cognitive and physiological determinants of emotional state. In P. H. Leidermann & D. Shapiro (Eds.), *Psychobiological approaches to social behavior*. Stanford: Stanford University Press, 1964.

Schachter, S., & Singer, J. E. Cognitive, social and physiological determinants of emotional state. *Psychological Review*, 1962, *69*, 379–399.

Schmidt, R. A. The schema as a solution to some persistent problems in motor learning theory. In G. E. Stelmach (Ed.), *Motor control: Issues and trends*. New York: Academic, 1976.

Seligman, M. E. P. *Helplessness*. San Francisco: Freeman, 1975.

Semmer, N., & Pfäfflin, M. *Interaktionstraining: Ein handlungstheoretischer Ansatz zum Training sozialer Fertigkeiten*. Weinheim: Beltz, 1978.(a)

Semmer, N., & Pfäfflin, M. Streβ und das Training sozialer Kompetenz. In R. Bösel (Hrsg.), *Streβ: Einführung in die psychosomatische Belastungsforschung*. Hamburg: Hoffmann & Campe, 1978.(b)

Skell, W. Analyse von Denkleistungen bei der Planung und praktischen Durchführung von Produktionsarbeiten in der Berufsausbildung. In Ders (Hrsg.), *Psychologische Analysen von Denkleistungen in der Produktion*. Berlin (DDR): Deutscher Verlag der Wissenschaften, 1972.

Solomon, R. L., & Turner, L. H. Discriminative classical conditioning in dogs paralyzed by curare can later control discriminative avoidance responses in the normal state. *Psychological Review*, 1962, *69*, 202–219.

Stadler, M., Seeger, F., & Raeithel, A. *Psychologie der Wahrnehmung*. München: Juventa, 1975.

Susskind, D. J. The idealized self-image (ISI): A new technique in confidence training. *Behavior Therapy*, 1970, *1*, 538–541.

Ulich, E. Das Lernen sensumotorischer Fertigkeiten. In R. Bergius (Hrsg.), *Handbuch der Psychologie* (Bd. 1, 2). Halbbd.: *Lernen und Denken*. Göttingen: Hogrefe, 1964.

Volpert, W. *Sensumotorisches Lernen*. Frankfurt a.M.: Limpert, 1973.

Volpert, W. *Handlungsstrukturanalyse*. Köln: Pahl Rugenstein, 1974.

Westmeyer, H. Verhaltenstherapie: Anwendung von Verhaltenstheorien oder kontrollierte Praxis? Möglichkeiten und Probleme einer theoretischen Fundierung der Verhaltenstherapie. In H. Westmeyer, N. Hoffmann (Hrsg.), *Verhaltenstherapie: Grundlegende Text*. Hamburg: Hoffmann & Campe, 1977.

Wiggins, J. S. *Personality and prediction*. Reading, Mass.: Addison-Wesley, 1973.

Wohlleben, B. *Esperimenteller Vergleich zweier therapeutischer Ansätze zur Behandlung von sozialen Ängsten bei Studenten*. Unveröff. Dipl.-Arbeit. Institut für Psychologie d. Freien Universität Berlin, 1974.

Zimmer, D., & Fiedler, P. A. *Verhaltenstherapeutische Gruppen,* Vortrag, 6. Verhaltenstherapie Kongreβ der GVT und DBV in München, 1974.

6

Problem Solving and Cognitive Therapy

FERDINAND KÖNIG

1. Introduction

Within the cognitive-therapeutic approaches, the ability to solve problems is more and more regarded as a central goal of therapy and is thus seen as a result of successful therapy. The significance of problem-solving thought as both generator and regulator of action is being taken into consideration for the theoretical foundation as well as for the practical realization of cognitive-therapy concepts, even if often in an unsystematic way.

Which results of basic scientifically oriented and applied research relating to problem solving can be significant or can be made useful for the formulation of therapeutic goals and strategies? Through the clarification of this question, statements have been substantiated concerning the conditions under which, the means by which, and the purpose for which it might be possible to make problem-solving behavior the object of therapeutic interventions. Such clarification would presuppose insight into a taxonomy, albeit tentative, for the activity of the human intellect in solving problems. All the more would this insight seem to be required, in that thinking has for a long time been shunted aside as the object and means of therapeutic endeavors owing to the one-sidedness of behavioristically oriented behavior theories and of the therapeutic principles derived from them.

Under these conditions, to investigate existing approaches of cognitive therapy with exclusive regard either to their consideration of problem solving, or the stringency with which they include features relevant

FERDINAND KÖNIG • Institut für Psychologie, Freie Universität Berlin, D-1 Berlin 41, Bundesrepublik Deutschland.

to problem solving, would represent an unreasonable limitation. It seems more important, rather, to systematize the insights and results of problem-solving research, in order to derive from them the consequences for a cognitive therapy. The structure of this paper is already marked out by these considerations. We classify problems and characterize the particularities of their different types. We discuss general characteristics of situationally specific facts and actions which must be taken into account in problem solving. We analyze cognitive structures and the manner of cognitive functioning with respect to their significance for the processes of gaining and processing information during problem solving. We outline a generalized plan for problem solving, characterize the various distinguishable phases in the total problem-solving process, and describe heuristic procedures which facilitate, or make possible at all, the continuation of the problem-solving procedure, both within its individual phases and through its different phases. We discuss the connection between psychological disorders and the lack of ability to solve problems, and raise questions as to how the development of problem-solving ability can be encouraged and realized under therapeutic conditions.

2. Problem-Solving Skills as the Therapeutic Goal

Personality development has frequently been equated with the acquisition of knowledge and special skills. This overevaluation of *what* a person learns has led to neglect of *how* he learns, gains, and processes information. Sudden changes in the circumstances of life require that the individual be capable, as much through insight into the procedure and forms of gaining and processing information as through the ability to acquire independent knowledge and to judge critically, adapting to new kinds of situations (at the moment perhaps not even conceivable), of productively translating what was previously learned, and of applying this translated knowledge to new realities. The decisive insight is that there are common requirements, beyond the specificity of particular areas of reality, as to how, when faced with concrete problems, one can isolate the conditional variables of a problem situation, collect new information, generate alternative views, make decisions, carry them through, and evaluate their consequences. It is a matter of equipping the individual with intellectual skills that can be generalized and that make it possible to deal with the changing demands of the environment in an effective way. The ability to solve problems in a productive way occupies a central position among these generalizable skills. The individual is supposed to learn to generalize procedures beyond the specific conditions of the problem context in which he acquired them, that is, to develop comprehensive strategies for solving problems. The attainment of a high degree of intellectual mastery of the environment as well as of individual problems represents significant progress in the development of personality (cf. König, 1976).

These considerations and demands, directed at the improvement of problem-solving skills, are, to begin with, not specific to therapy. They become relevant for therapy whenever an individual, whether through deficits relative to knowledge and/or action, through the absence of intellectual requirements specific to problem solving, or through specific experiences, anxieties, or conflicts, becomes incapable of recognizing, working at, and solving personally significant problems. The deficient ability to solve problems, necessitating therapy, may relate to many different aspects of a problem situation, problem-solving process, or problem solution. In order to identify these aspects and to recognize their significance in order to be able to apply measures which might make directed progress possible, one has to gain relatively comprehensive insight into the requirements, conditions, procedures, and forms of information processing which go on during problem solving. The most essential of these insights are characterized in what follows.

3. Problems and Their Classification

To visualize adequately the problematics of a situation requires the ability not only to recognize the various types of problems and to differentiate between them, but also to take into account the possible characteristics of both the facts specific to the problem and the actions relative to solving it. Following Dörner (1976), then, I shall next present *the* information of most essential importance for the characterization and classification of problems.

A problem is defined by an undesired initial state, a desired end state, and a barrier preventing the transformation from actual to desired state. In order to solve a problem, certain external (concrete) and internal (cognitive) operations must be carried out in such a way as to overcome the barrier. Whether a given situation represents a problem or a task—a demand requiring means and methods that are both suitable and familiar in order to be met, and thus also requiring the availability of quasi-automatic reaction capacities—depends on a person's previous experiences. Since the barrier preventing conversion from initial to end state can be of different kinds, different methods are required for overcoming it. The possible barriers, and hence the various types of problems, can be classified according to the categories "clarity of the initial state," "degree of familiarity with means," and "clarity of the goal state." These categories define essentially four kinds of problems:

1. Problems which relate to clarification of the initial state. The problem lies in the general attitude toward problematic situations, in the tendency to deny or to lack sensitivity to problems, which entirely prevents a situation from being recognized as problematic, unsatisfying, and in need of change. Or, rather, the problem lies in a subjective misinterpretation of the condition, which misinterpretation can, in principle, be described objectively by an assortment of features. The objective structure of the initial state is interpreted incorrectly, or accentuated in such a way that an adequate solution to the problem becomes more difficult or impossible.

2. Problems which relate to the application of means. The problem lies in the fact that although the operations which lead from the initial to the end state are known, they cannot be brought into a reasonable temporal or spacial arrangement; that is, there is no success in forming or realizing the proper combination or sequence out of a series of known operations.

3. Problems which relate to the finding of means. The problem lies primarily in the fact that one possesses or is familiar with no suitable means which permit the transfer from a known initial state to a known goal state. The means have to be systematically developed or found.

4. Problems which relate to the finding of goals. Such problems are mostly characterized by the fact that one merely knows that a situation is to be (must be) changed without having clear criteria for knowing how the goal state is to be constituted. This entails designing a goal state, making it concrete, and, if necessary, modifying it in accord with the clarification of both its internal and external contradictions and its possible consequences.

This classification does not mean that each problem can contain only one of these barriers. In complex problem situations, as they exist for the most part in real-life situations which prove to be new, uncertain, and full of conflict, all the barriers are usually present together. Initial and goal states must be made concrete and defined, external (concrete) and internal (cognitive) operations must be found, organized, and realized, in order to overcome the given barriers.

Every problem is attached to a concrete situation which can be described by means of a series of situationally specific facts. These situationally specific facts do not stand unconnected; on the contrary, they are not only connected, but conditional on one another, exhibiting an internal structure. Independent of their differences, such facts have general characteristics which must be considered in the course of explaining and solving problems:

1. The facts can be of varying complexity, so that their features can only be grasped through measures which reduce this complexity. The complexity of the facts depends in turn upon the number of their dis-

cernible components and the number of connections and relations between these components.

2. The facts can be meshed with one another to varying degrees, that is, the features of the situation depend on each other to a high degree, so that to influence one feature brings in its wake changes in a series of other features, necessitating an analysis of the secondary effects.

3. The facts can be transparent to different degrees, in that a variable number of features in the situation will not be directly observable and identifiable, and recourse to symptoms will be necessary, that is, to observable features which covary in different intensities with the supposed latent features and allow an inference to the supposed features.

4. The facts can present dynamics in various degrees, in that they may undergo changes even without the help of the person in question, may put him under time pressure if he wants to intervene correctively in the situation at all, and may require him to appraise the development of a situation.

If, in the course of solving a problem, the facts of a situation are to be changed by means of external and internal operations—the concrete realizations of action plans—then one must take into account what effect such actions have. In a way similar to the situationally specific facts, and independent of their differences, general characteristics of action performances and their effects can be shown, which must be taken into account in solving problems:

1. The actions relating to solving the problem can be effective to various degrees, that is, influence a variable number of features of the facts or several sets of facts of a situation in a way which changes them, so that the total spread of possible effects must be taken into account.

2. The actions and their effects can be reversible to varying degrees, in that the effects can be undone again with various degrees of difficulty, in case they should prove to be undesirable or not wanted as they exist.

3. The actions can be connected with a variable number of conditions and prerequisites, so that their area of application is of variable range, and poses the question as to what extent it is meaningful and possible to create the necessary prerequisites or, on the other hand, to switch over to using other actions which are tied to fewer conditions.

4. The effectiveness of the actions can be certain to a variable degree, in that there is variable probability of their realization under the given circumstances leading to an entirely particular, defined consequence, and only to this consequence. The less probability there is for this, the greater the risk taken with this action.

5. The performance of an action can require various amounts of effort, so that the question arises as to what extent its pursuit is worthwhile in relation to the supposed advantage.

However important the insights into the variety of problem situations, however significant the consideration of general characteristics of situationally specific facts and actions related to problem solving, they are not sufficient to give an adequate picture of the facts relevant for solving problems. Equally important is insight into the possible modes of cognitive functioning and their requirements; insight through which the processes of gaining and dealing with information can be described. The most essential insights gleaned from research into the activity of thought during problem solving are outlined in the following section, again in accordance with Dörner (1976).

4. Cognitive Structures and Cognitive Operations

The cognitive apparatus, the intellectual equipment necessary for problem solving, can be characterized, as to its function, in two respects:

1. The person solving the problem needs certain knowledge about the area of reality in which the problem is to be solved, and knowledge about possible actions by the aid of which the facts specific to the problem can be changed in the direction of the solution for which the person is striving. This knowledge is more or less organized, and corresponds to the picture which a person has regarding the respective area of reality, or to the picture he forms of it. This structure of knowledge would in principle be sufficient to carry out a task, where it is simply a matter of applying known means and procedures for solution, in a reproductive manner, to particular facts, in order to change them.

2. Beyond the knowledge necessary for carrying out a task in a reproductive manner, the person solving a problem requires an arsenal of procedures of construction (heuristics), which allow him systematically to develop action plans when—as is the case with genuine problems (in contrast to tasks)—these cannot be directly recalled from memory. Heuristic methods are, consequently, plans for the construction of action plans with whose help a given state can be productively converted into a desired state. The number of all the heuristic methods which a person has at his disposal for solving a problem characterizes his own heuristic structure.

The process of thought and problem solving consists of a succession of distinguishable cognitive operations whose selection and coordination are regulated by heuristic methods. The problem-solving process will be carried out effectively and systematically to varying degrees, corresponding to the heuristic structure of the person solving the problem. The most essential of the distinguishable intellectual operations significant for the problem-solving process can be assigned to four groups:

1. The group of explications of state. With its aid the given state is analyzed.

2. The group of operations of change. With its aid given facts are converted into new ones.

3. The group of testing operations. With its aid statements about the suitability and the progress of the problem solution become possible.

4. The group of goal explications. With its aid the intended goal state is made concrete.

The sequence of these operations is, as a rule, not arbitrary. It seems preferable that an operation of change follow an explication of state, and a testing operation follow the former; this, however, only when a systematic phase, prepared for by a goal explication, follows after a phase of relatively unsystematic searching.

The heuristic structure can be characterized as a system of heuristic methods which contains the procedures for linking intellectual operations together in order to solve certain problems. The cognitive operations which come into question can be of the most diverse kinds. Without going into a systematic presentation, as has been attempted by Lompscher (1972) for instance, a few can be arbitrarily selected, such as drawing a logical consequence, making abstractions, concretizing, testing, reflecting, understanding something, or having ideas. Every person is equipped with a great number of intellectual programs to meet a number of demands. They can relate to the way in which one analyzes the features of a situation, settles an argument, deals with conflicts, or composes a letter, or how one generally approaches the solving of problems. One of the most important principles for the formation of intellectual programs is the TOTE-unit formulated by Miller, Galanter, & Pribram (1960), which presents itself as the sequence of explications of state, operations of change, test operations, and goal explications. It signifies that when a test (T) reveals that a state does not correspond to a desired value, an operation (O) changing the state is employed, and is continued or varied until a new test (T) reveals that the goal state has been achieved and the problem-solving action, thereby, achieves its end (E). The question concerning the development of heuristic methods can be answered in accordance with classical learning principles. The most primitive form of heuristic method could represent a TOTE-unit in which some action is indiscriminately completed during the operational phase; whereas in the test phase one tests whether satisfaction of a particular need has been achieved. In so doing, one learns that certain operations have a greater chance for success than others (instrumental conditioning), and thus that certain situations have the characteristic of advance notice for other situations (classical conditioning); in this way, schemata are constructed (plans developed) which have the effect that in the future not just any action will be performed, but the particular one by means of which an undesired state is converted into a desired state in the most effective way. The shaping of behavior outlined here is one possibility for the formation and differentiation of heuristic methods; but what is most likely a far more important possibility is the conscious new combination of means and steps toward problem solution.

On the basis of the information about various types of problems with their essential characteristics; about general features of situationally specific facts and actions relating to solving problems, which must be taken into account in the problem-solving process; and finally about methods of cognitive functioning and their prerequisites with which the processes of information processing used in problem solving can be described; the attempt will be made in the next section to outline a generalized act of problem solving. This action represents the development of a solution as a process in the course of which individual phases can be differentiated. These process phases are characterized according to content, and heuristic procedures are presented by the aid of which the progress of the problem-solving process within the individual phases and beyond the various phases is either facilitated, or becomes possible at all.

5. Heuristic Procedures in Problem Solving

In spite of the unlimited number of problems and the diversity of abilities and skills which play a part in the problem-solving process, a general schema of the process can be designed which more or less corresponds to the solution of any number of problems. Previous models for the description of behavioral organization during problem solving have been conceived linearly, describing in steps the sequence of events which take place in the time between the emergence of a problem and the accepted solution. More recent, cybernetically oriented models (Guilford, 1966; Miller, Galanter, & Pribram, 1960; Newell & Simon, 1972), on the other hand, advocate the interpretation that problem solving, particularly in concrete life situations, seldom takes place in an exact sequence of steps; rather, the phases of the process overlap, interact, and are connected through feedback loops.

Both linear and standard circular models show a striking uniformity in spite of the assumption of various numbers of phases and in spite of variously detailed descriptions and labeling of the phases. Thus, Guilford, for instance, describes a problem-solving action as an ordered sequence of events in a system, composed of a memory reservoir and a series of operations which are taken over from his structural model of the intellect: cognition, divergent production, convergent production, and evaluation. The latter characterize decisive stations in the problem-solving process, such as: registering a difficulty or a need, becoming conscious of a problem, defining the given state and the intended goal, actualizing goal-related knowledge, developing possible alternative solutions, assessing the alternatives, deciding on a possible solution or a combination of possible solutions, realizing the cognitively prepared solution, and comparing the result of the action with the intended state in order, if necessary, to enter into a new problem-solving process. The model conceived by Guilford makes it clear that the course of problem solving corresponds, as a rule, to the listed sequence; however, many events can arise simultaneously, or the person solving the problem can be compelled to return to problem-solving activities which were considered to have been already concluded.

In consideration of the diversity of problems (problem types), a series of procedures and rules (heuristic methods) was suggested within problem-solving research which is supposed to facilitate the problem-solving work and by the aid of which progress within the individual phases of the problem-solving process and beyond the various problem-solving phases is achieved with greater certainty than if one were not to apply them. The most essential of the procedures will be presented next.

We defined a problem by the given initial state, the intended end state, and the barrier which prevents the transformation from the present to the desired state. We did not exclude the possibility that the decisive barrier may lie in the unsatisfactory clarification of the state itself, or in the inadequate clarity of the goal. When we limit ourselves in what follows to the presentation of heuristic procedures which relate to overcoming barriers within the framework of the application as well as the finding of means, we do so because the latter always imply the clarification of initial and goal states as well.

If the problem lies in the fact that, although the operations leading from the initial to the end state are known, there is no success in forming or realizing, out of the series of known operations, the combination or sequence which would be decisive for solving the problem; then the following procedures seem meaningful:

1. First of all, one tries to obtain an exact picture of the characteristics of the initial and the goal situation. This can be systematically acquired using the situational analysis proposed by Duncker (1935), composed of a material analysis ("What is given?") and a conflict analysis ("Why doesn't it work?"), and by analyzing the goal ("What do I actually want?"). For a successful analysis of the material, it is necessary to formulate a large number of questions which are asked about the situation and the replies to which are often already helpful in removing supposed difficulties. The same holds true for analyzing the conflict. Furthermore, it is decisive that the intended goal be formulated as precisely as possible.

Clarifying the question as to what is not required is also a part of an exact goal analysis. The decisive effect of analyzing the situation and the goal lies in the ascertainment of the essential features of the given and the intended state. By comparing the characteristics of the initial and the goal situation, one gains insight into the similarities and differences in their characteristics, and obtains clarity about which characteristics of the initial situation must be changed for the purpose of attaining the goal. From the situational and goal analysis there emerges a list of demands that must be met regarding the intended goal.

2. Once the given and the desired state have been defined by means of the situational and goal analysis, the next task lies in searching for means (operations) which allow the conversion from the initial to the goal state. In selecting these means, it is crucial to take their specific characteristics and effects into consideration. In this, particular attention must be paid to the extent to which the application of means can lead to undesired side effects, the assumptions to which particular actions are connected, and the degree to which particular actions preclude others, or make them impossible.

3. Once the person solving the problem has decided on an operation, or a series of them, which he thinks will reduce or eliminate the differences between the initial and the goal state, then he will realize his plan in the next step. It seems meaningful to prepare cognitively for the concrete conversion by using "internal" rehearsals in order to become more secure in the handling and performance of an action or a series of actions. It must also be asked to what extent the execution of the total plan is facilitated by attempting to achieve the intended goal by way of various intermediate goals. The significance of forming intermediate goals lies, above all, in the fact that their formation requires a previous total organization of the problem-solving process, because the problem solver must know the relationship of intermediate goals to each other and the relationship of each respective intermediate goal to the end goal. Such a cognitive preparation for a problem-solving action prevents, for the most part, hasty and unsuitable reactions to an actual or supposed problem, and thereby forces the problem solver to think—a crucial requirement for an adequate problem solution.

4. If the intended goal is not met in spite of the preparatory action or series of actions, this failure forces the problem solver to reorient himself. If the total plan for action has been outlined too roughly, or if the intermediate goals have been too vaguely formulated or set too far apart, it is necessary to refine the formation of intermediate goals, that is, to prestructure exactly the path to solution through a closely meshed network of intermediate goals. The reorientation can also relate to for-

mulating alternative actions and developing new action plans from them, or to setting the originally formulated intention (the goal) more closely, or, if necessary, to settling for the attainment of a particular intermediate goal.

The above-mentioned reorientation in the direction of formulating and developing alternative actions then becomes a central principle if the concern is to find solutions to problems in situations for which, at first, no means and ways allowing the conversion of initial state to goal state are known to the problem solver. For this case, the consideration and use of procedures are important as they have been formulated particularly in creativity research, to the extent that it has dealt with the requirements and conditions for creative problem solving. The following knowledge seems significant:

1. The ways and means suitable for solving a problem are often not seen because the space in which one searches for the problem solution is smaller than the area in which the solution really lies. The problem solver is compelled to enlarge the space of his search and thereby discover new and suitable solution possibilities. He has frequently learned from previous situations that very particular facts can be successfully changed by very particular actions, and is therefore incapable of applying these actions or similar ones to facts of a different kind or to new situations. In this connection, Duncker speaks of the heterogeneous dependence of thinking and acting, that is, the solution value of a possible action for a new situation is not recognized, on account of its grounding in some specific previous situation. Osborn (1963) proposed the method of brainstorming, with its principles of letting thoughts and ideas run their course, formulating as many solutions as possible and variously combining them with one another, and postponing the assessment of the obtained alternative solutions, that is, making a clear separation between the gaining and the evaluating of information. This method, above all, seems suitable for breaking open excessively narrow views regarding the usefulness of particular possible solutions for particular problems. Precisely this fluid and flexible production of ideas, together with the amount and variety of information which one can actualize in a problem situation, has proven significant for effective problem solving. The relationship between the number and variety of ideas produced and the capacity to solve problems is seen, above all, in the fact that the person who can point to a larger number of possible solutions has, under otherwise equal conditions, the greater chance of developing solutions that are realizable and adequate to the problem. A number of other so-called creativity techniques also seem suited for overcoming the heterogeneous interdependence of thinking and acting.

2. Another important way of proceeding in the attempt to extend the search space and to restructure available knowledge for the purpose of discovering possible new solutions is analogous thinking and the use of models. The significance of analogous conclusions is emphasized, above all, in connection with the discovery of new scientific findings (Mendeleev, Kekulé). The analogous conclusion, which serves, in particular, to fill out only partially known circumstances, usually goes through the following substeps: one forms abstractions from the individual characteristics of a given set of facts, looks for a model which in another way corresponds to the abstract facts, transfers characteristics of the model back onto the original facts, and in this way enriches the image of this set of facts and examines whether the new, hypothetically adopted characteristics are, in fact, significant for the original facts (cf. Dörner, 1976, p. 82). One of the well-known creativity techniques, the method of synectics stemming from Gordon (1961), attempts systematically to point out new solutions to problems through the search for analogies. The synectic process follows these principles: first, the problem is to be defined and analyzed; subsequently, proposals for solutions are to be named, which then generally lead to the insight that the problem obviously cannot be solved with the incidental *ad hoc* means; analogies of a direct, a personal, and a symbolic kind are to be found; the new ideas discovered through the use of analogous thought are to be confronted with the original problem, at which point one must ask to what extent these ideas can be made useful for a solution. This synectic process may be illustrated by an example. Suppose one is confronted with the problem of developing procedures which can be applied to prevent automobile headlights from getting dirty. Everyone thinks first of windshield wipers as an obvious possibility. If we initiate direct analogies regarding the question of what functions in a way similar to windshield wipers, we perhaps get answers such as: vacuum cleaner, electric fan, sandblast unit, and curtain of air, among others. If we initiate personal analogies to the question of how might one feel if one were a vacuum cleaner, answers such as the following are conceivable: loosening, crushing, altering, disintegrating, among others. If we initiate symbolic analogies by making concrete, for example, all the things that "changeable" can mean, then answers such as the following are possible: process of disintegration through chemical or physical effects, shredding, bursting, corroding away, among others. The confrontation with the original problem of ideas and answers gained in this way could lead to problem solutions, such as: an automobile headlight consisting of a great number of transparent layers, which, for example, dissolve one after the other through the influence of light, and in this way constantly provide for a clean headlight; a strong current of air (curtain of air) in front of the headlight preventing it from becoming dirty, for which the stream of air created by

driving could be utilized; a fan powered by the air stream and attached in front of the headlight allowing the passage of light but preventing small pieces of dirt from reaching the headlight.

The effect of using analogous thinking lies in the fact that it facilitates the concretizing of indefinite facts and supplies possible new solutions for problems by way of transfer.

6. Approaches for the Enhancement of Competence in Problem Solving

From the presentation of cognitive and action-oriented requirements significant for the problem-solving process one comes upon much, almost as a matter of course, to which a further development of competence in solving problems can be relevant, and upon those means and ways of proceeding which come into question for this development. In the following section, we present a number of suggestions as to how further development of competence in problem solving can be pursued.

We have shown that problem solving is, in principle, connected with two cognitive requirements. On the one hand, the person solving a problem needs particular knowledge about the area in which the problem lies, and, on the other hand, he needs an arsenal of heuristic strategies by the aid of which plans for action which permit a given state to be converted into a desired state in a reproductive and productive way can be developed and organized. Enhancing competence in problem solving must, therefore, relate both to the expansion of knowledge about a particular area of reality and to the improvement of the heuristic strategies. An individual's ability to solve problems can be improved through the expansion of knowledge to the extent that more information, especially information which has a greater probability of being relevant, is available to him for solving the problem, thus guaranteeing a more comprehensive and, therefore, adequate clarification of the state, definition of goals, selection of means, and/or discovery of means. The fundamental disadvantage of this form of enhancement lies in the fact that the problem-solving competence is improved within that specific area alone. It is only the additional improvement of the heuristic structure that allows the individual also to design action plans (strategies for solution) productively for those situations which are new and which demand that previous experiences in dealing with problems be handled more flexibly and be transferred to the concerns of new situations. Some of the most fundamental findings significant for improving the structure of knowledge and the heuristic structure are outlined in the following:

1. The goal of improving the structure of knowledge about particular areas of reality is to exchange undifferentiated knowledge for differentiated and integrated knowledge. Above all, the theory of conceptual complexity (Schroder, Driver, & Streufert, 1967) has supplied interesting hints as to how different structures of knowledge influence a person's perception, thought, judgmental behavior, and action, and how given structures of knowledge can be influenced in the direction of more differentiated and more integrated structures. The authors advocate the view that a person's mode of interaction with a defined area of his environment depends, among other things, on the structure of knowledge which is available to him in this area. The structure of knowledge particular to the individual and specific to this area is characterized according to the dimensions of differentiation, discrimination, and integration. Differentiation is defined by the number of categories of difference and of evaluation which are available to a person for analyzing facts belonging to a particular area. The degree of discrimination depends on the extent to which the categories of judgment themselves allow further differences and gradations. Integration means the degree of coordination between these categories and the number of possible alternative connections. A minimum of differentiation and discrimination is required for a higher degree of integration. In order to determine the degree of conceptual complexity, the dimensions of differentiation, discrimination, and integration are simultaneously taken into account. The authors distinguish between various levels of conceptual complexity, by which they mean particular points on a continuum which ranges from a slight degree to the highest level of complexity. The theory also presents a model for change, in that it proceeds on the basis that a certain level of complexity is attainable only by way of the stage that precedes it. The respective degree of complexity is brought into close relationship with general characteristics of perceiving, thinking, judging, and acting. The person with a low level of conceptual complexity has no alternative possibilities for judging and therefore tends toward stereotypical judgments. A small number of categories of judgment lying adjacent to each other but unconnected, produces a judgmental behavior with a high claim to absoluteness. The environment is experienced in categories of opposites. Information that does not fit into such simple categories is ignored or interpreted incorrectly. Behavior and judgment are strongly dependent on external conditions. The behavior of a person with a high level of complexity is, on the other hand, distinguished by a high degree of autonomy based on the self-designed categories of judgment. In addition to a series of graduated dimensions of judgment, the individual is equipped with a number of rules which specify when and under what conditions the one or the other behavior represents the most adequate reaction to particular situations.

The relationship between conceptual complexity and problem solving is seen in the fact that through the differentiation of knowledge and the combinatory rules, which are available to a person for structuring this knowledge, the informational categories on which to base the interpretation of a situation are also stipulated. The capacity to take the greater part of the available information into consideration in clarifying a situation, to develop alternative interpretations while giving weight to the information commensurate with the situation, makes it possible for the individual to acquire feasible alternative solutions even in complex problem situations. The more comprehensive the available information is in a problem situation, the greater the chance to carry on a situational and a goal analysis adequate to the problem, and to determine the means suited to solving it.

The function of improving the structure of knowledge, therefore, must be to support a person both in expanding the categories of judgment (differentiation and discrimination) available for the assessment of a situation and in elaborating the possible references and relationships between these known facts (integration). Particularly in the area of educational psychology programs have been developed to deal, among other things, with the differentiation and integration of the structure of knowledge (Covington, Crutchfield, & Davis, 1966; Karlins & Schroder, 1967; Suchman, 1960). A detailed survey of such programs has been presented by Davis (1973).

2. The goal of improving the heuristic structure is to expand the inventory of heuristic procedures, facilitate their availability, and promote the capacities which allow new heuristic procedures to be made available *ad hoc*. On the basis of the heuristic procedures already described, a few suggestions will be given as to how the facility of the usage and the availability of such procedures can be promoted.

One possibility consists in trying to promote the processes of dealing with information and the skills necessary for it which are known to be of particular significance for the problem-solving process. One such procedure involves practicing individual cognitive operations or series of operations which do not usually appear in isolation, and which relate only to specific activities connected with problem solving. We have characterized the explication of states and goals and the operations of change and of testing as significant subprocesses. In order, for example, to be able to determine the facts of the given and desired states with sufficient clarity in the framework of the situational and goal analysis, cognitive operations such as actualizing knowledge, describing facts, classifying, comparing, defining, making concrete, and abstracting, seen among others to be significant. In order to discover or to develop operations for change, cognitive operations as described, above all, in connection with so-called techniques of creativity, seem to be important: formulating ideas, generating alternative views, developing alternative possibilities for action, discovering implications, and restructuring, among others. In order to select out of the large number of possible solutions to problems, or alternative actions, those which are likely to be most effective and most adequate to the problem, such cognitive operations as assessing facts, drawing logical conclusions, calculating consequences, and estimating developmental tendencies are significant, among others. Such tactical training related to the enhancement of different distinguishable cognitive operations presumes not only that one is acquainted with the possible operations significant for solving problems but also that one tries to practice and apply them to the most varied problem situations.

A second possibility consists rather less in trying to practice the important cognitive operations in the individual phases of the problem-solving process than in making the entire behavioral organization of problem solving the central focus. A requirement for this is that the person solving the problem can recognize the specific character of a situation, that is, can categorize problems and differentiate them from one another, that he knows about heuristic procedures which can be useful in solving specific problems, and that he is acquainted with the structural features of heuristic methods and knows how heuristic methods are constructed out of individual components as in the sense of the TOTE-unit, for example. On this basis, and in consideration of each situation and the specificity of the problem, it seems possible to design strategies which relate to the total behavioral organization during problem solving, to apply these strategies, and to verify them in various situations.

7. Problem Solving in Cognitive Therapy

We have shown that a problem or problematic situation exists when no sufficiently effective possibility for response is available to the individual within a situation. The events requiring a response are not of external origin only. A substantial part of an individual's stimulative environment consists of the feedback (the internal cues) which result from the individual's behavior, including his thoughts and emotions, which prove themselves to be new, indefinite, and full of conflict, and which must be clarified within the meaning of the problem-solving process. We have designated as problem solving, or problem-solving behavior, the behavioral process through which a given initial state and a desired end state are made concrete. On the one hand, this behavioral process makes available one or several effective possibilities of response which are suited to overcoming the problematic situation; on the other hand, it increases the probability that the most effective behavior will be selected from the number of possible behavioral patterns. Of importance for this are the knowledge and the type of approach to cognitive strategies which enable the individual also to develop solutions for new, unfamiliar problems. The solution to the problem was finally characterized as the reaction which changes the situation in such a way that it is no longer problematic for the individual, optimizing the consequences resulting from the problem-solving behavior, that is, maximizing positive consequences and minimizing negative consequences. Here consequences are the short- and long-term results of the action of a personal and social kind.

With this it becomes clear that the structuralization of a problem-solving process and the decisive goals of therapeutic influence are largely identical. In both cases it is a matter of enhancing and supporting behavior which leads to positive and avoids negative consequences. If attempts to solve problems frequently fail, owing either to lack of the intellectual requirements specific to problem solving or to deficits in knowledge, or if the only result of specific experiences in dealing with problems is the avoidance of such situations and therefore of confronting problem situations in general, then the individual's capacity for action—a decisive requirement for actively organizing his life—is restricted. Since situational demands can no longer be transformed into action plans, at least not in any clear-cut way, a cognitive and experiential disorganization ensues, which the individual experiences as anxiety and which restricts his capacity for action even further. Processes of avoiding anxiety compel the individual to distort stimuli and to adhere to inadequate views, because anxiety is thereby reduced, at least for a short time. As a result, he either totally gives up on activities relating to problem solving, or takes refuge in aimless and stereotypical behavior which is regulated cognitively only to a small extent.

If, on the other hand, conditions and requirements are created which allow the individual repeatedly to experience the solution to personally significant problems, and if he learns through experience that solutions to problems are achieved through one's own actively pursued attempts toward solving them, he will to an increasing degree adopt an open attitude toward his environment. This openness to new experiences, the possibility of being able to take in environmental stimuli in an unobstructed and objective way, enables the individual to perceive changes in his environment and to become sensitive to inconsistencies, and thereby to problematical facts.

Psychological and action-related impairments of this kind, which derive from ineffective problem solving, exist in the majority of the disorders—even albeit to varying degrees—considered to require therapy; whereas the placing of patterns of experience and action into conjunction with the definite capacity to solve problems more or less corresponds to the formulation of every therapeutic goal. In this respect, it was inevitable that precisely within the cognitively oriented therapeutic approaches not only has the theoretical connection between a lack of capacity in problem solving and a series of psychological and behavioral disorders been discussed, but also means and ways have been sought to explicitly or implicitly include problem-solving activities in the therapeutic process. The majority of such attempts relate to the consideration of specific forms of thought which can be obstructive or encouraging in the individual stages of the problem-solving process, as, for example, in clarifying the situation, in finding the goal, in formulating the problem, in applying the means, in discovering the means, or in deciding on a particular behavior. From the cognitive-therapy approaches, which have as their central focus the individual conditions relevant to the problem-solving process, we mention as examples the processes of cognitive restructuring which Ellis (1969) considers significant, and the procedures in self-instruction emphasized by Meichenbaum (1973). Other authors try to do justice to the organization of problem-solving behavior which is achieved through the realization and practice of general strategic courses of action related to problem solving. In this connection, the problem-solving activities which D'Zurilla & Goldfried (1971) have included in the therapeutic process seem most important.

It would make little sense to give once again a detailed survey of the explicit or obscure cognitive and problem-solving aspects that can be found in the various therapeutic approaches (cf. Mahoney, 1974). Our intention has been to suggest and persuade the reader of the extent to which it can be meaningful, in investigating psychological and/or behavioral impairments, to give consideration to a lack of capacities specific to problem solving, and to overcome such handicaps, if necessary, through the directed enhancement of problem-solving competence.

8. Problem Solving under the Conditions of Therapy

Since problem solving and the enhancement of competence in solving problems are explicitly or implicitly the focus (although to varying degrees) of every educational or therapeutic influence, it does not at first seem difficult to impart either the information important for clarifying a problematic situation, or the tactical or strategic procedures decisive for the solution to the problem. Research in the field of education has already shown, however, that to abruptly confront learners with such information and procedures has little effect. The effectiveness of imparting such knowledge, rather, depends decisively on taking into consideration the individual experiential and intellectual requirements, on starting out from these requirements and systematically broadening the range of experience. What is valid here in a purely educational-didactic respect proves all the more significant for the therapeutic situation. We have shown how specific experiences, anxieties, or conflicts can make a person incapable of solving problems when relevant information is avoided or not used to the maximum, or if the individual has no urge to experience anything new. In such a situation, the first step in the direction of constructing effective problem-solving behavior will have to consist in helping the client to reduce conflicts and anxieties, so as thus to create the requirements for dealing more adequately with information—the necessary condition for solving problems effectively.

Enhancing competence in problem solving can, in principle, be included in the therapeutic process in two ways:

1. The therapist discloses the cognitive and behavioral operations or series of operations which are important for the individual stages of the problem-solving process and the requirements which are necessary for their integration in the sense of strategic action plans. He shows the advantages of tackling problems successively and systematically, develops with the client a sample problem-solving process by way of illustration, and over the further course of therapy supports tbe client's problem-solving activities only in a reinforcing way.

2. When, in the course of therapy, the client begins to develop particular activities significant for problem development and solution, the therapist reinforces these activities and makes proposals in such a way that the client carries out successive situational and goal analyses appropriate to his problem, develops possibilities for solution, assesses alternative actions with regard to their possible consequences, makes a decision, and finally carries it through.

The two modes of procedure differ in their degree of explicitness. Which form of therapeutic interaction is chosen will depend to a large extent on which form of therapy is favored. In principle, however, it seems possible, without feeling obligated to one therapeutic direction, to make the enhancement of problem-solving competence a focus of therapy. In any case, however, it is decisive that the therapy enhance the client's own initiative. This must continually be strengthened when the client is attempting to explore his situation and develop possibilities of solution for his problems. The therapist must not become the professional problem solver of the client's concerns; rather, he must create the conditions which will eventually permit the client to tackle his problems himself.

When problem solving is included in therapy, the therapist and the client are compelled to differentiate between the cognitive process of finding and developing a solution and the concrete translation of the solution into action. Since most problems and their mastery ultimately require action, the problem-solving process must include this action. On the other hand, within the development and support of effective problem-solving behavior it seems dubious to place the main emphasis on developing overt behavior. The new systematic handling of problems now demanded presupposes an extensive cognitive restructuring and change in attitude toward problems. The connection between cognition and action which is required here clarifies the limits of various therapeutic "schools" which strain the one or the other aspect to excess.

References

Covington, M. V., Crutchfield, R. S., & Davis, L. B. *The productive thinking program. Series one: General problem solving.* Berkeley: Brazelton, 1966.

Davis, B. A. *Psychology of human problem solving: Theory and practice.* New York: Basic Books, 1973.

Dörner, D. *Problemlösen als Informationsverarbeitung.* Stuttgart: Kohlhammer, 1976.

Duncker K. *Zur Psychologie des produktiven Denkens.* Berlin: Springer, 1935 (1963).

D'Zurilla, T. J., & Goldfried, M. R. Problem solving and behavior modification. *Journal of Abnormal Psychology,* 1971, *78,* 107–126.

Ellis, A. A cognitive approach to behavior therapy. *International Journal of Psychotherapy,* 1969, *8,* 896–900.

Gordon, W. J. *Synectics.* New York: Harper & Row, 1961.

Guilford, J. P. Basic problems in teaching for creativity. In C. W. Taylor & F. E. Williams (Eds.), *Instructional media and creativity.* New York: Wiley, 1966.

Karlins, M., & Schroder, H. Discovering learning, creativity and the inductive teaching program. *Psychological Reports,* 1967, *20,* 857–876.

König, F. Die Verbesserung der Problemlösefähigkeit durch gesprächspsychotherapeutische Reduktion internal motivierter Konflikte. In P. Jankowski *et al.* (Eds.), *Klientenzentrierte Gesprächspsychotherapie heute.* Gottingen: Hogrefe, 1976.

Lompscher, H. J. (Ed.). *Theoretische und experimentelle Untersuchungen zur Entwicklung geistiger Fähigkeiten.* Berlin: Volk & Wissen, 1972.

Mahoney, M. J. *Cognition and behavior modification.* Cambridge, Mass.: Ballinger, 1974.

Meichenbaum, D. Cognitive factors in behavior modification: Modifying what clients say to themselves. In C. M. Franks & G. T. Wilson (Eds.), *Annual review of behavior therapy theory and practice* (Vol. 1). New York: Brunner/Mazel, 1973.

Miller, G. A., Galanter, E., & Pribram, K. *Plans and the structure of behavior.* New York: Holt, Rinehart & Winston, 1960.

Newell, A., & Simon, H. A. *Human problem solving.* Englewood Cliffs, N. J.: Prentice-Hall, 1972.

Osborn, A. F. *Applied imagination.* New York: Scribner, 1963.

Schroder, H. M., Driver, M. J., & Streufert, S. *Human information processing.* New York: Holt, Rinehart & Winston, 1967.

Suchman, J. R. Inquiry training in the elementary school. *Science Teacher,* 1960, *27,* 42–47.

7

Cognitive Therapy in the Treatment of Depression

AARON T. BECK AND RUTH L. GREENBERG

1. Overview

The cognitive model of depression originated in a series of studies of clinical depression conducted by Beck in the late 1950s. Although these studies arose from the desire to secure empirical evidence in support of psychoanalytic theories of depression, the psychoanalytic model proved difficult to confirm empirically. Rather, the data suggested an alternate formulation, namely, that the depressed patient was characterized by a particular kind of thinking: he tended to regard himself as a "loser." The dreams he reported, his early memories, his responses to projective tests, and the material he generated in a clinical setting all tended to reflect certain stereotyped themes: he saw himself as a person who was continually deprived, frustrated, and thwarted, whose prospects were dim, and who had little chance of improving them. Beck also observed that depressed patients made certain logical errors—among them overgeneralization, arbitrary inference, and selective abstraction. Beck concluded that the negative thinking typical of the depressed patient—his negative bias in interpreting events—might underlie his depressed moods. It followed that correcting this thinking might then improve the mood and other symptoms of depression (Beck, 1967/1972).

In the 1970s, Beck initiated a long-term study of suicide, examining both completed suicides and suicide attempters. In its results to date, the study has implicated hopelessness, a cognitive factor, as a major determinant of suicidal behavior. Beck and his colleagues found that a person's

AARON T. BECK AND RUTH L. GREENBERG • Department of Psychology, University of Pennsylvania, Philadelphia, Pennsylvania 19104.

subjective expectations about the future were highly correlated with the seriousness of his suicidal intent (Beck, Kovacs, & Weissmann, 1975). Again, these findings focused interest on the way a person conceptualizes himself and his future, and suggested that suicidal intent might be modified if the patient were helped systematically to revise his views.

In other writings, Beck (1963, 1964, 1976) suggested further that emotions in general follow from the meanings attributed to events, and that emotional disturbances result when events are given distorted meanings. An individual's interpretation of an event is encapsulated in fleeting "automatic thoughts" which are often at the fringes of consciousness, and mediate between an event and the affective response. A patient, Beck argued, can be trained to observe his maladaptive thoughts and formulate alternate interpretations. The "automatic thoughts" also provide a clue to the identification of an individual's underlying belief system, which is ultimately responsible for the way he assigns meaning to events. Beck hypothesized that many forms of psychopathology besides depression, such as anxiety, phobias, and obsessions, may be associated with characteristic cognitive distortions, and that these disorders too would respond to therapy aimed at the correction of the distortions.

"Cognitive therapy" for depressed and suicidal patients has been developed intensively by our research group, and has been the subject of ongoing comparative outcome studies. A recent study (Rush, Beck, Kovacs, and Hollon, 1977) found cognitive therapy to be more effective than pharmacotherapy (imipramine) in the treatment of 41 unipolar depressed outpatients. Increasingly, the effectiveness of cognitive therapy in dealing with anxiety and other disorders is also being examined. Further, empirical studies supporting the cognitive model of depression have been accumulating.

2. The Cognitive Model of Depression

Depression can be viewed in terms of the activation of three major cognitive patterns which induce the patient to see himself, his experiences, and his future in an idiosyncratic, negative manner. These patterns have been termed "the cognitive triad" (Beck, 1967/1972).

The first component of the cognitive triad concerns the patient's negative view of himself. He sees himself as deficient, inadequate, or unworthy, and he tends to attribute his unpleasant experiences to his physical, mental, or moral defects. In his opinion, he is undesirable and worthless because of his presumed defects; he tends to reject himself because of them. Furthermore, he regards himself as lacking in those attributes that he considers essential for the attainment of happiness or contentment.

The second component of the triad is the patient's distorted interpretation of experience. He tends to see the world as making exorbitant demands on him, as presenting insuperable obstacles to his achieving his life goals, or as devoid of pleasure or gratification. He consistently construes experiences in a negative way. He interprets his interactions with the environment as representing defeat, deprivation, or loss.

The third component of the triad consists of viewing the future in a negative way. The depressed patient anticipates that his current troubles will continue indefinitely. As he looks ahead, he sees a life of unremitting hardship, deprivation, and frustration. Furthermore, whenever he contemplates undertaking specific tasks, he expects to fail.

Depressed patients systematically interpret situations in negative ways even though more plausible interpretations are available. When a depressed patient is asked to reflect on alternative explanations, he may realize that his initial interpretation is biased, or rests on an unlikely inference. He may then be able to recognize that he "tailored the facts" to fit his preformed negative conclusions. Also, the depressed patient typically commits a number of logical errors: (a) *Arbitrary inference:* the process of drawing a conclusion in the absence of evidence to support the conclusion, or when available evidence is contrary to the conclusion; (b) *Selective abstraction:* focusing on a detail taken out of context, ignoring other, more salient, features of the situation, and conceptualizing the whole experience on the basis of this element; (c) *Overgeneralization:* to drawing a general conclusion on the basis of a single incident; (d) *Magnification and minimization:* these affect evaluation of the relative importance of particular events; (e) *Personalization:* the proclivity to relate external events to himself when there is no basis for making such a connection (Beck, 1967/1972). These errors lead to and reinforce his characteristically negative, distorted views.

In the cognitive model, other phenomena of depression are considered consequences of the activation of the negative cognitive patterns. The affective group of depressive symptoms—feelings of sadness, loneliness, or boredom—is seen as a direct result of these negative concepts. If a patient incorrectly thinks that he is being rejected, he will react with the same negative affect that occurs with actual rejection. If he erroneously believes that he is a social outcast, he will feel lonely.

Motivational and behavioral changes are similarly related to negative thinking. "Paralysis of the will" results from the patient's pessimism and hopelessness: since he expects that his endeavors will end in a negative outcome or failure, he is reluctant to commit himself, and his activity level drops. Since he believes that he lacks the ability to cope with situations he may meet, he experiences avoidance and escapist wishes. In the cognitive model, suicidal wishes are seen as an extreme expression of the desire to escape from what appear to be insoluble or unbearable problems. Believing himself a worthless burden, the depressed patient believes that everyone—including him—will be better off when he is dead. Increased dependency is also attributable to negative concepts. The patient sees himself as inept and undesirable; he tends to overestimate the difficulty of normal tasks in life, and expects things to turn out badly. Under these circumstances, many patients seek help from other persons whom they consider to be competent. Similarly, indecisiveness is derived from the patient's belief that any decision that he makes will be wrong.

Some of the physical correlates of depression may also be related to cognitive patterns. Profound motor inhibition appears to be associated with a negative view of the self and negative expectancies: when a patient is encouraged to initiate an activity, the retardation and the subjective sense of fatigue are reduced.

2.1. The Development of Depression

The cognitive model presumes that concepts that predispose an individual to depression are formed early in life, and that they derive from his personal experiences, from his identification with significant others, and from his perception of the attitudes of other people toward him. Once a particular concept is formed, it may influence subsequent concept formations; if it persists, it becomes an enduring structure or "schema" in the individual's cognitive organization.

Though the schemata may be latent at a given time, they are activated by particular kinds of circumstances. Situations analogous to the experience responsible for embedding a negative attitude may trigger a depression. For instance, if an individual lost a parent as a child, disruption of a marriage may activate the concept of irreversible loss that was implanted by that early experience. Other types of precipitating events include failing an examination, losing a job, acquiring a disease or physical abnormality, or encountering serious difficulties or frustrations in meeting important life goals. It should be noted that depressions do not always occur in relation to specific stress situations, but may be reactions to a series of nonspecific stresses. In practice, the precipitating event may be hard to identify.

Although any of these events might be painful to the average person, they are not expected to produce depression unless the person is especially sensitive to the situation because of a specific predepressive constellation. Whereas the average person exposed to such a trauma might be able to maintain interest in other aspects of his life, the depression-prone person experiences a change in his view of every aspect of his life. As the depression deepens, his thinking is increasingly saturated with typical depressive themes, even though there may be no logical connection between the actual situation and the interpretations at which he arrives. He gradually loses his ability to view his negative thoughts with objectivity. The dominant schemata seem to interfere with the operations of those involved in reality testing and reasoning. The systematic errors which lead to distortion of reality (arbitrary interpretation, selective abstraction, etc.) are attributable to the action of these hypervalent schemata.

A feedback model provides a more complete explanation of depressive phenomena. In this model, an unpleasant life situation triggers cognitive schemata related to loss, negative expectancies, and self-blame, which in turn produce the related affects of sadness, apathy, loneliness, or disappointment. The affect itself is then taken as another sign of loss or failure—"I'm feeling bad, so things must be bad"—and reinforces his negative attitudes. Stated differently, the affect itself is processed as a stimulus, and its interpretation is subject to the same biases as are external events. Thus, the depression seems to spiral downward until it "bottoms out."

2.2. The Cognitive Model of Depression: Empirical Investigations

Since we find that these studies are not widely known even among those actively interested in cognitive approaches to treatment, we should like to summarize briefly a few of the investigations which support the cognitive model of depression.

A number of studies suggest that particular patterns of negative thinking characterize the depressive. Weintraub, Segal, and Beck (1974) devised a test to measure the cognitive process in depression. The test consisted of hypothetical story introductions, with the stories to be completed by the subject. Each of the incomplete stories involved a principle figure, with whom subjects were asked to identify. They were then to complete the stories by selecting one sentence from each of four sets of sentences following each story. Each group of sentences pursued one of the following themes, drawn from Beck's description of the cognitive triad: expectation of discomfort, expectation of failure, negative interpersonal relations, and low self-concept. Within each group, sentences varied in depressive content.

The story-completion test and a measure of depressed mood were administered to 30 normal male undergraduates on five occasions over a two-month interval. The authors found a time-specific relationship between cognition and mood: subjects who were thinking more negatively, as measured by responses to the story-completion test, were feeling more depressed. The four aspects of cognitive content were highly intercorrelated; also, each aspect correlated with the total cognitive-content score, and was positively associated with depressed mood.

These results seemed to indicate that the cognitive content is a unified, cohesive entity, with a stable relationship to depressed mood. Further, the cognitive content appeared to be a relatively enduring characteristic, whereas depressed moods were more transient. Weintraub *et al.* argue on this basis that a negative attitudinal set, rather than depressed affect, may be the primary factor in depression.

Hammen and Krantz (1976) developed a similar story-completion test which, in addition to cognitive content, also focused on the tendency of the negative cognitions to show certain logical distortions. The subject was asked to read a paragraph describing a woman in a problematic situation, put herself in the woman's place, and select one of four possible responses for each of several items following each story. Each group of responses contained a depressed-distorted response, a depressed-nondistorted response, a nondepressed-distorted response, and nondepressed-nondistorted response. The depressed-distorted responses were constructed on the basis of Beck's (1967/1972) typology of cognitive distortions; each distortion represented an instance of overgeneralization, arbitrary inference, selective abstraction, magnification, or minimization.

The Hammen-and-Krantz test was administered to 33 depressed and 34 nondepressed women. The authors found that depressed women selected significantly more depressed-distorted responses, and significantly fewer nondepressed-nondistorted responses, than nondepressed women.

Hammen and Krantz also assessed life stress for all subjects. There were no significant differences in life stress between the depressed and the nondepressed groups. Within the depressed group, however, high-stress women had more positive expectations and fewer cognitive distortions than low-stress women. It is interesting to note that the most depressed and distorted cognitions were displayed by depressed women with low life stress. This evidence argues against the presumption that depressed thinking is only a feature of "reactive" depression.

Component parts of the "cognitive triad" have also been subjects of empirical investigation. An experimental study by Loeb, Beck, and Diggory (1971) supports the hypothesis that depressed patients suffer from a negative view of the self. Depressed outpatients and nondepressed controls were asked to estimate the probability that they would succeed at a card-sorting task. Although the depressed patients indicated that they would try as hard, and subsequently performed as well, as nondepressed patients, they were significantly more pessimistic regarding their chances

of success, and rated their performances as poorer than did the nondepressed subjects.

Earlier studies by Loeb and his colleagues demonstrated that depressed patients are particularly sensitive to failure. After inferior performance in a word-completion test, high-depressed patients showed a
greater drop in mood level and in level of expectation than low-depressed
patients (Loeb, Feshback, Beck, & Wolf, 1964). Loeb, Beck, Diggory,
and Tuthill (1967) found that depressed subjects reacted to failure on a
card-sorting task with significantly greater pessimism and lower levels of
aspiration than did nondepressed patients.

Strongly associated with low self-concept are the depressed person's
self-criticism and self-blame. Experiments by Rizley (1976) confirm that
the depressed person tends to hold himself and his own inadequacies
responsible for negative outcomes. In one experiment, Rizley had depressed and nondepressed subjects perform a task in which they were to
predict the order of numbers presented. Numbers were actually in a random order, and the experimenter controlled which subjects "succeeded"
and which "failed." Subjects were asked to judge the amounts of luck,
task difficulty, effort, or ability responsible for the outcome. In assessing
the reasons for failure, depressed subjects ascribed more causal importance to internal factors—effort and ability—than nondepressed subjects
(yet in assessing reasons for success, they rated effort and ability as *less*
important factors than the nondepressed group).

Results consistent with the hypothesized negative "mental set" were
obtained in an investigation of memory in depressives. Lishman (1972)
found the tendency to recall more positive than negative material less
marked in overtly depressed patients than in hypomanics and patients
recovered from depression. The author attributed this result to the higher
negative tone of material which depressed patients recalled. In a later
study, Lloyd and Lishman (1975) demonstrated a highly significant relationship between degree of depression and speed of recall of pleasant and
unpleasant experiences: increasing depression was associated with a pro-
gressively diminishing ratio between the speed of recall of pleasant and
unpleasant memories. These studies seem to indicate a tendency to selective recall of negative experience during the depressive episodes.

In a laboratory feedback study, Wener and Rehm (1975) found un-
expectedly that more depressed subjects frequently underestimated the
percentage of "correct" feedback they had received in a laboratory task.
These results were consistent with the hypothesis that depressed patients
tend to interpret their experiences in a negative way. Following in the
footsteps of Wener and Rehm, a number of experiments have examined
the recall of reinforcement in depression. Nelson and Craighead (1982)
used the technique of predetermining reinforcement received by subjects

performing a task. They predicted that, although all subjects received the same amounts of reinforcement and punishment, depressed subjects would recall less reinforcement and more punishment than nondepressed subjects. They also predicted that this effect would be greatest in high-reinforcement and low-punishment conditions, since these reinforcement schedules would be least consistent with their expectations. The predictions were confirmed. The authors also found that depressed subjects self-reinforced significantly less frequently than nondepressed subjects.

DeMonbreun and Craighead (1982) used a similar technique in an experiment with psychiatric outpatients. Again, they found that depressed patients underestimated the amount of reinforcement received when asked to recall previous performance. Their recall of reinforcement was more inaccurate in the high-reinforcement condition than in the low-reinforcement condition, at which time they were fairly accurate. In comparison, nondepressed psychiatric patients overestimated reinforcement; and nondepressed, nonpsychiatric subjects were almost completely accurate in their recall.

In a very different type of investigation, Hauri (1976) found evidence that depressed patients tended to see themselves as thwarted, frustrated, deprived, etc., even after acute depression had remitted. Hauri compared dreams of 11 patients remitted from reactive depression with dreams of 11 matched normal controls. Dreams of remitted patients were "subtly atypical." Combining results on a number of measures, Hauri concluded that remitted depressives "see their world as much more violent and threatening than do controls."

Another group of studies supports the contention that major symptoms of depression—sadness, lack of motivation, suicidal wishes, dependent and avoidant behavior—are consequences of the negative cognitive set.

In an effort to demonstrate that negative thinking can produce sad affect, Velten (1968) examined the ability of self-referent statements to induce mood changes. After reading self-referent statements that progressed from neutral to depressive mood, normal subjects were significantly more depressed on a number of self-report and behavioral measures. Opposite effects were produced by reading statements that progressed from mood neutrality to elation. Coleman (1975) modified the Velten procedure so that subjects read statements of self-evaluation which avoided mention of mood. A subject read either positive or negative statements. Again, the positive statements produced significantly greater levels of elation, and the negative statements produced a more depressed mood.

A second demonstrated consequence of negative thinking is suicidal preoccupation. The statistical association between hopelessness and suicide is supported by several studies (see Beck, 1972). Also of interest is a study by Melges and Weisz (1971), in which a soliloquy technique was used to reevoke subjective experiences preceding suicide attempts. These authors found that suicidal ideation was related to a hopeless, helpless, and narrow view of the personal future.

Several studies by our own research group have indicated that hopelessness, defined as a cognitive factor involving negative expectations, may represent the link between depression and suicide. Minkoff, Bergman, and Beck (1973) administered the Beck Depression Inventory, a "Generalized Expectancy" Scale, and a Suicidal Intent Scale to 68 suicide attempters. The Suicidal Intent Scale assesses factual circumstances surrounding the attempt and the patient's intentions during the attempt, based on his self-report. A highly significant positive relationship was found between hopelessness and suicidal intent; hopelessness appeared to be an even stronger determinant of suicidal intent than did depression itself. This study was replicated by Beck et al. (1975), who studied 384 suicide attempters. Both clinical and psychometric ratings confirmed that hopelessness is more highly correlated with suicidal intent than is depression, and accounts for the variance in the relationship between depression and suicidal behavior. This relationship appeared to hold for schizophrenics as well as depressives.

At another research center, Wetzel (1976) replicated the findings of Minkoff et al. in a sample of 48 suicide attempters, and extended the inquiry to a group of 56 patients who had planned, but not carried out, suicide attempts. Findings for the "ideators" also showed hopelessness to be the mediating variable between depression and suicidal intent.

We suggest, then, that we can attribute considerable empirical validity to the concept of a "cognitive triad" that plays a central role in the psychology of depression. In addition, there is some experimental evidence that negative cognitions and their negative effects can be altered. Loeb et al. (1967) showed that, though depressed patients were particularly sensitive to failure, they also were encouraged by success. Depressed patients who had previously succeeded at a card-sorting task were more optimistic, showed higher levels of aspiration, and performed better on a second task than depressed patients who had failed.

Beck (1974) conducted a study in which depressed inpatients were presented with a hierarchy of verbal tasks. The tasks ranged from reading a paragraph aloud to improvising a short speech on a chosen subject and attempting to convince the experimenter of their point of view. Patients began with the simplest task, and progressed to the most difficult items in the hierarchy. After successfully completing the assignment, they showed significant improvement in global ratings of optimism and self-concept. Beck has employed graded task assignments in a clinical setting: the patient is encouraged to use the success experience as evidence that he can achieve specified goals. This procedure is a cornerstone of the cognitive therapy of depression.

3. Cognitive Therapy of Depression

3.1. Behavioral Techniques

The fundamental goal of cognitive therapy with the depressed patient is to train the patient to alter the thoughts that maintain his depressed mood and underlie his lack of motivation, low activity level, and other symptoms. Both cognitive and behavioral techniques are used to achieve this end. In the initial stages of therapy, the severely depressed patient is typically convinced that his thoughts are realistic, and will resist the therapist's efforts to convince him that they are incorrect. Consequently, the therapist concentrates on behavioral methods at this stage. In order to "mobilize" the patient, the therapist may schedule activities with him in advance; hour-by-hour scheduled may give the patient a better sense of being able to control his time. Often the therapist has the patient list his actual daily activities in some detail, and may assign the keeping of written activity lists as "homework." He may also ask the patient to rate the amounts of "mastery" and "pleasure" he has obtained from each activity.

These behavioral records provide factual information to the therapist about the patient's actual activities, which may differ radically from the patient's oral report ("I did nothing," "I just sat around"). More important, they constitute evidence to counter the patient's idea that he has done nothing: actually he has gotten up, dressed himself, drunk coffee, chatted with friends, paid bills, etc. If he has given even low ratings of mastery or pleasure to any activity, this information counters his idea that he *always* feels terrible and that *nothing* he does will give him pleasure or satisfaction. These are the first steps in the process of changing the patient's tendency to think in broad extremes: "all-or-nothing" thinking.

If the level of activities is low, or the patient reports obtaining little gratification from them, the therapist may assign particular activities, such as preparing a dinner or attending a movie. The patient's reaction to the assignment may provide a clue to his thinking; if he does not volunteer his reaction, the therapist inquires specifically about it. Often the patient will be reluctant to undertake the assignment, because he is sure that he will fail at it, or thinks that he is too weak or incompetent to take even the first step; or he will believe that there is no point in doing things that he used to enjoy, because they no longer give him satisfaction. At this point, the therapist may suggest that the patient carry out the assignment as an experiment, the purpose of which is to determine whether or not he is capable of accomplishing the task or gaining pleasure from it. Since the goal of the experiment is just to gather information, there is no way the patient can fail—any outcome will provide information to patient and therapist. Generally, the patient will agree to such an experiment, and will indeed discover that he can do and enjoy more than he expected. The success encourages the patient, and often causes an improvement in affect. More important, it provides the therapist with an occasion to point out that the patient's beliefs and expectations differed from reality.

When the patient is reluctant to attempt any activity, the therapist may introduce a graded-task assignment. This method breaks an activity into a hierarchy of small steps, ranging from simple to more complex. The task is arranged so that the patient is very likely to accomplish each step, but again it is understood that "failure" is acceptable, because it too provides needed information. A severely depressed professor, for example, believed that he should take his life because he could no longer lecture; in fact, he had stopped making even routine efforts to care for himself. Therapist and patient agreed that the patient would begin to increase his activities by cooking an egg for breakfast the next morning; this goal too was broken down into specific segments, such as buying the eggs, finding the pan, boiling the water, etc.

Although the patient is likely to feel better after these small successes, he also tends to disparage the accomplishment. To avoid giving himself credit for an accomplishment, he may use the most convoluted logic. A teenager who found that smoking marijuana made her feel "down" made sure that she had no available supply one weekend. Although she achieved her goal of not smoking "grass" for a few days, she took no credit, because, after all, "there was no marijuana around to smoke." The patient must be encouraged to evaluate his achievement realistically: that is, to compare it to his previous level of activity when depressed and to his incorrect estimate of what he could accomplish, rather than the levels of achievement he was accustomed to before he became depressed. This focus on small satisfactions and achievements is aimed at altering the all-or-nothing thinking—the tendency to think that if an achievement is not perfect, it is entirely worthless. Since in the graded-task assignment the criteria for success and failure have been clearly defined, the procedure also provides an opportunity for the patient to observe his tendency to evaluate himself negatively, even when he has met objective criteria for success.

A number of obstacles may prevent a patient from achieving a given goal, and it is helpful to envision these problems and develop possible solutions before the patient actually encounters them, becomes frustrated, and once again labels himself a hopeless failure. To facilitate this process, a method called "cognitive rehearsal" is used. The patient is asked to imagine going through all the steps necessary to achieve a goal. One woman, for example, intended to take an exercise class the following day, but in using this technique recognized that she lacked the proper shorts, might not have access to the car, etc. Solutions were devised for these difficulties, and she was able to take the class. Rather than being overwhelmed with a sense of futility and frustration, as she often was in trying to achieve simple goals, she was able to define discrete problems and work out solutions.

This procedure, like others described here, redirects the patient's attention from the abstract to the concrete. Although the patient's abstract conceptualizations may be pervaded by negativity, his concrete problems are often solvable. He can secure *some* relief from the painful, depressed mood. Encouraged by small successes, and made increasingly aware that his negative expectations are not necessarily borne out, the patient becomes more receptive to the suggestion that there may be systematic distortions in his perceptions of reality. At this point, more directly cognitive methods may be introduced.

3.2. Cognitive Strategies

The essential first step in the use of cognitive methods is to explain to the patient the major premises of the cognitive model. Quite explicitly, the patient is told that the cognitive model presumes that the way people feel depends on the way they think, that they have *learned* to think the way they do, and that they can train themselves to think differently. A number of examples are offered to illustrate the basic idea that thinking determines feeling. In one case, the therapist asked the patient how he would feel if he heard a crash in the next room, and believed a burglar had entered; the patient replied that he would feel anxious, but agreed that he would *not* be upset if he thought the wind had merely blown over an inexpensive object. Or the patient may be receptive to examples drawn from his own experience. Or he may agree that people can make themselves feel sad or angry by thinking of certain subjects. In any case, the therapist looks for signs of assent or at least tentative agreement with the model. Further, he introduces the concept of the "automatic thought"— the feeling, instantaneous interpretation of a situation which is presumed to intervene between an event and the individual's emotional reaction, and may take a verbal or a pictorial form. The concept of the negative cognitive set, which directs the depressive's attention to highly selected features of his experience, is also explained.

This explanation of the cognitive model provides a rationale for the specific techniques to be employed, but it also underscores the collaborative nature of the relationship between the cognitive therapist and his patient. The therapist tries to correct the patient's frequent impression that he will be passively "cured" by an all-powerful authority figure who conceals his working premises from the patient. Rather, consistent with his reality-oriented approach, the therapist places his "tools" on the table, and offers to work *with* the patient toward specific goals which both agree on. Since this procedure elicits the patient's preconceptions regarding what treatment will involve, it allows the therapist to take these into consideration. For example, the patient may believe that therapy inevitably involves exhaustive discussion of childhood experiences. In this case, the therapist can reassure the patient that relief from the condition may be obtained even without looking into its probable origins—that thinking can be altered just as any other habit can be changed. Or the therapist may decide to allow somewhat more than the usual time in therapy to the discussion of past experiences, based on evidence that therapy is more successful when the patient's expectations about it are fulfilled.

In the initial stages of therapy, the therapist has observed the way the patient himself conceptualizes his problems, what areas he believes are the most important to work on, and the way he tends to approach and solve his own problems. In this second stage of therapy, patient and therapist direct their attention to whether the patient's conceptualization of his problems is accurate, and, subsequently, to finding better ways of solving them.

In the therapy session, the therapist asks questions that are designed to point to the way the patient arrives at particular conclusions. For example, a middle-aged housewife complained that she was depressed because her teenaged children no longer wanted to spend time with her. At the therapist's inquiry, it became apparent to both therapist and patient that she had reached this conclusion largely because of preconceived ideas, and in the face of evidence that would have suggested just the opposite to an impartial observer. Another woman concluded, when her lover left her, "I'll always be alone." The therapist, however, does not assume from the outset that the patient's conclusion is wrong, nor does he try to persuade the patient that he is wrong based on the therapist's own perception of the evidence. Rather, he uses a Socratic method of questioning to elicit from the patient himself the statements of fact that lead to a more accurate conclusion.

The patient's own participation in the reasoning process tends to make the more realistic conclusion more credible to him, but, further, it provides experience in reality testing which he can draw on in situations outside the psychiatrist's office. At times, patients require active instruction in how to validate a conclusion. A student who was convinced that a mediocre grade on an exam indicated a low class standing was induced to telephone his professor from the therapist's office and inquire about the meaning of the grade. The professor informed him that he had received the average grade and that it would not necessarily affect his standing in the class, and he offered constructive suggestions on how the young man could improve his performance. The student was relieved at the more accurate appraisal, but had also learned a way of gathering information directly that was helpful on subsequent occasions. Further, the experience served to *disconfirm* his negative cognitive set.

The purpose of these methods is to arrive at an accurate assessment of the patient's problems, in order to supplant the distorted view with which he entered therapy. In other words, the first step is to "get the facts straight." At a later stage, the patient's attitudes may also be questioned. For example, let us assume that the housewife above really did find that her children no longer desired her company on frequent occasions. In that case, the therapist looks into the meaning she assigns to the fact: possibly, "I'm no longer needed as a mother," or "My only pleasure in life is unavailable." She will be encouraged to look for alternate interpretations ("I should be proud of my success as a mother, because I've helped my children achieve independence"), to examine the underlying beliefs that give rise to her spontaneous interpretations ("My purpose in life is to care for my children"), and to modify the underlying beliefs ("My purpose in life is to find personal satisfaction, for which my family is only one possible source"). Similarly, if the student described were indeed in poor academic standing, he would be asked to identify the thoughts elicited by evidence of inferior performance or the possibility of flunking out. If he thinks "I'm worthless if I fail as a student," or "My parents will be disappointed," these premises too are reconsidered. Of course, the "thoughts" indicated are hypothetical; patients' actual belief systems vary widely.

3.2.1. Automatic Thoughts

A basic method of cognitive therapy is to train the patient to identify and evaluate his automatic thoughts. In the therapy session, the patient may be asked to recollect an event that has upset him—to replay it step by step in his imagination—and to look for the thoughts that actually gave rise to his distress. Or a "cognitive rehearsal" method may be used, in which a *potentially* upsetting event is imagined and related thoughts identified.[1] But what occurs in the session itself is only a small part of therapy, for the cognitive therapist continues to depend to a large degree on "homework" assignments in which the patient carries his observational and evaluative skills into daily-life circumstances. The therapist emphasizes that the patient will benefit from therapy in direct proportion to the amount of homework he does—although in some cases, where the homework is seen as burdensome in itself or as having unpleasant associations, this rule may be modified. In fact, the basic "data" which therapist and patient use to construct and refine their strategy are the written records which the patient compiles as "homework." "Homework" is also the setting in which the patient learns and overlearns a new set of responses.

The major thrust of cognitive homework in the early phase is to observe the actual cognitions or "automatic thoughts." Patients are asked to record them, or sometimes simply to count them. In either case, the patient is immediately helped by "distancing" himself from his thoughts— observing them as psychological events. To illustrate the process of "catching" the thoughts, the therapist may ask the patient what was "passing through his mind" while he was sitting in the waiting room. The patient may recall musing that the therapist might be late, or that he might not want to see him; these thoughts are counted as cognitions.

The patient may use changes in affect as cues to look for the cognitions that precede them. Although the optimal time to record cognitions is at the time they occur, a second method is to have the patient set aside a short period each day to "replay" the distressing events of the day and record recollected thoughts.

A slight variation on these methods is to have the patient attend to automatic thoughts specifically in situations, or at times of day which are known to be problematic. The therapist may even assign the patient as "homework" an activity that is somewhat distressing to the patient, so that the patient can "catch" the cognitions that are evoked. Really upsetting events that occur naturally are fully exploited—even welcomed— as opportunities to observe the thinking–feeling sequence and to articulate better the underlying conceptual system. When it is apparent that a particlar theme is common to many of a patient's thoughts, he may be asked to collect thoughts on that theme for a given period.

[1]An experimental study by Wade, Malloy, & Proctor (1977) supports the validity of the cognitive-rehearsal procedure as a model for real-life reactions in a therapeutic setting. Snake-phobic subjects reported experiencing a stream of aversive thoughts and images as they approached a caged snake. When they simply *imagined* approaching the snake, they also experienced these cognitions. Most phobic subjects could not complete the hierarchy of behaviors that was to culminate in lifting the snake from the cage. It is relevant that the point at which they stopped was the same both in imagination and in vivo.

3.2.2. Testing Hypotheses

When enough data have been collected, the therapist may construct an hypothesis. If, for example, many of a patient's thoughts contain the theme of rejection, the therapist may suggest that the patient sees himself as a person who is often rejected by others and consequently avoids social situations in which there is a chance that he may be rejected or disapproved of; this in turn brings isolation and loneliness. The patient is asked to consider whether this conceptualization of his problem seems to fit his past experience, and with his feedback the original hypothesis may be discarded or modified. He is also asked to consider whether future experiences seem to confirm the hypothesis.

3.2.3. Alternative Explanations

At the same time, he is trained to alter his thinking. To a great extent, this takes the form of providing alternate responses to the distressing automatic thoughts. He is asked systematically to consider alternate ways of conceptualizing an event or solving a problem. The depressed person seems to have "tunnel vision"—to have so constricted his view of reality that he is blind to other possibilities. For example, a young mother recently abandoned by her husband believed that she could not survive without him, and was constantly troubled by thoughts such as, "I'll never be able to pull through." Her evidence for this point of view was that she had never managed on her own before; that she had no training in managing finances, and was poor at disciplining her children; and that she felt helpless and unable to cope. Although this "evidence" was perhaps an accurate report of past experience, it did not mean that she was incapable of learning to handle things in the future—a possibility that she had not considered. It was then established that she had in fact resented her husband's domination, and was capable of looking forward to the chance to acquire new skills and more independence. Because her particular cognitive set was so powerful, she had failed to observe these equally relevant aspects of her situation, or seriously to consider pursuing possible solutions to her problems, such as acquiring short-term financial help. The therapist had her consider all her possible courses of action and the objective evidence for and against each one. When he returned to the original belief that she "couldn't survive," she was able to view it with more circumspection.

In severe cases, the patient may be unable to conceive of any solution to his problem except suicide. One by one he has eliminated all alternative solutions from consideration—some, perhaps, because they arouse severe anxiety which he cannot imagine being able to tolerate. In these cases, the therapist must cautiously reopen these possibilities for consideration.

These principles of cognitive therapy lend themselves to a type of written homework assignment which uses the "column technique." Although the form may vary, basically the technique involves recording a distressing event and subsequent reactions in a predetermined format. Generally, in the first column the patient records the event itself—a critical comment by a boyfriend, rejection by a graduate school, a daydream or fantasy. He then makes note of the resulting emotion, and writes down the intervening thought or image. In a final column he reports his "rational response" to the original, dysfunctional thought. More complex homework forms require the patient to rate numerically his original emotional response, and identify and rate his subsequent emotional response; they also ask for ratings of belief in the dysfunctional thought and the rebuttal. Since ratings of disturbed affect generally drop after the "rational response," they can later be used to demonstrate to the patient that he *can* assert control over his emotions.

3.2.4. Analysis of Dysfunctional Thoughts

The analysis of dysfunctional thoughts can take at least three general approaches. *Logical* analysis involves examining the types of inference used in reaching a conclusion. Although the automatic thought is instantaneous, it may compress a complex reasoning process, which can then be recapitulated. The patient asks whether it has involved such logical errors as overgeneralization, arbitrary inference, or selective abstraction, which would cast doubt on the validity of the conclusion. For example, a woman recognized her arbitrary inference when she concluded that a man disliked her because he had failed to telephone. Patients may conclude that something is wrong simply on the basis of their own feeling states. They can learn to recognize and terminate the "cognition–affect spiral." A second approach is *empirical* analysis: the patient considers whether the thought corresponds to factual reality. If the facts are unknown to him, he determines how the relevant information might be obtained. The woman above might have reviewed other evidence of her friend's attitude, and considered calling him herself to acquire firsthand data. *Pragmatic* analysis answers the question, "What are the practical consequences of holding this belief?" If the effects are likely to be self-defeating, this in itself constitutes reason to search for alternatives. In our example, the woman's arbitrary interpretation made her feel sad and dispirited.

With practice, the patient begins to observe patterns in the kinds of events that distress him, and to note that he has stereotyped cognitive responses to these events—an interpretational bias. He recognizes that his beliefs also lead to behavior which may in turn reinforce the belief; an instructor who believed that he could not give a lecture did not attempt to prepare it, leading to failure and confirmation of his low self-image. The patient also becomes aware that particular "rational responses" are especially helpful to him, and he may develop his own shorthand devices to remind himself of useful strategies. One woman, who formulated a helpful distinction between "Task-Interfering Cognitions" and "Task-Orienting Cognitions," would signal herself to dismiss the former by the mnemonic device "TIC–TOC."

3.2.5. Maladaptive Beliefs and Assumptions

Whereas many automatic thoughts are simply distortions of reality and are relatively simple to evaluate, others derive from basic belief systems which may be very firmly entrenched. Yet these too may be subjected to review. A physician strongly believed that professional accomplishment was all that made her life worthwhile, and felt extremely threatened by any sign that her status might be imperiled. She was encouraged to assign more importance to her personal and family life. Another patient, a middle-aged divorcee who was quite secure and untroubled about her career, was nevertheless convinced that a woman's worth depends on having a man: she felt inadequate, inferior, and hopeless wben she was "between relationships." In therapy, her belief was challenged directly: "Do you want your happiness to depend on the whim of another person?" "Do you need parenting, as you did when you were a child?" "Is your friend Sally inferior because she doesn't have a man?"

Many people believe that conspicuous signs of success or social approval are essential for their happiness; or that the world should be fair or just; or that it would be "terrible" or "awful" if certain eventualities came about. Ellis (1962) and others have noted that any statement that contains the word "should" probably is an "irrational" belief that causes distress or discomfort (e.g., "I should be a perfect mother, superior student, high-ranking executive," "I should worry about my parents' opinions of me," etc.). Whether or not they are "irrational," they are seen in cognitive therapy as deserving of careful scrutiny. One therapist asks patients, "Suppose you really *are* inferior. What then?" His purpose is to demonstrate that it is not necessary to be perfect or superior or to meet others' criteria for success.

The cognitive therapist expects that a patient will benefit from a relatively short course of treatment; study patients (Rush *et al.*, 1977) who were initially moderately to severely depressed were seen for a maximum of 20 psychotherapy sessions, and all were substantially improved at the end of treatment. But recovery that is "too quick" is immediately suspect: the patient is cautioned that real change requires long periods of practice. "Feeling better" is distinguished from "getting better." Relief that is based on simply removing environmental stresses—getting a job or finding a boyfriend, for example—will be short-lasting, for the next time the patient loses a job or a man or encounters other stresses to which he or she is sensitive, the relevant cognitive schema will be mobilized again.

3.2.6. Goals of Therapy

From the outset the therapist is realistic in his goals, and ascertains that the patient's expectations are also realistic: the therapist does not attempt to reconstruct the personality in a few weeks or to set right complex interpersonal relationships, nor does he try to eradicate the cognitive schema that have guided the patient's responses for most of his life. He does aim at recovery from the depressive episode and the establishment of new thinking habits that can help prevent future episodes and eliminate mild and chronic discomforts between episodes. To save time, patient and therapist agree on "target symptoms" which will be the major focus of effort: they may be inertia and fatigability, avoidant or dependent behavior, hopelessness and suicidal wishes, perfectionism, self-criticism and self-blame, painful affect, or exaggeration of external demands (see Beck, 1976). In Beck's experience, improvement in one area of functioning leads to improvement in other areas—lessened self-criticism may relieve the sense of fatigue, for example. Also, solving one set of problems implants skills which the patient can then apply to other problems. The patient is trained to become his own therapist: eventually he may be asked to picture future stresses and how he will deal with them on his own.

3.2.7. Specialized Techniques

In addition to the general methods described above, a wide range of more specialized techniques is employed, of which a few will be outlined here. "*Reattribution*" attacks the patient's self-blame and self-criticism, and looks for more balanced, realistic ways of attributing responsibility. A bank manager who complained that he was depressed because of ineffectiveness at his job blamed himself for approving a loan which had fallen through. Questioning established that he had followed good banking procedures and approved the loan on the basis of the best information available at the time. Blaming himself entirely for the negative outcome was a distortion of reality (and had also complicated the original problem by causing him to neglect corrective measures). In this case, the therapist countered the patient's self-blame by (1) reviewing the facts; (2) demonstrating that the patient applied different criteria to his own performance than to others'—he would not have blamed a colleague for approving the loan in question; and (3) directly challenging the belief that he was solely and wholly responsible for the outcome.

A number of approaches are used to counter dichotomous ("all-or-nothing") thinking—the tendency to see things as good or bad, black or white, success or failure. When the patient takes a one-sided view of a situation, the therapist may have him *list advantages and disadvantages,* pros and cons, and weigh both sides until he has achieved a more balanced view. Since he tends to take a one-sided, hopeless view of his own condition, the therapist repeatedly emphasizes the experiences that disconfirm that view, and reminds the patient that setbacks do not "wipe out" the gains he has made. Another tactic is to have the patient *rate various qualities* on a graded scale. He may find it hard to defend the proposition that he is 100% miserable, or helpless, or hopeless, and that nothing the therapist can think of—torture, bankruptcy, paralysis—could make him feel any worse. In this way, he may be induced to give a more moderate, realistic rating of his condition, and to acknowledge and credit himself for small gains.

Some specialized techniques (see Beck, 1970) involve the use of *induced fantasy.* In order to put his current situation in perspective, the patient may be asked to project himself forward in time, and envision a period of greater contentment. If he has had an unpleasant spontaneous fantasy, the therapist may have him deliberately repeat it, changing it so that it is less unpleasant. Or he may simply have him repeat the original fantasy several times, until he is desensitized to it—can experience it without negative affect.

Labeling is another target of the cognitive therapist. Since we are affected by the very words we choose, he observes the way the patient describes himself and his experiences, and may require the patient to find substitutes for (*relabel*) inaccurate or affectively "loaded" words or phrases. If the patient calls an event "depressing" or a comment "insulting," it is likely his feelings will match the description. When an obese woman criticized herself for eating "like a pig," it was suggested that she use the words "hungrily" or "greedily" instead. The patient who calls himself a "loser" is asked to define "loser" in operational terms. If he says, for example, that a loser is a person who fails at everything he tries to do, whether or not he is a "loser" can become an empirical question.

A patient who feels that it is futile to try to solve his problems may benefit from *redefining his goals.* The therapist helps him set reasonable, realistic goals, and, moreover, goals which he can achieve directly, through his own behavior. Since a student cannot control the grade he receives, for example, his goal should not be to receive an A, but simply to complete the required coursework. Similarly, an appropriate goal for an obese patient is not to lose weight, but to follow a diet for a period of time. This method is more likely to provide success experiences and a sense of mastery and control. It also serves as a model for setting realistic, achievable goals in the future.

3.2.8. Approach to Anxiety

Anxiety has a special relationship to depression, and is an important secondary focus of cognitive therapy. Often it appears that a patient's sense of loss, deprivation, or loneliness stems from behavior patterns that are severely circumscribed because of anxiety. A graduate student, new to the metropolitan area, feared to walk in the city streets. He restricted his activities to necessary classes, and became depressed because of social isolation and lack of recreation. Interpersonal anxieties can produce the same result. Frequently, patients do without things they want and need because of paralyzing anxiety that prevents them from asserting themselves to spouses, parents, employers, shopkeepers, and others with whom they come in contact; further, meekness and submission reinforce the "loser" self-image. It never occurs to these patients that they might learn to master their anxiety and avail themselves to these closed-off behavioral options; but doing so can have a profound effect on their negative expectations, and for this reason anxiety-management training has a major function in the treatment of depression.

The cognitive approach to anxiety is eclectic, and draws heavily on behavioral techniques, but it emphasizes the patient's beliefs about the feared situation and its consequences. Two levels of question are asked: First, what is the actual likelihood that the snake will bite, the employer will scold, the blind date will embarrass the patient in public? Second, what is to be feared if the employer *does* scold or the date *does* reject, embarrass, or criticize? Generally, the patient experiences a stream of cautionary, anxiety-provoking self-statements which reflect an unrealistically high assessment of the likelihood of a negative outcome; when the airplane takes off, the patient momentarily regards it as a virtual certainty that the plane is going to crash. He also "catastrophizes" about the potential outcome: "It would be *terrible* if he makes fun of me." Again, these self-statements involve basic beliefs (e.g., "It is important never to look ugly, awkward, stupid, inept, or incompetent to other people"). As in dealing with depressed affect, patients are instructed to observe, record, count, and challenge the cognitions. Techniques drawn from Ellis's rational-emotive therapy extend and vary this approach.

To counter the belief that he cannot cope with anxiety, the patient is coached in practical ways of handling anxiety, and encouraged to practice them in vivo. He is reminded that an age-old method for coping with severe anxiety is self-distraction: performing a task, talking to someone, outlining emergency measures, doing deep-breathing or relaxation exercises. "Thought-stoppage" and structured "flooding" may be suggested; and assertive training might be deemed appropriate. Since the patient fears the feeling of anxiety itself, it helps him to keep in mind that acute anxiety peaks and then decreases. Further, he is taught to recognize that the anxiety itself is not a signal of danger.

Central to cognitive therapy is the assumption that the individual need not be a passive victim of anxiety and depression, but has at his disposal a broad range of problem-solving skills that can be brought to the task of solving his emotional problems. In appraising areas unrelated to his special sensitivities, the depressed patient continues to have clear and unbiased perceptions. If he consciously uses this undistorted reasoning to deal with his emotional problems, we argue that he has a good chance of solving them.

One final point: cognitive therapy is technically eclectic within its conceptual framework, and uses the entire range of current psychotherapeutic strategies, from role playing to marriage counseling and relaxation training. But each technique is chosen as a means of expanding the depressed patient's perceived range of options and altering his negative views of himself, the world, and the future. Further, although the cognitive therapist may identify the same phenomena as a psychotherapist using a different model, he is apt to interpret them in cognitive terms. Thus, "transference" and "resistance" phenomena are utilized as opportunities to observe and correct the patient's unrealistic cognitions about his relationship with the therapist or his distorted perceptions about therapy itself and the nature of change.

As we have noted above, Rush *et al.* (1977) found that cognitive psychotherapy was even more effective than antidepressant medication in the treatment of a group of 41 depressed, suicidal outpatients. Follow-up results to date indicate that the difference in improvement is maintained for nine months after treatment is terminated. We continue to be involved in expanding and reformulating the principles and methods of cognitive therapy, studying its efficacy for various subgroups of depressed patients, and refining our understanding of the psychology and psychotherapy of depression.

References

Beck, A. T. Thinking and depression: 1. Idiosyncratic content and cognitive distortions. *Archives of General Psychiatry*, 1963, *8*, 324–333.

Beck, A. T. Thinking and depression: 2. Theory and therapy. *Archives of General Psychiatry*, 1964, *10*, 561–571.

Beck, A. T. *Depression: Clinical, experimental, and theoretical aspects.* New York: Harper & Row, 1967. (Republished as *Depression: Causes and treatment.* Philadelphia: University of Pennsylvania Press, 1972.)

Beck, A. T. Role of fantasies in psychotherapy and psychopathology. *Journal of Nervous and Mental Disease*, 1970, *150*, 3–17.

Beck, A. T. The phenomena of depression: A synthesis. In D. Offer & D. X. Freedman (Eds.), *Modern psychiatry and clinical research: Essays in honor of Roy R. Grinker, Sr.* New York: Basic Books, 1972.

Beck, A. T. The development of depression: A cognitive model. In R. Friedman & M. M. Katz (Eds.), *The psychology of depression: Contemporary theory and research.* Washington, D. C.: Winston-Wiley, 1974.

Beck, A. T. *Cognitive therapy and the emotional disorders.* New York: International Universities Press, 1976.

Beck, A. T., Kovacs, M., & Weissman, A. Hopelessness and suicidal behavior: An overview. *Journal of the American Medical Association,* 1975, *234*, 1146–1149.

Coleman, R. E. Manipulation of self-esteem as a determinant of mood of elated and depressed women. *Journal of Abnormal Psychology,* 1975, *84*, 693–700.

DeMonbreun, B. G., & Craighead, W. E. Perception and recall of evaluative feedback by depressed and nondepressed persons. *Cognitive Therapy and Research,* 1982.

Ellis, A. *Reason and emotion in psychotherapy.* New York: Lyle Stuart, 1962.

Hammen, C. L., & Krantz, S. Effect of success and failure on depressive cognitions. *Journal of Abnormal Psychology,* 1976, *85*, 577–586.

Hauri, P. Dreams in patients remitted from reactive depression. *Journal of Abnormal Psychology,* 1976, *85*, 1–10.

Lishman, W. A. Selective factors in memory. Part 2: Affective disorder. *Psychological Medicine*, 1972, *2*, 248–253.

Lloyd, G. G., & Lishman, W. A. Effect of depression on the speed of recall of pleasant and unpleasant experiences. *Psychological Medicine,* 1975, *5*, 173–180.

Loeb, A., Feshback, S., Beck, A. T., & Wolf, A. Some effects of reward upon the social perception and motivation of psychiatric patients varying in depression. *Journal of Abnormal and Social Psychology,* 1964, *68*, 609–616.

Loeb, A., Beck, A. T., Diggory, J. C., & Tuthill, R. Expectancy level of aspiration, performance, and self-evaluation in depression. *Proceedings of the 75th Annual Convention of the American Psychological Association,* 1967, *2*, 193–194.

Loeb, A., Beck, A. T., & Diggory, J. Differential effects of success and failure on depressed and nondepressed patients. *Journal of Nervous and Mental Disease,* 1971, *152*, 106–114.

Melges, F. T., & Weisz, A. E. The personal future and suicidal ideation. *Journal of Nervous and Mental Disease,* 1971, *153*, 244–250.

Minkoff, K., Bergman, E., Beck, A. T., & Beck, R. Hopelessness, depression and attempted suicide. *American Journal of Psychiatry,* 1973, *130*, 455–459.

Nelson, R. E., & Craighead, W. E. Perception of reinforcement, self-reinforcement, and depression. *Journal of Abnormal Psychology,* 1982.

Rizley, R. C. *The perception of causality in depression: An attributional analysis of two cognitive theories of depression.* Unpublished doctoral dissertation, Yale University, 1976.

Rush, A. J., Beck, A. T., Kovacs, M., & Hollon, S. Comparative efficacy of cognitive therapy and pharmacotherapy in the treatment of depressed outpatients. *Cognitive Therapy and Research,* 1977, *1*, 17–37.

Velten, E. A laboratory task for induction of mood states. *Behaviour Research and Therapy,* 1968, *6*, 473–482.

Wade, T. C., Malloy, T. E., & Proctor, S. Imaginal correlates of self-reported fear and avoidance behavior. *Behaviour Research and Therapy,* 1977, *15*, 17–22.

Weintraub, M., Segal, R., & Beck, A. T. An investigation of cognition and affect in the depressive experiences of normal men. *Journal of Consulting and Clinical Psychology,* 1974, *42*, 911.

Wener, A. E., & Rehm, L. P. Depressive affect: A test of behavioral hypotheses. *Journal of Abnormal Psychology,* 1975, *84*, 221–227.

Wetzel, R. D. Hopelessness, depression, and suicide intent. *Archives of General Psychiatry,* 1976, *33*, 1069–1073.

The Applicability of Cognitive Components of Behavior in Diagnosis and Therapy

Practical Approaches for a Cognitive Theory[1]

PETER A. FIEDLER

In recent years there has been a noticeable increase in practical behavior therapy as compared to cognitive approaches to therapy. This increase parallels the development of fundamental research in clinical psychology which has demonstrated the significance of cognitive variables in modifying deviant behavior (cf. Mahoney, 1974). Research stemming from behavior therapy never disputed the idea that internal variables have a decisive influence on human behavior; it has simply not been concerned with this problem, mainly because of the methodological difficulties which arise in the investigation of conditions which are not directly observable. Recently, however, the more what one might almost call the "rediscovery of the thinking and feeling human being" becomes a part of behavior

[1]Translation by Gayle Ayn Vickery, revised by Elizabeth Z. Lachman.

PETER A. FIEDLER • Psychologisches Institut, Abteilung für Klinische Psychologie, West. Wilhelms Universität, D-44 Münster, Bundesrepublik Deutschland.

therapy, the more often mention is made in the same breath of certain limitations of the therapeutic process based on behavior-theory models of operant and respondent conditioning (Jaeggi, 1976; Westmeyer, 1976). These limitations become especially clear when research attempts to understand the structures conditioning the entire therapeutic situation rather than confining itself only to factors which influence particular applied techniques (Scheele & Groeben, 1976).

This will also have to be made clear again in the present paper, in which the possibilities and limitations of a cognitively oriented behavior therapy will be discussed. Stress is laid on two main points:

1. First, in a primarily *theoretical section,* we shall discuss characteristics brought forth by the individuality of analysis and modification of cognitive components of behavior. Thus, the necessity for expanding and completing strict behavioral approaches will be emphasized, and some possibilities for achieving this will be pointed out and discussed.

2. In a second, *practical section* we shall concretely demonstrate the applicability of cognitive components of behavior in both diagnosis and therapy. It will be made clear in the process that a therapeutic study of clients' cognitions has significant consequences for the entire therapeutic process.

Since this study was written primarily for practitioners, it is thus limited, in that the necessary theoretical considerations have been given only brief, provisional treatment. We trust, however, that they will still make sufficient contributions toward an understanding of the practical suggestions for diagnostic and therapeutic case work.

One further preliminary comment: The concern of this study is to expand the approach of behavior-therapy to methods of cognitive analysis and cognitive therapy, and not at all to present alternative procedures. We shall therefore illuminate areas of the therapeutic process traditionally neglected by behavior therapists and by the therapeutic methods which behavior therapy has to offer. In particular this means the area of *diagnostic* and *therapeutic dialogue,* which is the primary concern of this study.

Above all, this section reflects the author's concern for promoting discussion within the field of behavior therapy for an *integration of various therapeutic directions.* We hope that this paper will provide a modest beginning toward that end. In what follows the attempt is made to develop some pragmatic prescriptions for therapy which should make it easier to organize and subdivide the whole therapeutic process in such a way that the adoption of the most varied intervention strategies in therapy can also be immediately accounted for. Inspirations for this have come in particular from studies by Bastine (1976) and Kaiser (1975).

1. Therapy as a Cognitive-Social Problem-Solving Process

One practical formulation of the therapeutic process entails attempts to present therapy as an ongoing process of individual problem-solving (by client *or* therapist) and of interpersonal problem-solving (by client *and* therapist). It is becoming more widely accepted to view clinical practice as a problem-solving process. This has also led to interesting innovations in the development of behavior therapy (Bromme, 1977; Kaminski, 1970; Marquis, 1976; Schulte, 1973; Urban & Ford, 1971; cf. also individual contributions in the volume by Kanfer & Goldstein, 1977). Bastine (1976) proposes that the problem-solving approach be made the basis for an integrated therapy.

Here we proceed under the assumption that therapy can be viewed as a problem-solving process guided by feedback. This process can be subdivided into at least the following six stages:

1. *Subphase of problem description:* Therapeutic conversations and activities directed to *searching for* and *identifying* the problem as well as illustrating and describing variables concerning its nature; this phase of data investigation is generally carried to the point at which therapist and client can proceed together in the problem-solving process.

2. *Subphase of problem analysis:* Here we are concerned with the therapist's (and client's) attempts so to *organize* the data related to the problem, which were gathered in the first stage, that clear statements about the origin and conditions responsible for the problem behavior can be generated. Usually the client will have a layman's naive conceptions for explaining the problem behavior, which should be taken into account (cf. Laucken, 1974). In his analysis of the conditions, however, the therapist should rely on his theoretical knowledge of the conditions of learning and strive for a *(functional) behavior analysis* of the symptoms.

3. *Subphase of goal analysis:* The search for and definition of goals for *possible changes in behavior* as generated by the conversations and activities of the client and therapist. The (functional) conditioning analysis can be an aid to an initial orientation. During therapy sessions clients often express explicit desires for changing themselves and their behavior. The client's social partners often have a strong influence on the determination of goals. Staying close to the client's wishes, the therapeutic processes should mediate between these various elements and possibilities for goal determination.

4. *Subphase of plans for change:* Subsequent to goal determination the client and therapist decide on (tentative) general directions of change. These proposed directions are formulated as explicit *plans for change.*

5. *Subphase of motivation for action:* Attempts by the client and

therapist to translate problem solving from the cognitive-verbal level to the level of concrete action and changed behavior. This is facilitated by *practice* sessions in the therapeutic setting, as well as intentional *alternative behavior* under natural conditions.

6. *Subphase of evaluation:* This step entails comparison of the expected results with the actual conditions both during and after Step 5 (Motivation for Action). This final step will possibly engender a new phase of problem description (Step 1), in which case the *problem-solving sequence* continues until a satisfactory evaluation can be achieved.

It is beyond doubt that this therapeutic framework for problem solving contributes to the understanding of the development of individual processes in therapy. Diagnostically, however, the question remains *which* cognitive conditions are elements of the (cognitive-social) problem-solving effort. Furthermore, *how* can cognitive components of behavior be investigated and presented in such a way as to provide access for a functional behavioral and conditioning analysis?

2. Diagnostic Applicability of Cognitive Components of Behavior

It is generally assumed that subjective verbal components of behavior, the internal dialogue, the individual's "inner circumstances," have a clear influence on manifest behavior. These cognitive components of behavior characterize

> a system that mediates in the individual between stimulus and response, between properties of the surroundings and his active reply to them, and chooses and predisposes, that is, makes probable, specific ways of ordering and orienting action in concrete situations. (Schmidt-Mummendey, 1974, p. 2)

As such, cognitive components of behavior are useful in explaining deviant behavior (behavioral disorders).

Attempts both to describe cognitive components of behavior in a unified way and to evaluate them have met with great difficulty. This is due, on the one hand, to their variability and their diverse applicability in diagnosis and therapy, and, on the other, to the limitations of theoretical explanations, which most often have their empirical basis in laboratory experiments alone. In the course of personality development, cognitive learning processes are influenced by stimuli and reinforcement conditions whose complexity is beyond the scope of current laboratory methods (cf. Mischel, 1973; Neisser, 1974; Seiler, 1973). This is especially true of the development, growth, and change of cognitive components of behavior: for the *predictability of changes* in cognitions (*prognosis*) is decisively determined by the *peculiarities of their development* (*genesis*). An investigation of cognitions as *dispositions* to behavior is essential if the significance of the learning history and variability of an individual's current behavior is to be seen clearly. Technically, "disposition" should refer to the fact that cognitive components of behavior remain stable over time, in the extreme case throughout an entire lifetime, and therefore have a constant function as determinants of behavior.

Under given circumstances, elements of these persisting cognitive realities (generally because of their stimulus dependency) become apparent in verbal form (as *subjective verbal components of behavior*). In this form cognitions can be *perceived* within the social environment, and thus their conditioning structure can be *influenced*, thus essentially inhibiting their continuation. A cognitive-oriented therapy makes use of this. Cognitive determinants of behavior are subject to constant change. They are altered when environmental circumstances "force" a change in the value of cognitive dispositions (for example, by reconditioning).However, they can also change in the course of "thought processes" (i.e., during careful weighing of the consequences of a given behavior in the problem-solving process), and can therefore lead to a reinterpretation of the individual's immediate situation.

Cognitive components of behavior are then *relatively constant dispositions to behavior*. They structure the space within which the individual's interactions are defined. Incoming stimuli are filtered by these dispositions as by a cognitive screen. This determines what kind of evaluation the individual makes of the situation and how he assesses the competence of his responses and manner of experiencing. On the basis of cognitive dispositions, possible responses and their predictable and context-dependent consequences may be (cognitively) examined. Ultimately they serve also as standards for a variety of assessments (of one's actions, of changed environmental conditions, etc.).

Yet how can cognitive components of behavior be investigated and presented comprehensively enough to become susceptible of analysis and change?

Approaches, possibilities, and suggestions for *investigation* and *systematization* should be presented and discussed with this question in mind. We shall proceed on the assumption that *motor* and *physiological problem behaviors* should be examined further, perhaps with the assistance of the (S–O–R–K–C) *behavior equation* (cf. Kanfer, 1969). The respondent and operant parts of the behavior-adjusting model of Schulte (1974) is also applicable to this investigation. In our opinion, the form for analyzing cognitive determinants of behavior presented in what follows adapts favorably to traditional therapeutic analysis of behavior.

2.1. Problem Description: Data Investigation and Organization

It is hardly possible to get anything like a universal grasp of all cognitions basic to the problem behavior, regardless of the amount of time spent on the effort. While such universality is not essential for therapeutic intervention, this diagnostic constraint makes it necessary to proceed in a very specific way during the investigation phase: it is essential, in the combined effort of client and therapist, to work out what components of behavior are determining the problem to set out from the client's own perspective. We have already alluded to the necessity for a specific form of diagnostic dialogue which closely follows the client's wishes. This will be explained in more detail below.

To formulate an analysis of conditions, a comprehensive *inventory* is necessary, and is therefore initiated at the onset of therapy. This inventory can be (and usually is) taken during the course of conversations between client and therapist (analytic exploration of behavior). It further serves as both informational resource for the therapist and as (renewed) reassurance for the client concerning his own point of view on the problem behavior. Observations of behavior and questionnaire probes can also be used, but a discussion of these is beyond the scope of the present study (see however Belschner, 1978; Lutz & Windheuser, 1974; Schulte & Kemmler, 1974). To insure a comprehensive inventory, it is important to offer the client a *structure* which facilitates his self-exploration. At this point we should like to suggest a *framework for exploration* which is rooted in the general structure of the therapeutic problem-solving process. Early in therapy, ascribing the subjective verbal components of the client's behavior to general concepts provides further direction for diagnosis and therapy. This generates six points of orientation for exploring cognitive behavior components:

1. Subjective verbal communication reflecting the client's perspective on the symptoms (problem description)
2. Client's assumptions concerning the causes and determinants of the symptomatic behavior and their assessment (*problem analysis by the client*)
3. Client's assumptions concerning possible directions for change and assessment of these goals (*goal analysis by the client*)
4. Client's previous attempts to achieve the goals already set up, as well as assumptions concerning possibilities already considered

or being considered for the achievement of self-appointed goals (*client's past and present plans for change*)

5. Accounts and descriptions of previous successes and failures in attempts to change behavior (*client's previous attempts to change*)
6. Summarized evaluation of the current problem and the client's attempts at prognosis, which takes into consideration the conditions, assumptions, and assessments previously reported (*client's system of evaluation*)

In this phase the client should be encouraged to make subjective verbal communications. These should take the form of evaluations, fears, attitudes, emotional experiences, dogmas and beliefs, expectations (as compared to the instability or constancy of material, social, and personal conditions) which are further considered to be subjective internalized norms, goals, plans, experiences, and parental and educational behavior rules.

Owing to economic considerations, this problem description must at first remain limited to its subjective verbal components, even if this means it is fairly tentative and crude. The description of the problem will be continuously broadened in the therapeutic process. Problems of a more general nature brought about by the symptom will also be included if the client is interested and feels competent, or if this is necessary to therapy (cognitive testing of the entire life situation).

2.2. Analysis of Conditions: Systematization and Evaluation

As the first step it was recommended that the investigation of cognitive determinants of behavior be client-oriented. A general problem-solving schema was used as the basis for preliminary organization. However, in the course of the diagnosis, the *exact* relationship between the cognitions communicated by the client and the emergence and maintenance of the symptomatic behavior must be determined. The following examples should clarify the possibilities for the evaluative analysis of all influencing conditions.

2.2.1. Behavior Rules a a Guideline for Diagnosis

In order to systematize the cognitive components already investigated, one should bear in mind a possibility already presented by various authors, although it has been employed in various ways within diagnosis and therapy: the transfer of subjective verbal behavior components into the more general form of behavior rules (Fiedler, 1976; Innerhofer, 1974; Kraiker, 1974; cf. Mischel, 1973).

Behavior rules occupy a central position in the following outline. An attempt systematically to understand the various components underlying the problem behavior should be made by way of these behavior rules. They emphasize certain aspects of behavior and refer to the subjective value of experience which is associated with the social and cognitive problem behavior. A typical example is as follows: *"When you do this or that under such and such circumstances, then such and such are the consequences!"*

This formulation is typical in that clients generally do not verbalize cognitions in a very comprehensive way in the behavior exploration. Usually, however, *rule components* or *rule aspects* are communicated, from which a prototype for rules of behavior can be derived. Ideally, the therapist should understand the subjective verbal components of behavior as they are communicated by the client, because of the behavior-guiding functions attributed to them. These components can be differentiated in the following six tentative points:

Evaluations: These are the individual's emotional and rational attitudes toward external and conditioned stimuli (also values, evaluations, interpretations, etc.). The person's relationship to specific stimuli and groups of stimuli is characterized in his evaluations. On the basis of these subjective evaluations, perceived stimuli are assessed in terms of their threat and/or appeal. Evaluations have a significant influence on the emotional state, which can in turn influence involuntary physiological reactions.

Examples:
Unwashed fruit causes cancer.
This room boxes me in!
Disgusting, so much fish!
You as a therapist are patient; I can't say the same of my friends.

Stimulus Expectations: These are the client's expectations concerning the *regularity* and the *contiguity of stimulus associations* as he experiences them (anticipations about stimulus associations based on past experiences). Thus person and behavior are often repeatedly experienced as "inseparable," and later expected to occur together (for example, "Paul never talks about things like that!", or "My mother just doesn't understand things like that!"). The genesis of some stimulus expectations can be explained in terms of the classical conditioning paradigm; (as a laboratory example, the paired association of a light signal and shock in aversive conditioning). Many socially conditioned conflicts lead to stimulus expectations which emphasize their "insolubility" (the "inability to influence" the association of stimuli). Other stimulus expectations are hypotheses about the susceptibility of associated stimuli to influence and change.

Examples:
Whenever Paul is there, Peter is there, too.
Through therapy everything will be different!
Either he is there and doesn't pay attention, or he isn't there. You can't call him up, either.

Behavior Evaluations: One's potential motor and cognitive responses are determined in the process of one's learning history by the development of a "cognitive security" (or "cognitive insecurity"). Such *evaluation of one's (social) competence to respond* depend on previous experiences in various structured situations, the behavior being followed by reinforcers. They also depend on demands which the individual either was or was not in a position to meet. In this sense, for example, motor limitations such as blindness, paralysis, or hereditary motor impairments, as natural limitations, set quite direct restraints on motor behavior; as evaluation of one's competence to act, however, they will always have an indirect cognitive influence as well. Because behavior evaluations are influenced by previous behavior and the resulting conditions, it is logical to divide them roughly into *stimulus-directed* and *consequence-dependent* behavior evaluations.

Examples of stimulus-directed behavior evaluations:
You can't talk when your mouth is full!
I just can't do anything in the morning.
When Peter is with us, I can't get a word in edgewise.
When he yells at me, I feel paralyzed.

Examples of consequence-dependent behavior evaluations:
Once I pound on the table everything is all right again for a few hours.
I don't want to exaggerate, but my jokes always make everyone laugh.
No one listens to me, because I stutter!

Experience Expectations: As compared to evaluations, which emphasize one's attitude toward stimuli and stimulus associations, experience expectations summarize the *emotional-affective experiences* of a person in relation to internal and external stimuli. Experience expectations are anticipations of continuance or change in emotional state in view of present or anticipated stimuli.

Examples:
When I have to eat everything that is on my plate, even when I don't want anything, I feel sick.
Just remembering the test sends cold shivers down my back.
Screaming children will be the end of me yet.
There's no more hope for me.

Condensed Rules: Many of the intelligible cognitive components of behavior already have significant behavior-regulating properties from their semantic makeup alone. These concisely formulated, condensed rules of behavior are based for the most part on either *previous* or *expected* stimuli. Here we reiterate the necessity of the division into stimulus-directed or consequence-dependent condensed behavior rules.

Examples of condensed stimulus-directed rules:
When dad is home, I'm better off if I keep my mouth shut!
We're only allowed in the formal living room on Sundays.
Because of dogs I always make a detour around Garden Street.
No alcohol during the day!

Examples of condensed consequence-dependent rules:
I'm better off being on time; otherwise there is trouble when I get home.
No rewards without work!
To avoid infection I wash my hands as often as possible.

Behavior Plans: Behavior rules or rule components are the reservoir from which the individual can choose appropriate behavior. To deal effectively with problematic situations, it may be necessary to *cognitively actualize* ("mentally note") certain behavior rules or rule components. Behavior plans are those behavior rules eventually chosen or reconstructed out of the rules or rule components available for dealing with problematical situations. A behavior plan is typically something of this sort: *"When I behave in such and such a manner under the present conditions because of this or that experience* (rules and rule aspects), *I can anticipate this or that!"* Behavior plans are *self-produced contingency specifying stimuli* (Grawe & Dziewas, 1978; Kanfer, 1973).

Examples:
After thoughtful consideration I have decided to discuss everything peacefully tomorrow
    afternoon with my wife, to settle it once and for all.
From now on I am through smoking!
If I can hold out for two months, I'll take a vacation in Greece. If not, I'll stay in Germany
    this year.

Behavior rules, rule components, and behavior plans do not necessarily involve observable behavior and experience. There are also behavior rules for the *gathering* and *transfer* of information, rules, and rule aspects; that is, behavior rules which include the purely cognitive aspects of behavior. These metarules usually determine the cognitive relationship between behavior rules and rule components.

2.2.2. The Rule System of the Problem Behavior

The diagnostic ordering of behavior rules provides a useful instrument for describing cognitive determinants of behavior in a *communicative* form. Rule components, rule aspects, and behavior plans are integral components of behavior rules in that they essentially provide the determining viewpoints and grounds for behavior regularities. As a system for clarifying cognitive components of experience and behavior, behavior rules are suggested here as a *supplement* to traditional behavior analysis, which is still pertinent to the individual case (e.g., Schulte, 1974). In the form of behavior rules the (subjective-verbal) components of the problem behavior will be investigated as comprehensively as possible within the framework of such a behavior analysis. The first step is to *transcribe*, on the basis of exploratory and observed data, the rules and rule components communicated by the client. A basic *list of explored behavior rules and/or rule components* may be generated from the problem-solving schema presented in Section 2.1. Each recorded rule (rule component) is to be evaluated according to the rule categories (described in the preceding section) to which it can be ascribed. The therapist should refrain from making any further evaluations and comments; this is reserved for the next step, the evaluation phase.

The client interprets the *cause of the problem* from such a list of behavioral rules, which incorporates his system of reference. This rule system of the problem behavior is the basis for a cognitive-oriented therapeutic approach, or for the therapy of the cognitive components of the problem behavior. In such a therapeutic process a *rule system for changing problems* will be developed. The first list is generally the result of an exploration at the beginning of therapy; it serves as a basis for an analysis of conditions, a goal analysis, and basic therapy planning, and results in concrete decisions for therapy and change.

2.2.3. Cognitive Conditions of the Problem Behavior

In preparation for goal analysis and therapy planning, the extent to which the rule system of the problem behavior is responsible for the continuation of the symptomatic behavior must be determined. This (functional) analysis of conditions influencing cognitive determinants of behavior will become the basis for further indications of method through the *formulation of hypotheses* which stress the relationship between symptoms and aspects of conditions. The analysis should also allow for statements concerning the stability of and possibilities for changing the contexts of conditions. This forms the basis for *prognosis*. It thus becomes clear that this analysis of conditions influencing cognitive determinants of behavior serves as a significant supplement to and verification of the hypotheses connected with the behavior-analysis through which the respondent and operant components of the problem behavior are determined (see the schema suggested by Schulte, 1974). The (functional) relationship between cognitive components of behavior and the problem behavior will be explained below:[2]

Question 1: To what extent is the rule system of the problem behavior characterized by (obvious) uncertainty about rules?

To clarify this question one must determine whether the client exhibits *obvious gaps in knowledge* concerning behavior rules in relation to the problem behavior and its social determinants. Specifically, are rules absent? And is the absence of rules a possible reason for the existence of the problem behavior? Gaps in knowledge are often detected only by a comprehensive analysis and evaluation of the rule system of the problem behavior. However, there are also rules and components of rules which indicate gaps in knowledge; (e.g., "I've never tried that," or "I prefer not to get involved in that," or "I've already tried everything"). It is noteworthy that such "cognitive gaps" are often filled by the client's own hypotheses concerning appropriate behavior. Examples of such *substitute behavior rules* can be found in obsessive-compulsive behavior and superstitious reactions (cf. Belschner, Dross, Hoffmann, & Schulze, 1972).

Uncertainty about rules is primarily reinforced by the general form rules take: the rules are too *abstract* to be transformed into concrete behaviors which are socially acceptable (e.g., when a young person attempts to follow the parental mode of upbringing without ever having directly learned which behaviors constitute social and sexual propriety). Further examples of behavior rules with a high degree of abstraction are: "My child should have it better than I did," or "You should love your parents," or "By 'good partnership' I understand both partners always having time for themselves," or "I'm not good for anything."

States of increased *emotional tension* can be interpreted as further indications of uncertainties about rules. As a consequence, (cognitive) rules of behavior which emphasize *behavior rigidity* can be found, especially in the perception of situations (see Question 3). Escape and avoidance rules may indicate possible fears (e.g., "I refuse to take part in that," or "I will not go out of the house alone"). They may also indicate a lack of rules for appropriate behavior in (anxiety-producing) situations.

---

[2]The following points are excerpts from theoretical works (general and clinical psychology) and from practical behavior-diagnostic and therapeutic works and investigations. The former include Klix (1971), especially Chapters 7 and 9; Neisser (1974), especially Chapter 11; Laucken (1974); and Watzlawick, Beavin, and Jackson (1972); other references are given in the text. The latter include Fiedler (1976) and Fiedler and Standop (1978), especially Chapter 5. Various theoretical considerations which still need further empirical proof are included.

The quality of uncertainties about rules can be indicated by examining the rule systems for completeness: Can value orientation, situation and behavior evaluations, experience expectations, and condensed rules yield a model for behavior rules from which possible plans of behavior can be derived? The existence of contradictory rule components often causes uncertainty in making decisions. This brings us to the next question.

Question 2: Are there detectable conflicts in the rule system of the problem behavior that can be taken into consideration as possible causes of the problem behavior?

The entire system of rules for behavior generally serves to maintain adequate functioning in society. Actualizing these rules (rule systems) depends decisively on the external social conditions. Actualized rules substantially determine one's *social role* if translated into socially perceived behavior. The continuity of the social role is endangered when intrapersonal rules contradict each other (*intrapersonal rule conflicts*).

When rules for behavior contradict each other, cognitive and emotional conflicts arise. Deciding to act on inconsistent behavior rules necessitates *rule rejection*: a situation develops in which the person can no longer behave so that punishment can be avoided and praise won. Such situations produce a greater or lesser degree of neurosis, depending on the amount of punishment (cf. Innerhofer, 1974). For example: "If I eat my cream of wheat mother won't punish me. But sometimes I have to throw up afterward. If I don't eat it, I am punished, but I don't throw up."

Intrapersonal rule conflicts can be traced to consequences of behavior that were experienced as inconsistent, yet recurred regularly. As recurring experiences they become rule components, and as such constitute the inconsistency of behavior-guiding rules. Intrapersonal rule conflicts often *reflect social-rule conflicts*, as may have become clear above. During the interpretation and evaluation of rules it should be noted that these rule conflicts can be changed by cognitive dispositions as a result of subjective perception (i.e., by the existing behavioral rules and rule components which guide the process of perception): seen in this way, intrapersonal rule conflicts are the subjective interpretation of social rule conflicts (a sort of mirror of reality "broken" by the evaluation of one's experience). This does not in any way lessen the accountability of contradictory social rule systems for *inter*personal conflicts. On the contrary, social conflicts affect cognitive social behavior in two ways. First, social (rule) conflicts affect the range of the client's behavior. Second, a possible source for behavior problems (as *interpersonal rule conflicts* between client and environment) lies in the discrepancy between objective reality and the cognitive image of reality.

In analyzing the conditions of the rule system we can proceed from three possible determinants of conflict: we must discuss the individual role and interdependence of (1) *intrapersonal,* (2) *social,* and (3) *interpersonal rule conflicts.* First of all, the rule conflicts in each area must be worked out individually. Next, their interdependence must be clarified. Contradictory rules are to be presented simultaneously, and their usefulness for the client evaluated.

Clients are often unable to determine social and interpersonal conflicts more precisely. Their ability improves as they come to terms with personal and social difficulties. In order to illuminate social and interpersonal conflicts separately, it would prove beneficial in many instances to initiate an early exploration of the rule system, within the client's social environment. Innerhofer (1974) suggests three spheres for analysis of the rule system: the *intimate sphere* (family and spouse), the *achievement* and *work sphere* (school, classes, co-workers, colleagues, etc.), and the *social sphere* (peer group, friends and acquaintances, etc.). This analysis could, however, be expanded into still other spheres, especially when they dictate norms of behavior (for example, narrower and broader *social settings,* or *religious affiliation*).

In situations where a person is unable to function owing to conflicts which are difficult to solve, behavior-rule conflicts lead to a whole sequence of *physiological side effects* which should be taken into consideration during behavior analysis. Thus, intrapersonal rule conflicts can lead to arousal states, which are manifested as changes in pulse, heartbeat, and blood pressure, vascular contractions, reduction in skin resistance, and other such involuntary reactions (cf. Birbaumer, 1975). Careful analysis of basic cognitions is essential to the determination of the extent to which particular problem components can be attributed to particular conflict situations. Therapy needs to proceed not only from the conflict-producing social determinants, but also from the conflicting rules of the intrapersonal cognitive system. Rule systems are often characterized by a stability which persists even after the social stimuli have changed (see Question 3). Thus, although unnecessary on the grounds of external circumstances, an intrapersonal rule conflict may persist and lead to rigidities in behavior, as for example in so-called "superstitious reactions." The *significance of rule conflicts* in the analysis of conditions must be discussed.

It should be noted that rule conflicts which the client subjectively perceives as insoluble could prevent him from becoming habituated to the conditions maintaining the conflict. This situation leads to the intensification of arousal states and stress reactions, to which a whole sequence of psychosomatic illnesses can be attributed (general activation syndrome, Birbaumer, 1975).

Question 3: Can indications as to whether the client is prepared to change be found within the rule system of the problem behavior (rule stability)?

In the question concerning insecurity about rules, as well as in the clarification of rule conflicts, we indicated that each rule system includes rules which directly affect the stability of the other existing rules. Such rules interfere with rule modification. It then becomes necessary to investigate and even to modify these system-stabilizing rules. They may be *problem-descriptive* and *problem-forming behavior rules* (e.g., "You are never allowed to talk back," or "I don't dare make myself appear unpleasant"). On the other hand, they may be *metarules* (in part to be interpreted by the therapist) which *determine the cognitive relationship with the behavioral rules* (e.g., "It's better for me to think for a long time before attempting to solve a problem," or "The first ideas are always the best ones," or "One should always be conscientious," or "I've already considered everything; there's no solution for my problem"). It is primarily these metarules that determine the stability of a rule system. They, too, must be changed if the client is to learn to solve problems on his own.

Whether the client is presently prepared to change (i.e., the stability of his rule system) will be evaluated in terms of two aspects of the fixation on dispositional rules, aspects which reflect rule stability even within the person:

1. *Rule fixation following uncertainties about dispositional rules:* Such rule fixations are frequently *disguised* as *gaps in knowledge* (see Question 1) and/or, in a case of helplessness at decision making, as an *inability to make decisions*, resulting from rule conflicts (see Question 2). Rule fixations are manifested as an extremely stable system of tendencies to avoidance and flight, and behaviors whose verbal (rule) components are characterized by rationalizations and irrational "logical" assumptions (e.g., "I don't dare leave my wife alone for a minute, otherwise she'll be running around with other men" or "I prefer to stay at home because outside I feel as if I'm constantly being watched. Besides, I have plenty to do at home"). Frequently this form of rule fixation, which follows uncertainty about rules, appears as a result of one or more traumatic experiences, and justifies behavior patterns that often deviate from the norm. Depressive and compulsive behavior is exhibited in extreme forms of rule fixation. The same is true for clients exhibiting phobic reactions.

2. *Rule fixations following the successful application of rules.* Here we shall proceed on the assumption that clients apply rules *on the basis*

of positive consequences of behavior, the modification of such reinforced behavior provokes resistance precisely because of the positive experiences in the client's learning history. When the client retains previously successful rules, though the social context has changed and the rule behavior (according to measures of social comparison) is inadequate, problems may arise within the therapeutic process. This may also be the case when successful rules are applied to a social setting in which their application or maintenance also deviates from the norms. Rule fixations in this sense can be found in very typical rule components (e.g., "Why should I change?" or "After all, it has always worked up to now," or "I never get upset with other people, but they always get upset with me"). The degree to which the client is fixated on what appear to be successful behavior rules probably plays a part in determining how rule components may be employed in a way which the client considers socially acceptable. Now and then, too, it may happen that just *one* significant event leads to rule fixation. Repeated coincidences can also condition a rule fixation, usually because they are misinterpreted by the client (so-called superstitious reactions). The extent to which the client is prepared to change is decisively influenced by fixations in the rule system of the problem behavior. For the purposes of therapeutic planning and prognosis, it should be precisely ascertained to what extent clients are employing rules which have been retained despite both a change in objective circumstances and an ongoing process, contingent on internal variables, of invalidating the hypotheses. Let us simply say that clients are not always able to perceive and evaluate their own rule fixations. As the therapist has often already been delayed in disclosing and interpreting problem-determining rule fixations during the diagnostic phase, this situation further confuses the therapeutic process (cf. Section 3). This is especially true of metarules, which determine the (fixated) relationship between the individual's rules and rule components.

2.3. Determination and Analysis of Goals

The client's exploration will also generate this phase (see the schema for exploration in Section 2.1.). Here we shall highlight two areas: (1) the possibilities of evaluating the exploration data in order to analyze the goals, and (2) problems already revealed during the data investigation (exploration of the client's attitudes toward his goals).

2.3.1. Evaluation of the Exploration Data for Goal Analysis

If the initial exploration follows the guideline given in Section 2.1., then the client's provisional assumptions about possible directions of change as well as evaluations of these goals have been discussed (client's goal analysis and a provisional rule system of behavior change). The client's preliminary goal hypotheses and goal evaluations complete the analysis of the rule system of the problem behavior. They will undergo a closer analysis oriented to three areas for evaluating the analysis of conditions that influence cognitive determinants of problems:

1. *Rule uncertainty*. Are there gaps in knowledge which hinder the client in an accurate assessment of possible changes? Are the client's preliminary behavior plans concrete enough for a realistic assessment of the possibilities for change, etc.?

2. *Rule conflicts*. Are there intrapersonal, social, and interpersonal conditions of conflict which (could) hinder an acceptable plan for change?

3. *How prepared is the client to change?* Are rule fixations or metarules present that (could) inhibit a broadening and changing of the rule system?

In part this goal analysis will necessitate referring back to data from the rule system of the problem behavior, especially the metarules that determine the cognitive relationship with the behavior rules.

It should be stressed again that locating and analyzing goals tailored to the cognitive components of behavior is part of an extensive goal analysis in general therapeutic preparation. Such a general goal analysis takes into account the social partner's attitudes concerning the goal(s) as well as the consequences of a change in behavior for the client and his social environment (cf. Schulte, 1974).

2.3.2. Therapeutic Problems of the Goal-Diagnostic Phase

At the conclusion of the analysis of conditions influencing the client's behavior problems and goals for change, the symptoms should be evaluated and defined (by the therapist) in terms of their deviation from the norm: in discussing gaps in knowledge, degree of abstraction, whether or not he is prepared to change, intrapersonal conflicts, etc., the therapist is responsible for evaluating the symptoms and (here) cognitive-social determinants of the symptoms. As this can prove problematic, the therapist must (continually) guarantee that his interpretation takes into account both the client's subjective conceptions of the symptomatic behavior and the normative and evaluative systems of his social environment. Such a guarantee, however, demands a high measure of *insight* on the part of the therapist, even in the diagnostic phase of the problem-solving process.

As can be determined from the exploratory stages, behavior rules and rule components often change as they are clarified. This is all the more likely, the more clearly and emphatically the therapist emphasizes a comprehensive self-exploration by the client. In this sense, diagnostic dialogues always have a greater or lesser *therapeutic* effect, and can permanently influence and alter the client's plans for change and the goals he has projected. This phase of the goal analysis therefore demands from the therapist a high measure of empathy and adeptness, as it leads directly to the question of the "normality" and "deviance" of the interfering behavior. We must discuss the prognosis for behavior changes as seen from the client's "inner perspective." Further, the client's rules toward effecting change will be discussed. The "I cannot change, because . . ." rules enable the therapist, apart from determining fixations, to assess how the process of social stigmatization has affected the application of the rule and its modification, thus leading to a state of indecisiveness and learned helplessness.

During the goal-finding phase it is very important to encourage the client to an explicit *self-exploration* in the *problem-solving orientation*, thus to search not only for the conditions underlying the problem, but also for the conditions under which the problem can be solved. Clients can be encouraged to expand their rule systems of behavior changes (and problem determinants) by forming rules according to the following model: "I *can* change (quite certainly) in the following areas . . .". This or a similar model can be supplemented with several rules for change (compare this solution-oriented process with the useful ideas presented by Watzlawick, Weakland, & Fisch, 1974, or Peseschkian, 1977, even if different theoretical assumptions are made).

The combined effort of client and therapist in finding and establishing concrete goals is often critical for later successes. Although we do not wish to introduce practical suggestions here, we emphasize how important it is to inform the client that he alone must make the decision to change his own rules and actions, and that the therapist cannot relieve the client of this responsibility, though he can, of course, make suggestions and offer assistance. Decisions and transformations to change behavior and attitudes are the primary responsibility of the client, since he is the one who must also face the incalculable consequences and risks.

2.4. Basic Plans for Change

We have presented various viewpoints which enable the therapist to discuss both cognitive components of the problem behavior and the significance of the symptom's emergence and continuation. We also emphasize that the formulation of general goals presupposes an understanding of the client's goals and goal evaluations. The client's rule system should always be the focal point. In our opinion, this is especially crucial where the concrete realization of goals and the actualizing of behavior plans is concerned.

Early in therapy the analysis of conditions influencing the problem behavior essentially allows general strategies for further therapy to be derived. This is also true when the phase of cognitive problem-description (self-exploration) and the goal analysis are extended to allow the client to become more comfortable and certain about making decisions. The therapist should consider at an early juncture, immediately following the first exploration if possible, how the symptomatic behavior might, in principle, be changed (here the cognitive determinants of behavior are components of the whole problem). Schulte (1974) suggests early consideration to prevent a "blind" eclectic method. Early consideration has the further advantage of allowing the therapist to feel more at ease with the problem and its potential for change, and thus to be better prepared for therapy.

Which therapeutic approaches for effecting change in cognitive components of behavior can be derived from the suggested model of analysis and conditions? This model will be presented schematically. The following list of possibilities (in principle) for intervention respects both the evaluation of the problem behavior and the analysis of goals. To this, in each instance, we will first relate the approaches which are possible in principle, then occasionally, the more concrete approaches of therapeutic plans for change which have already been mentioned. The outline of therapeutic possibilities for intervention will be more thoroughly discussed in Section 3.

1. *Possible steps for therapy when rule uncertainties are present:*

General:

- Extending and broadening the rule system.
- Redefining and reevaluating rules and rule components.
- Reassessing stimuli and stimulus connections.

When gaps in knowledge are present:

- Principles for broadening knowledge, advancing information, gathering information, and comparing knowledge and information.

When rules are too abstract:

- Approaches for concretization in conversation and behavior.
- Attempts to complete rules by adding rule components.

2. *Possible steps for therapy when rule conflicts are present:*

General:

- Principles of cognitive problem-solving, such as:

- Practicing the (cognitive) skills of perception, interpretation and evaluation of stimuli and stimulus connections, behavior planning, transforming and concretizing behavior plans in actions, as well as evaluating behavior and behavior sequences.
- *This in addition to* a client-centered therapeutic dialogue.
- *Further,* models for solving problems and conflicts.
- Exercises in creativity and flexibility.
- *If possible,* the introduction of strategies and methods for minimizing and/or ignoring neurotic conditions and conflicts.
- *Or,* additionally, exaggerating and making fun of conflicts.
- *Finally,* possible attempts by the client to accept the existence of conflicts, especially where insoluble.

In social and interpersonal conflicts:

- Role playing.
- Discussion of rules.
- Discussion of conflicts.
- Examination of conflicts in a social context.
- Reality testing.
- Above all, therapeutic work in a social context that includes persons and conditions contributing to the conflict (e.g., parents and social partners).
- Working out the differences and similarities of interest of those involved in the conflict.

3. *Possible steps for therapy in the presence of rule stability, or, unwillingness of the client to change:*

General:

- Therapist's acceptance of rule fixations as learned/unsuccessful attempts at problem-solving by the client.
- (Client-centered) understanding of the rule system of the problem behavior.
- Helpfulness and use of persuasion techniques and instructions on the part of the therapist if possible only when the client desires their application.
- Necessary openness (genuineness) on the part of the therapist concerning his personal feelings, thoughts, and considerations as to whether the problem behavior can be changed.
- Modification of the client's inner dialogue, self-instruction, self-dialogue, etc.

When rule fixations are present because of rule uncertainties:

- Setting the limits of difficulties, emphasizing rule aspects and rule

components, completing and broadening rules, subdividing and concretizing rule systems in the therapeutic dialogue.
- Simulating actual situations, role playing, psychodramatic approaches to problem-solving, imitating fear behavior, etc., in the therapeutic process.

When rule fixations are present because of rule success:

- Conflict and uncertainty-producing communication, confrontation with and presentation of behavior consequences; the therapist directly addressing the rule fixation in therapeutic dialogue.
- Role playing, role exchange, modeling the problem behavior and other alternative behaviors, contrast exercises, video-playback during behavior exercises in the therapeutic process.

2.5. Inducing and Evaluating Behavior

In order to realize the basic possibilities of the cognitive therapy outlined above, a *concrete plan for treating* the entire problem should be established. The requirements for this will be thoroughly discussed in Section 3, along with concrete suggestions derived from the problem-solving model and the behavior-rule approach. In addition, cognitive components of behavior are part of a comprehensive methodology developed by behavior therapists (e.g., Goldfried & Goldfried, 1977; Kanfer, 1977; Mahoney, 1974; Meichenbaum, 1977). They are part of this methodology, however, only to the extent that the methods employed coincide with the basic goals and plans for therapy. In this case, concrete planning may be limited to questions concerning methodological form.

Further, the *sequence* according to which individual measures will be introduced into therapy should be established. Thus we reiterate that a therapy for cognitive components of behavior is only a partial treatment of the client's behavior problems, in which physiological and motor components of the symptomatic behavior are equally included. It is only possible to establish priorities for treating one of these three areas (physiological, motor, or subjective-verbal) after careful consideration of these different symptom determinants and their interdependence and after the establishment of a meaningful temporal sequence (cf. Schulte, 1974).

An *evaluation* of the introduced and completed behavior changes also requires some consideration during the therapy-planning phase. It is possible to evaluate the actual behavior changes only by measuring the changes which accompany therapy as well as those which anticipate and follow it. General references may be found in the works of Schulte (1974), Schulte and Kemmler (1974), and Lutz and Windheuser (1974). Special aids for measuring the effects of a cognitive therapy may be found in

Morganstern (1976), Bellak and Schwartz (1976), Meichenbaum (1976), Belschner (1978), and in Chapter 5 of Mahoney (1974). We shall discuss a few possibilities toward the end of the following section (such as behavior-rule lists and self-observation by the client). A more comprehensive discussion of diagnostic measures of change is, however, beyond the scope of the present study.

This concludes the establishment and presentation of possibilities concerning the diagnostic application of cognitive behavior components. We have presented a possible framework, which has resulted from practical application in a larger number of individual and group therapies. Essentially it aids the therapist in orientation and provides a framework for making decisions by means of which he can adjust the cognitive problem-solving process with the client. However, in taking this framework for decision-making as a basis, a careful assessment of the effects of the practical therapeutic work is essential, since no information about the interpretative objectivity is available at the present time (cf. van Eickels, Fiedler, & Schäuble, 1978). Only in this way can incorrect decisions be recognized in time to remedy them in therapy.

3. Therapeutic Applicability of Cognitive Components of Behavior

We have suggested a framework for comprehensively describing and analyzing cognitive component of behavior and for their use as a theoretical foundation for therapeutic planning. This third section is concerned with the therapeutic applicability of cognitive determinants of behavior; within its framework we shall reiterate the central importance of the client's participation in all steps of analysis, planning, and decision making. The client must understand what happens in the therapeutic process, as this is the only way he can beneficially participate in finding goals and making firm decisions for change. This basic requirement for the process of generalization must be fulfilled by the client. The behavior-therapy work requires a client-centered therapy enabling the client to codetermine the course of therapy. Such a therapeutic requirement is pragmatically and technologically based (goal: the client should become his own therapist), and is also supported by numerous empirical results. The following section emphasizes the need for a client-oriented understanding form of communication to take place in the methodological transformation of possibilities which result from the problem-solving and behavior-rule approach. First we include the approaches of psychotherapeutic dialogue (Bommert, 1977; Martin, 1975; but also Bastine, 1976). General implications and concrete references will also be extracted from studies which examine the specific and general effects of therapeutic communications (e.g., Haley, 1973; Watzlawick, 1977; Watzlawick, Weakland, & Fisch, 1974). The problem-solving process presented is also a useful guide for the selecting, systematizing, and initiating of dialogue techniques.

3.1. Therapeutic Dialogue: Necessary Framework for a Cognitively Oriented Therapy

Nearly all psychotherapeutic approaches emphasize the *client–therapist relationship* for promoting positive changes in the client. In the therapeutic sense a "positive" relationship may be defined as the cooperative effort of therapist and client toward developing mutual openness, support, and trust. In particular, the approaches of client-centered psychotherapeutic dialogue have unanimously generated certain behaviors on the part of the therapist which promote this relationship. We introduce them briefly as follows:

- *Openness* on the part of the therapist as to his goals and desires for therapy and for the client.
- *Honesty* on the part of the therapist with regard to evaluating the problems and the client's attitudes toward change.
- *Empathy* as the therapist's living understanding of the client's problems and the expression of his endeavors to find solutions with the client.

Certainly therapists could be trained to realize these characteristics to a great extent within their own behavior (Martin, 1975). An important prerequisite for acquiring and maintaining therapeutic competence in promoting relationships is the therapist's *personal therapeutic experience,* which should be part of every therapist's practical training.

Aside from these basic attitudes, which should be reflected in the therapist's behavior, is a series of concrete forms of communication directly derived from the behavior-rule model and the general model for therapeutic problem solving already introduced. If behavior rules are the focal point of therapeutic intervention, these forms of communication should be integrated into therapeutic dialogue following the behavior analysis. There are five basic dialogue variations, as follows.

3.1.1. Rule-Reproduction as the Central Variant in Dialogue

In dialogue with the client, the therapist should attempt to have empathy in his effort to understand the rule system of the problem behavior. This is the first step in the problem-solving process, offering the client and the therapist the possibility of making the rule system of the problem behavior accessible to a goal-oriented problem-solving process. Rule reproduction serves the therapist as a verbal mirror of the client and shows that he has been understood; further, it facilitates the client's reexamination of the dialogue. To attain a high level of empathy, we recommend going beyond the verbalization of the emotional contents of experience as suggested, for example, by Tausch (1970) within the framework of psychotherapeutic dialogue, and intensifying the reproduction of *behavior-regulative aspects* and *behavior tendencies* as well as internalized norms and attitudes. This verbalization process, especially as based on new advancements in therapeutic dialogue (Bommert, 1977), is highly therapeutic, in that through a continuing description of problems the client gains (new) insight into his problems. Through (new) insight the original rule system of the problem behavior (problem change) may be modified. The therapist can support the problem-solving process with further dialogue variations.

3.1.2. Completion and Expansion of Rules

In many cases clients find it difficult to discuss their problems and to explain their rule system. Here the therapist should astutely employ his competence in verbalization (empathy), and help the client by advancing carefully into areas of the rule system which the client has, up to the present, been unable to express. Perhaps clients lack words (because they have never learned them) for designating their feelings, evaluations, and impulses; in which case they might welcome the therapist's assistance. Perhaps the client is also so inhibited by negative experiences and/or the expectation of negative consequences that an understanding approach (by the therapist) through the use of *modeled problem designation* can have a disinhibiting and liberating effect on him. This second dialogue variation is also highly therapeutic.

The therapist can prepare and introduce a *cognitive restructuring* which employs therapeutic verbalization (rule completion and expansion), especially when new rule aspects are stressed; thus he can make speculations concerning the inception and change of difficulties. Through verbalization he can single out various aspects of rules and rule systems, and thus shift the emphasis; evaluations can be transformed into *reevaluations,* thereby removing the threat, as, for example, with threatening environmental stimuli. Finally, the therapist may *simplify* the problem rules by translating complex situations and experiences into simple, soluble units comprehensible to the client.

3.1.3. Putting Intentions for Change and Plans of Behavior into Words

Therapeutic dialogues should not only broaden information and perceptions concerning the problem behavior, but should also extend to the intended behavior changes. The client's participation in the behavior analysis through self-exploration, however, does not always immediately lead to an active plan for change. The therapist's role of stimulating and encouraging the client is foremost, as clients often suppress goals and plans for change. Clients often resign themselves to helplessness, and rely strongly on external sources for help. In either case, the therapist must be the motivating force. It is difficult to decide whether it is therapeutically beneficial to follow up the client's request for help with suggestions (therapeutic techniques), or to wait for the client actively to pursue a self-initiated plan for change. Generally, however, encouraging the client to act is a more valuable approach both for changing behavior and for generalization; and, in fact, constant intervention by the therapist can make the naturally uncomfortable road to self-modification more difficult. The therapist must be sensitive and patient. The client's verbalizations of behavior impulses often have further implications. Nevertheless, suggestions and assistance are sometimes more beneficial (for example, in the form of individual therapeutic techniques).

3.1.4. Activating Efforts in the Rule System of the Problem Behavior

In our opinion this is both the most important and most difficult part of therapeutic dialogue. Questions concerning the integration of both intentions to change and of plans for behavior into new activities and modes of behavior (for overcoming problems in therapy and employing them outside therapy) are presented to both client and therapist in any therapy. The limited value of suggestions and instructions soon becomes apparent, as well as the fact that therapeutic practice sessions and role-playing, etc. often do not guarantee the practice and use of these new methods by the client in his natural environment. On the basis of therapeutic training and experience, some strategies and rules may be suggested:

- Extensive exclusion of suggestions and assistance unless specifically requested by the client.
- Emphasis on the client's self-definition in determining goals and concrete approaches to problem solving, as the symptoms permit.
- Motivating the client to translate noncommittal plans (such as "I would surely like to") into decisions ("I will") and eventually into behavior commitments or even behavior contracts (e.g., the client's written intentions).
- The therapist's active support and helpful direction both during and after the client's decisions (active rule reproduction such as "You want to ask your mother whether she can cope with your moving away from home . . . then do it! It's best if we try it right now. Go ahead. I'll be your mother.").

The goal of these and similar therapeutic strategies is to motivate the client actually to realize intentions and plans for changing behavior. Here the therapist must equally *empathize* and *guide*. The translation of plans into behavior may be significantly hindered by rule fixations (unreadiness for change). In this phase clients frequently express rules containing feelings of helplessness and an inability to act. When it appears that the client is unable to initiate changes, the therapist should not be reluctant to demand steps for change from the client (tentatively, through practice, in role-playing, ongoing, etc.). This becomes possible when the client comes to understand the necessity of taking risks. Venturing into the unknown is the only real way to experience success (or failure) and to continue to build competence.

3.1.5. Behavior Evaluations (Feedback) and Redefinition of Rules

The client's ability to *evaluate his behavior* and to utilize these evaluations in changing and reconstructing behavior rules is an important step in therapy. The therapist has several functions in this. He may attempt to explore the client's self-evaluations, encourage him to make such evaluations, both overt and covert, and also encourage him both by attempting to understand his tendencies toward self-evaluation, and by putting them into words. It has proven less desirable when the therapist simply presumes to evaluate the client prior to determining whether the client desires such an evaluation. This is also true for positive feedback (cf. Fiedler, 1975). Positive feedback—introduced by the therapist in the "classical" behavior-therapy sense as a "reinforcer"—can even produce opposite effects, as when the "reinforcement" contradicts the "inner experience" of the client's self-evaluation. Many reinforcements experienced by the client as contradictory and unsuitable may generate questions concerning the therapist's competence, and may often lead to rejection of the therapist. It is therefore advisable to proceed from the client's experience of behavior evaluations. The therapist should note the client's "negative verbalization" and self-degradation and transform them as directly as possible into a new plan for change (for example, "You are upset because you contradicted your friend so strongly. How might you have done better in this situation?"). Once this can be accomplished, the plans for change should be integrated into therapy (still tentatively, e.g., in role-playing) as soon as possible, and reevaluated from time to time.

The therapist, in so far as this is possible, should make positive or negative evaluations only if the client so desires. Thus, although in most cases negative feedback may be helpful (such as feedback concerning the client's faults), the therapist must not rely solely on negative feedback, as by itself it could unintentionally produce insecurity in the client. Therapists should make it a point to combine negative feedback with helpful suggestions, to speak less about the negative feedback and more about the possibilities for behavior improvement.

Behavior evaluations enable the therapist to *redefine behavior rules* with the client. It is often useful not just to say behavior rules (once), but to put them in writing, and encourage the client to reflect on them between sessions. This increases the probability that the client's rule system will actually be reconstructed, even if the written rules are modified in later sessions.

3.2. Therapeutic Strategies to Modify Cognitive Determinants of Behavior

In the preceeding section, the transformation of the behavior-rule concept into possibilities for therapeutic dialogue was presented. In this section, a therapeutic method which is the basis for both the problem-solving model and the behavior-rule approach will be discussed, with examples.

3.2.1. Training in Alternative Monologue

We are concerned here with *systematically* integrating the client's alternatives to symptomatic behavior as useful, acceptable rules of behavior. The following procedure is indicated.

1. *Client's demonstration of "symptomatic monologue."* The client is requested to immerse himself mentally in the problem situation (eyes shut), and to share his thoughts (internal dialogue) with the therapist. Assuring the client of his trustworthiness and confidentiality, the therapist should encourage him to go through anxiety-filled and difficult internal dialogues. When the client feels inhibited, the therapist sbould help him in his verbalization. Above all, a concise model suggested by the therapist to reduce the client's inhibitions is recommended. The client's internal dialogues, often already during the initial exploration, offer a useful first grasp on the rule system of the problem behavior.

2. *Therapist's preparation of models for alternative monologues.* The therapist should devise additional models for alternative monologues between therapy sessions. Several models serve to contrast the alternatives. The client's decision is made easier when alternative models suited to his problem are available.

3. *Therapist's model for alternative monologue.* In following sessions the therapist presents an alternative model for internal dialogue and briefly discusses it with the client.

4. *Client's random sample of experience*. The client is asked to repeat the model introduced by the therapist. It is helpful for the therapist to reiterate the model sentence by sentence (using mimicry and gestures), requesting the client in turn to repeat each sentence as closely as possible (using the same accentuation, mimicry, and gestures). The client is requested to observe his experiences carefully and exactly during the repetition of the behavior model, and to inwardly register his resistances or positive feelings.

5. *Discussion*. The random sample of experience is completed, and the client has the opportunity to reflect upon and evaluate with the therapist the inner experiences, feelings, and thoughts that have come to the surface.

This is followed by the therapist's presentation of further models for alternative dialogues, by the same procedure as in 3. through 5.

6. *Complete evaluation of the models*. As a basis for selecting a suitable model for alternative dialogues, it is necessary to reflect conclusively on and to evaluate all models.

7. *Integration of alternative monologue*. In closing, the client is again requested to imagine himself in the problem situation, and to verbalize the form of alternative monologue which seems most appropriate. The client should be encouraged to maintain the monologue for a considerable time, and not to hesitate in repeating entire passages. Careful concluding consideration of the client's experiences during this trial session is essential.

It is our experience that such training is especially useful in dealing with uncertainties about rules (dispositional behavior rules are too abstract, and may be more precisely formulated by using rule models) as well as with intrapersonal rule conflicts (contradictory rule components within the rule system of the problem behavior will be completed and expanded by these therapeutic rule models, giving the client new rules and rule components for behavior).

Conditions which the client considers threatening (anxiety-producing stimuli) can also be dealt with through this procedure (e.g., the therapist's presentation of an anxiety-free model for reevaluating the danger). Meichenbaum's *anxiety-copying strategies* (1974, 1977) are relevant here, as they also aim at modifying internal dialogues when anxiety is present. The following procedures are derived from the method suggested by Meichenbaum as a further process for integrating alternative monologue.

1. *Building a hierarchy of anxiety-producing stimuli*. This first step must be a joint effort of client and therapist, as in the building of a hierarchy of anxiety-producing stimuli in the framework of *systematic desensitization*. This hierarchy defines the parameter of behavior for a successive approach to anxiety-producing stimuli higher in the hierarchy during the actual training in Step 4 below.

2. *Putting alternative self-dialogues into writing.* Client and therapist together will work out and put into writing new, alternative assessments of threatening situations in a way acceptable to the client.

3. *Integration of various techniques for tentatively reducing anxiety.* During the actual integration of alternative dialogues, various techniques are utilized to assist the client in quieting and controlling rising stimulation in the presence of anxiety. These include relaxation techniques, breathing exercises, and self-instruction (e.g., "Take it easy!" or "I am calm and relaxed.").

4. *Training alternative monologues.* The client should make himself comfortable in an easy chair, and cognitively immerse himself in anxiety-producing situations. The therapist should help the client in practicing this (for example, from lower to higher anxiety-producing stimuli in the hierarchy). If the client is able successfully to imagine the anxiety situations, he will be requested to continue the internal dialogue previously worked-out, while the therapist intervenes supportively by referring to the written record, asks questions, offers suggestions, and gives instructions. In the presence of increasingly strong anxiety, the client will be requested to initiate the techniques practiced for regulating agitation; if the anxiety becomes too great, it is useful to retrace the steps in the hierarchy, as in desensitization. In contrast to desensitization, however, the client should be encouraged not to avoid increasing anxiety (i.e., not to go back in the hierarchy immediately), but to "get a grip on" the anxieties and bring them under control with the help of the integrated behaviors and dialogues: for the goal of this training is not to put an end to anxiety, but rather to learn competent ways of cognitively controlling anxiety, that is, to limit and thereby master anxiety with the help of learned alternative monologues.

Example from Therapy of a Client with a Fear of Swimming

A section from the beginning of the first training in alternative dialogue; *client* is in an easy chair.

THERAPIST: Can you tell me when you have imagined yourself on the street outside the swimming pool? (Pause. Therapist notices client's hands tightening on the arm of the chair.) Okay?

CLIENT: I notice that I'm getting tense when I picture the swimming pool, and then the image disappears. But I want to . . . *Maybe I need to get more comfortable.*

THERAPIST: Yes, take your time. (Pause. *Client* tries to breathe quietly and evenly.)

CLIENT: Well, I'm now in front of the swimming pool. I'm still tense, but it's not too bad! *I'm breathing slowly in and out.* (Pause.) I'm settling down. Yeah, the more I talk, the calmer I feel.

THERAPIST: Imagine yourself going to the counter and buying a ticket.

CLIENT: I'm already doing that. *I'm still very calm.* No, it's not really working.

THERAPIST: Explain what you mean. . . .

CLIENT: I notice that I'm starting to sweat, but I want to hold out. *Certainly I can stand some fear.*

THERAPIST: Hmm.

CLIENT: It's really silly to be so upset when I'm not even in the water.

THERAPIST: Yes, encourage yourself. Repeat again out loud: *It's important not to give up with every little fear.*

CLIENT: Yeah. . . .

THERAPIST: Go ahead and say it. (*Client* clears his throat.) Well?

CLIENT: It is important not to chicken out right away. I've got to go through with it sometime, and I want to. I want to be able to go swimming again. (*Client* opens his eyes and looks at *therapist.*) You know, I've said that so many times, then I always chicken out. Usually I just set out to do it.

THERAPIST: And now you finally want to go through with it?

CLIENT: Yes. (Shuts his eyes again. Pause.) I buy a ticket and just walk in. Strange that I can do it.

[The italicized expressions are parts of the previously practiced monologue.]

An additional example for changing inner monologues is found in Fiedler (1976, p. 156 f.). Such training takes up approximately 15–30 minutes of the therapy session. It is recommended that active verbalizing be required of the client. This is a little different from the process suggested by Meichenbaum, which, in our opinion, demands too strong a guidance function on the part of the therapist (mainly in behavior instruction).

3.2.2. Rule Training in Role Playing

Whereas the training possibilities explained in the previous section are intended for modification of the internal dialogue, monologue, self-instruction, and the like, the behavior practices about to be suggested emphasize a reexamination of the (changed) rule system in comparison with the social environment. The goal of these exercises is to come to terms rationally and argumentatively with the rule system of the problem behavior and behavior change. This goal includes:

- Making possible an objective discussion of rule systems and rule content (for example, by a detached observation of models); this should generate a differentiated and rational consideration, evaluation, and modification of rule systems.

- Presenting a broad spectrum of symptom-alternative and complementary rules of behavior and examining their usefulness.
- Clarifying contrasts and diversity, which should encourage creativity and flexibility in rule modification.

We have utilized suggestions by Schwäbisch and Siems (1974), Fiedler & Windheuser (1974), Belschner (1976), Flowers (1977), and Marlatt & Perry (1977) for integrating role playing and rule models toward the (flexible) modification of cognitive determinants of behavior. From our own experience we have found the exercises that follow especially helpful.

1. *Rule discussion with a client-centered argumentation: client as observer.* Two partners discuss the client's behavior rules and rule system. One plays the client as he has presented himself and his problems in the previous course of therapy. This role playing must be very carefully prepared and practiced prior to its integration into therapy. If there are no other participants, the therapist may use two chairs, moving back and forth and playing both the client and the fictitious partner (e.g., himself). Although this role playing helps the client to come to terms with his rules "from a distance," it is often astounding what clearly therapeutic effects (*great perplexity*) such a model produces on the client's cognitive emotional experience. The therapist must be prepared for this, and carefully discuss such effects with the client. Rule discussion using client-centered argumentation and with the client as non-participating observer can be employed when the client signals the least capacity for change, through a greater readiness to change ("I want to, but I just can't!" or "I should like to, but I don't see any possibilities!" etc.). Role playing is the more effective the nearer it approaches the client's viewpoint. This first exercise is concluded with a consultation.

2. *Rule discussion with client-centered argumentation: client as partner.* This exercise is especially valuable subsequent to the one just described, when used in conjunction with the client's desire for change. Like the first exercise, it can be employed as an attempt to become acquainted with someone's rule system from the perspective of an impartial observer. However, in this exercise the client is requested to interact and actively come to terms with himself and his own rules (from the viewpoint of a partner). This usually increases the client's perplexity and involvement. In this exercise, one participant (or the therapist) plays the client. The client in turn plays the part of the partner. As the client accepts this role playing, he can and should constructively come to terms with his behavior rules ("defended" by the partner). This exercise can be reorganized in many ways. The client may be requested to become active, even aggressive, in the discussion of his rules ("attitude-contradictory agitation"; cf. Cranach, 1965). The client may also play the role

of the therapist, and thereby directly experience some of the therapist's difficulties in working with the rule system. This produces, in some therapies, a clearly improved cooperative effort of client and therapist. These exercises must also be thoroughly discussed.

3. *Rule discussion in individual role playing.* In practice, role playing presents many problems. However, role playing is possible even without partners. Aside from role playing between client and therapist, one may engage in individual role playing, which is often employed in Gestalt-therapy exercises. Two or more chairs are placed side by side for the training of rules. The client is then asked to discuss the pros and cons of aspects of the rule system with himself. The *pro* position is presented in one chair, the *con* position in the other. Such role games are often quite successful as the client becomes more prepared to change. The therapist may thus more easily encourage the process of combined problem-solving Schwäbisch and Siems (1974, p. 86 ff.) supply a detailed example and a representation of the structure of individual role playing. Individual role games are suggested: (1) when the client's problem is very complex, and can be simplified by a discussion of major themes (e.g., by differentiating "pro" and "con" arguments); (2) as a substitute for other types of role playing, particularly since a high degree of empathy (and understanding) is demanded of the client when dealing with the partner's thoughts and contrary arguments; in this sense it is also suited to (3) as a key to various conflicts, in that the area of conflict in its possibilities for change can be illuminated by the client, or in that he can become familiar with the various positions in social or interpersonal conflicts.

4. *Rule disputes.* This form of rule discussion may be employed when several role players are available (e.g., in groups of clients). The goal of role playing here is a combined problem-solving effort between the partners and the client, who has previously presented the rule system of the problem behavior, a system whose parts have been made as explicit as possible beforehand, to the group. Rule disputes may be utilized for the examination, broadening, completion, reformulation, and evaluation of behavior rules. In ways clear to the client, role-playing partners may fulfill various assignments: Partner A could be challenging, pushing for a quicker reformulation of rules; Partner B (as assistant, so to say), more supportive, prompting the client to clarify rules. This role differentiation has proven useful in many cases (e.g., Fiedler, 1976, p. 158 ff.).

As the client can easily fall into the "crossfire" of the other partners during rule discussions, it is essential that they be recorded on a tape recorder or videotape. The therapist, who is participating as little as possible in the crossfire exchange, should directly conduct the discussion, as minor annoyances between partners may be left over from the rule discussion. The subject of the discussion may revolve around the content and formal peculiarities of role playing, and should deal with the relationship between role partners. Up to this point it has been essential to continue the discussion of rule content, and it is all the more so with the therapist's inclusion as a neutral observer. Some clients felt that it was in the discussion (the recordings of the role playing) that the most important changes in the rule system occurred.

3.2.3. Introducing Therapeutic Activities in Ongoing Therapy

In the course of building a therapy, the spontaneous introduction of actions, both diagnostic techniques and therapeutic behavior exercises, always raises great difficulties. Precisely because the problem-solving process is client-centered, the therapist must develop a feeling for: (1) when the client is ready for concrete behavior, instead of just talking about his problems; (2) how the client can best be motivated and persuaded to participate; and (3) how the activities may best be organized to coincide with the current diagnostic and/or therapeutic goals.

In the framework of discussing diagnostic applicability through the steps of the problem-solving process, *timing* is important. The *fundamental therapeutic steps* are a result of the determination of problem behaviors and goals in the analysis of conditions. General indications that the client is ready for some form of behavior-guiding *therapeutic communication* were given in Sections 3.1.3. and 3.1.4. Finally, suggestions have been given in therapeutic actions previously discussed.

A concrete example from therapy will now be used to illustrate how role playing may be utilized in ongoing therapy (transition from therapeutic dialogue to individual role playing). The example was chosen because it illustrates the therapist's effort to find a transition that is as client-centered as possible, in order to overcome clients' frequent reservations concerning role playing. This particular example concerns a 25-year-old male client's fears that his marriage may split up and his wife leave him.

THERAPIST: You are afraid of not knowing whether your wife still wants you and would like very much to discuss this with her. However, you don't want to bring it up for fear she will think you don't trust her, and you don't want that.

CLIENT: Yes.

THERAPIST: I can see how uncertain you are. You want to get things cleared up.

CLIENT: Hmm—sometimes I can't think about anything else and get nowhere. (Pause.) I don't see any solution.

THERAPIST: Hmm. (Pause.) I have just tried to put myself in your place and feel how depressing it is, and. . . .

CLIENT: Yeah, I just can't see any way through it, so. . . .

THERAPIST: Because there is no way of seeing through it. Maybe we need to think everything over again. I have an idea, but I don't know if you're ready.

CLIENT: Do you see a way?

THERAPIST: I sense that you really would like to discuss everything with your wife, but you don't know how she will respond. You could practice the conversation here so that you can judge her reaction. (Therapist, still talking, stands up and puts two chairs down.) We could try it with you sitting in this chair, and you begin the conversation with your wife. Imagine her sitting in the chair across from you. (Client remains seated.)

CLIENT: What good will that do?

THERAPIST: We can record everything and discuss afterwards how it could be improved.

CLIENT: I don't know if that will help much. You see, I'm afraid she will interrupt or not even listen.

THERAPIST: (Seated again): I suggested it because I saw you were looking for a solution. Somehow just thinking about it doesn't get you anywhere. I thought maybe just trying it would help you, where we could improve it afterwards. I see now how difficult it is for you. (Pause.) I was just thinking how you could find out what your wife thinks about your relationship. There are two options: wait until she brings it up, and in the meantime you are uncertain and depressed, or make a direct approach, even when what you say to each other is painful.

CLIENT: (Begins to cry): When you set the chairs down and I was supposed to talk to her, it all came back to me just as I had imagined it.

THERAPIST: Yes . . . (Pause.)

CLIENT: Really, I'm a fool not to take your suggestion. This is the only chance I could hope for.

THERAPIST: You want to, don't you? Go ahead. I'll help you!

3.3. Therapeutic Transfer

Still further possibilities for stabilizing, testing, and optimizing the changes in cognitive behavior determinants arrived at through dialogue and action, and for investigating the rule system for positive transfer under natural social conditions will now be presented by way of example: Behavior commitments, behavior contracts, behavior rule lists, and self-observation.

3.3.1. Behavior Commitments

These represent the goal of every problem-solving effort of client and therapist. One must insure that therapeutic dialogues always lead from a consideration of behavior change to a commitment to change. Therapy comes to a standstill when possibilities for change are discussed in the goal analysis. Therapeutic responsibility and control are extended when behavior plans are executed and evaluated. The client must not be left alone in his attempts to change. Notes prepared by the client and therapist have proven useful in stimulating the translation of attempts to change at the end of each session. Notes may be limited to the client's most important plans for change, written in the form of "I want to" sentences. The sentences must be concrete and complete. The client takes one copy of the notes home, and the other goes into the therapist's files.

3.3.2. Behavior Contracts

These are a continuation of the client's commitment to actually fulfilling his intentions to change (at least attempting to). As complete information concerning the outline, form, and function of therapeutic contracts is available (cf. Kanfer, 1977), we shall mention only a few basics. Contracts must be drawn up such that they are totally acceptable to the client. If new behaviors are to be performed socially, they should be practiced prior to their application outside of therapy. Reinforcements or punishments for keeping or breaking the contract should be agreed upon beforehand. The contract should state how the client can observe, measure, or record the application of his plans for change. Finally, the duration of the contract should be established (the same holds true for homework assignments; cf. Shelton & Ackerman, 1978).

3.3.3. Behavior Rule Lists

If cognitive components of behavior are the subject of therapeutic intervention (as described in this chapter), the prepared lists of behavior rules should be modified at the end of each session, on the basis of the experience of that session (see Section 2.2.2.). Additions or alternatives to behavior rules accepted by the client should always be added to the existing list. Outdated rules may be discarded; however, rules no longer accepted by the client may be kept to provide examples of variety and contrast. We suggested to our clients that they read through the lists two or three times a day at set times. In the process each rule was to be evaluated as to whether it represented an acceptable basis for guiding and modifying behavior. All rules accepted by the client are marked with a " + ". The client should pay no further attention to dubious or rejected rules. The goal is a gradual restructuring of negative behavior rules into positive ones. According to the principle of "overlearning" (cf. Bergius,

1971), we feel certain that clients can cognitively encode and apply many rules outside therapy if the rules are reviewed daily.

3.3.4. Self-Observation

Therapists should seek opportunities in every therapy to enable the client to observe, measure, and record changes in his behavior. Experience suggests that the introduction of self-controls is useful not only for diagnosis. The observation and recording of problem behaviors and their change also have a considerable therapeutic function. This is particularly the case when a clear-cut evaluative measure for the modification of the observed behavior is present in the recorded behavior samples. Kanfer (1977) recommends the following steps when introducing the self-observation method: (1) motivating the client to keep exact records (e.g., by considering and verifying the usefulness of rules); (2) clearly defining the recorded behavior and eliminating irrelevant behavior components; (3) choosing the easiest and most comfortable method of recording; and (4) introduction, if possible, of the notes during the session.

3.3.5. Further Reflections on the Success of Positive Transfer

The goal of the possibilities presented thus far for the transfer of learned behavior from therapy to the client's natural (learning) environment is to stabilize the cognitive skills acquired in therapy (behavior rules relating to social and internal conditions) by their *repeated application*. Hypotheses for further intervention alluded to in the first three sections and their relationship to transfer will be briefly summarized again here.

1. *Client's expectations from therapy*. This concerns how the client measures therapeutic success. The therapist may influence the client's expectations from the start by, in attempting to clarify the *course and structure of therapy*, indicating what he may or may not hope for (cf. Fiedler, 1974). In order not to hinder or completely eliminate the capacity for generalization, the client should never get the impression that therapy is a complete solution for his problems. Rather, therapy should (and can only) concentrate on making basic improvements. Sometimes therapy is helpful only to the extent that it prepares the client to cope better with his problems (self-control). Thus the occasional "programming" of the insoluble remainder of problems is recommended (as in hypnosis therapy). Watzlawick (1977) describes the usefulness of problems remaining unsolved in therapy:

> One realizes first of all that the idea of the transformation from the utopian black-and-white picture of complete success or total failure is reduced, and second that the client has the possibility of surpassing on his own what the therapist thinks is possible. (pp. 64–65)

2. *Locating goals in therapy*. In many behavior therapies, the therapist determines the goals on the basis of the results of behavior-analysis. We feel that the combined and longer reflection of both client and therapist concerning possible goals has substantial therapeutic value that should not be relinquished (cf. Fiedler, 1978/1979). This is not only an opportunity to combine the client's expectations and goals with new explanative associations and ways of experiencing in therapeutic dialogue through rule repetition, completion, and expansion; far more, this phase of acquiring cognitive skills for relating to one's problems (as personal attempts at problem solving) is part of the search for an understanding of the relationships between conditions.

3. *The subject of transfer*. The subject of transfer becomes a question in therapy when behavior commitments, behavior contracts, and lists of behavior rules are suggested as possibilities for stabilizing the target changes in the rule system of the problem behavior. In every session the therapist should again ask the client, "Can you be absolutely certain that you will employ your plans for change? How can we prepare you for that in today's session?" *Transfer is never only the concern of the final session.* It should be striven for from the onset of the mutual diagnostic and therapeutic work. Transfer is primarily the client's responsibility, and it will be achieved only when alternative behaviors are repeatedly realized under natural conditions and when these attempts at generalization are reinforced by continuous therapeutic evaluation.

4. *"Reviewing" the therapy*. Often so much occurs during therapy sessions that at the end of such a session both client and therapist are confused rather than clear about goals. The wish often arises to rework or reexperience more thoroughly and carefully what has occurred. One wishes to "take hold" and find a structure for further therapy. The use of technical aids is worth considering. Occasionally we give our clients *cassette recordings* of the therapy session, which they (as well as the therapist) can listen to again at home. This also facilitates transfer in that the client can continue to work on his problem between sessions. We have also set aside every second session for the therapist and client *together* to review sections of the previous session on a video monitor or tape recorder. Both methods of "reviewing" result in an improvement in the *openness* of the therapeutic process. This also has very positive effects on joint cooperation in the therapeutic process, because in this way the clarification of problems in the therapeutic relationship, which remained an undercurrent while the session was actually going on, can become a theme; or because the client may realize for the first time how hard the therapist is striving for progress, and how difficult it often is for him to motivate the client to change.

Searching for ways to facilitate transfer while preparing for and even during the sessions is valuable.

4. Final Remarks

This study has been concerned primarily with two questions: (1) How can cognitive determinants of behavior be presented so comprehensively that they are accessible to a conditioning analysis and therapeutic evaluation? (2) How can the entire therapeutic process be understood in the framework of a cognitively oriented behavior therapy, such that the appropriate goal-oriented therapeutic dialogues and activities may be determined and evaluated? Useful and practicable possibilities are opened up both by structuring therapy as a process of cognitive-social problem solving, and by attempting to understand cognitive components of behavior through the diagnostic-therapeutic system of behavior rules. This permits the inclusion of current and proven cognitive behavior-therapy methods, and redefines their relationship to therapy.

A therapy for cognitive components of behavior demands of the therapist a much higher level of competence in communication than does traditional behavior therapy. In the future, behavior therapists must become more competent in therapeutic dialogue than has previously been the case. Techniques for this have been advanced in the present study, and a way has been shown for the meaningful integration of any therapeutic technique (such as psychotherapeutic dialogues or communication therapy) that stresses therapeutic dialogue as a means of facilitating (cognitive) behavior changes in the client.

The approach presented here confronts behavior therapy with realms which it has previously been very reluctant to enter. The conflict revolves around the question whether the utilization of goal-oriented techniques, or the understanding of the client's problem behavior, plays a more decisive role in modifying behavior. We cannot attempt to answer such a question here. Let it suffice to say that complete empirical data is needed to determine whether the actual therapeutic effects lie in one's approach to therapy, in the choice of a goal-oriented method, or in the person of the therapist. We realize the limitations of the present study, as precise guides for making goal decisions have not yet been developed. Nevertheless, numerous possibilities for establishing a structure for therapy have been presented.

We hope that our contribution will prove fruitful for the discussion, which is now also going on among behavior therapists, concerning the search for ways to integrate disparate conceptions of psychotherapy.

ACKNOWLEDGMENTS

In concluding this work, I should like to thank all those who assisted by offering criticism and helpful suggestions as to basic changes in the first draft of this paper. They are Henriette Altmann (Passau), Hartmut

Berwald (Münster), Rainer Bromme (Bielefeld), Hans Deidenbach (Wiesbaden), Margarita Engberding (Münster), Karl Kaiser (Münster), Heinz Liebeck (Göttingen), Ulf Plessen (Münster), Waltraud Schäuble (Münster), Christa Schulte (Münster), and my wife, Zwannet Steenstra. However, without the cooperation and openness of patients and therapists from many areas, this study would not have been possible. I should like to thank them too.

References

Bastine, R. Ansätze zur Formulierung von Interventions-strategien in der Psychotherapie. In R. Jankowski, D. Tscheulin, H.-J. Fietkau, & F. Mann (Hg.), *Gesprächspsychotherapie Heute*. Bericht über den I. Europäischen Kongreβ für Gesprächspsychotherapie. Würzburg 1974. Göttingen: Hogrefe, 1976.

Bellack, A. S., & Schwartz, J. S. Assessment of self-control programs. In M. Hersen & A. S. Bellack (Eds.), *Behavioral assessment: A practical handbook*. New York: Pergamon, 1976.

Belschner, W. Kreativitätstraining als transferorientierte Behandlungstechnik. *Bildung und Erziehung*, 1976, *29*, 216–228.

Belschner, W. Subjektive Strukturierung und Bewältigung von Situationen. In *Fortschritte in der Verhaltenstherapie*. Kongreβbericht Berlin 1977. Sonderheft I/1978 der "Mitteilungen der Deutschen Gesellschaft für Verhaltenstherapie." Tübingen, 1978.

Belschner, W., Dross, M., Hoffmann, M., & Schulze, C. *Sozialangst und Normunsicherheit als Vorläufer von Zwangsverhalten*. Vortrag 4. Verhaltenstherapiekongreβ des DBV und der GVT, Münster, 1972. (Überarbeitung in Vorbereitung.)

Bergius, R. *Psychologie des Lernens*. Stuttgart: Kohlhammer, 1971.

Birbaumer, N. *Physiologische Psychologie*. Berlin: Springer, 1975.

Bommert, H. *Grundlagen der Gesprächspsychotherapie*. Stuttgart: Kohlhammer, 1977.

Bromme, R. Das Theorie-Praxis-Problem als Aufgabe der allgemeinen Psychologie. In J. Bergold & E. Jaeggi (Hg.), *Verhaltenstherapie: Theorie*. Sonderhelf I/1977 der "Mitteilungen der Deutschen Gesellschaft für Verhaltenstherapie." Tübingen, 1977.

Cranach, M. V. Meinungsänderung durch eigenes Handeln: Die Rückwirkung einstellungskonträrer Agitation. *Psychologische Forschung*, 1965, *28*, 89–151.

Fiedler, P. A. Gesprächsfuhrung bei verhaltenstherapeutischen Explorationen. In D. Schulte (Hg.), *Diagnostik in der Verhaltenstherapie*. München: Urban & Schwarzenberg, 1974.

Fiedler, P. A. *Zur Funktion der Verstärkung in Problemlösungsprozessen*. Phil. Diss., Münster, 1975.

Fiedler, P. A. Behandlung von Zwangsgedanken eines 22jährigen Klienten mit einem Kognitionstraining. In M. Reiss, P. A. Fiedler, R. Krause, & D. Zimmer, *Verhaltenstherapie in der Praxis*. Stuttgart: Kohlhammer, 1976.

Fiedler, P. A. Zur Theorie und Praxis verhaltenstherapeutischer Gruppen. In A. Heigl-Evers & U. Streek (Hg.), *Die Psychologie des 20. Jahrhunderts*. Band VIII. *Lewin und die Folgen. Sozialpsychologie - Gruppendynamik - Gruppentherapie*. Herausgegeben von A. Heigl-Evers und U. Streek. Zürich: Kindler, vorauss. 1978/1979.

Fiedler, P. A., & Standop, R. *Stottern: Wege zu einer integrativen Theorie und Behandlung*. München: Urban & Schwarzenberg, 1978.

Fiedler, P. A., & Windheuser, H.-J. Modifikation kreativen Verhaltens durch Lernen am Modell. Zeitschr. Entwicklungs-psychol. *Pädiatric und Psychologie*, 1974, *4*, 262–280.

Flowers, J. V. Simulation und Rollenspiel. In F. H. Kanfer & A. P. Goldstein (Hg.), *Möglichkeiten der Verhaltensänderung*. München: Urban & Schwarzenberg, 1977.

Goldfried, M. R., & Goldfried, A. P. Kognitive Methoden der Verhaltensänderung. In F. H. Kanfer & A. P. Goldstein (Hg.), *Möglichkeiten der Verhaltensänderung.* München: Urban & Schwarzenberg, 1977.

Grawe, K., & Dziewas, H. Interaktionelle Verhaltenstherapie. In *Fortschritte in der Verhaltenstherapie.* Kongreßbericht Berlin 1977. Sonderheft I/1978 der "Mitteilungen der Deutschen Gesellschaft für Verhaltenstherapie." Tübingen, 1978.

Haley, J. *Uncommon therapy: The psychiatric techniques of Milton H. Erickson.* New York: Norton, 1973.

Innerhofer, P. Ein Regelmodell zur Analyse und Intervention in Familie und Schule: Abänderung und Erweiterung des S–R–K-Modells. *Zeitschrift für Klinische Psychologie,* 1974, *3,* 1–29.

Jaeggi, E. Erleben und Handeln in der Psychotherapie. In J. Bergold & E. Jaeggi (Hg.), *Verhaltenstherapie: Theorie.* Kongreßbericht Berlin 1976. Sonderheft I/1977 der *Mitteilungen der Deutschen Gesellschaft für Verhaltenstherapie.* Tübingen, 1977.

Kaiser, K.-W. *Verhaltensmodifikation durch Änderung kognitivsozialer Lernvariablen.* Unveröff. Diplom-Arbeit, Münster, 1975.

Kaiser, K.-W., Berwald, H. Zur praktischen Anwendung kognitiver Therapieansätze in Gruppen. *Mitteilungen der Gesellschaft zur Förderung der Verhaltenstherapie,* 1975, *7,* 31–44.

Kaminski, G. *Verhaltenstheorie und Verhaltensmodifikation.* Stuttgart: Klett, 1970.

Kanfer, F. H. Verhaltenstherapie: Ein neues Theoriengerüst zur Lösung klinisch-psychologischer Probleme. *Psychologie und Praxis,* 1969, *13,* 1.

Kanfer, F. H. Die Aufrechterhaltung des Verhaltens durch selbsterzeugte Stimuli und Verstärkung. In M. Hartig (Hg.), *Selbstkontrolle.* München: Urban & Schwarzenberg, 1973.

Kanfer, F. H. Selbstmanagement-Methoden. In F. H. Kanfer & A. P. Goldstein (Hg.), *Möglichkeiten der Verhaltensänderung.* München: Urban & Schwarzenberg, 1977.

Kanfer, F. H., & Goldstein, A. P. (Hg.), *Möglichkeiten der Verhaltensänderung.* München: Urban & Schwarzenberg, 1977.

Klix, F. *Information und Verhalten.* Berlin: Verlag der Wissenschaften sowie Bern: Huber, 1971.

Kraiker, C. Bemerkungen über die empirischen und theoretischen Grundlagen der Verhaltenstherapie. In C. Kraiker (Hg.), *Handbuch der Verhaltenstherapie.* München: Kindler, 1974.

Laucken, U. *Naive Verhaltenstheorie.* Stuttgart: Klett, 1974.

Lutz, R., & Windheuser, H. J. Therapiebegleitende Diagnostik. In D. Schulte (Hg.), *Diagnostik in der Verhaltenstherapie.* München: Urban & Schwarzenberg, 1974.

Mahoney, M. J. *Cognition and behavior modification.* Cambridge, Mass.: Ballinger, 1974.

Marlatt, G. A., & Perry, M. A. Methoden des Modellernens. In F. H. Kanfer & A. P. Goldstein (Hg.), *Möglichkeiten der Verhaltensänderung.* München: Urban & Schwarzenberg, 1977.

Marquis, J. N. Ein zweckdienliches Modell der Verhaltenstherapie. In A. A. Lazarus (Hg.), *Angewandte Verhaltenstherapie.* Stuttgart: Klett, 1976.

Martin, D. G. *Gesprächs-Psychotherapie als Lernprozeß.* Salzburg: Müller, 1975.

Meichenbaum, D. *Therapist manual for cognitive behavior modification.* Unpublished manuscript, University of Waterloo, 1974.

Meichenbaum, D. A cognitive-behavior modification approach to assessment. In M. Hersen & A. S. Bellack (Eds.), *Behavioral assessment: A practical handbook.* New York: Pergamon, 1976.

Meichenbaum, D. Methoden der Selbstinstruktion. In F. H. Kanfer & A. P. Goldstein (Hg.), *Moglichkeiten der Verhaltensänderung.* München: Urban & Schwarzenberg, 1977.

Mischel, W. Toward a cognitive social learning reconceptualization of personality. *Psychological Review,* 1973, *80,* 252–283.

Meichenbaum, D. A cognitive-behavior modification approach to assessment. In M. Hersen & A. S. Bellack (Eds.), *Behavioral assessment: A practical handbook.* New York: Pergamon, 1976.

Meichenbaum, D. Methoden der Selbstinstruktion. In F. H. Kanfer & A. P. Goldstein (Hg.), *Moglichkeiten der Verhaltensänderung.* München: Urban & Schwarzenberg, 1977.

Mischel, W. Toward a cognitive social learning reconceptualization of personality. *Psychological Review,* 1973, *80,* 252–283.

Morganstern, K. P. Behavioral interviewing: The initial stages of assessment. In M. Hersen & A. S. Bellack (Eds.), *Behavioral assessment: A practical handbook.* New York: Pergamon, 1976.

Neisser, U. *Kognitive Psychologie.* Stuttgart: Klett, 1974.

Peseschkian, N. *Positive Psychotherapie: Theorie und Praxis einer neuen Methode.* Frankfurt a. M.: Fischer, 1977.

Seiler, B. (Hg.), *Kognitive Strukturiertheit.* Stuttgart: Kohlhammer, 1973.

Scheele, B., & Groeben, N. *Voraussetzungs- und zielspezifische Anwendung von Konditionierungs- und kognitiven Lerntheorien in der Klinischen Praxis.* Bericht aus dem Psychologischen Institut der Universität Heidelberg. Diskussionspapier Nr. 6, Heidelberg, 1976.

Schmidt-Mummendey, A. *Der Begriff der sozialen Einstellung in termini der funktionalen Verhaltensanalyse.* Habil. Vortrag, Münster, 1974.

Schulte, D. Der diagnostisch- therapeutische Prozeß in der Verhaltenstherapie. In J. C. Brengelmann & W. Tunner (Hg.), *Behaviour Therapy - Verhaltenstherapie.* München: Urban & Schwarzenberg, 28–39, 1973.

Schulte, D. Ein Schema für Diagnose und Therapieplanung in der Verhaltenstherapie. In D. Schulte (Hg.), *Diagnostik in der Verhaltenstherapie.* München: Urban & Schwarzenberg, 1974.

Schulte, D., & Kemmler, L. Systematische Beobachtung in der Verhaltenstherapie. In D. Schulte (Hg.), *Diagnostik in der Verhaltenstherapie.* München: Urban & Schwarzenberg, 1974.

Schwäbisch, L., & Siems, M. *Anleitung zum sozialen Lernen für Paare, Gruppen und Erzieher.* Reinbeck bei Hamburg: Rowohlt, 1974.

Shelton, J. L., & Ackerman, J. M. *Verhaltens-Anweisungen, Hausaufgaben in Beratung und Psychotherapie.* München: Pfeiffer, 1978.

Tausch, R. *Gesprächspsychotherapie.* Göttingen: Hogrefe, 1970.

Urban, H. B., & Ford, D. H. Some historical and conceptual perspectives on psychotherapy and behavior change. In A. E. Bergin & S. L. Garfield (Eds.), *Handbook of psychotherapy and behavior change.* New York: Wiley, 1971.

van Eickels, N., Fiedler, P. A., & Schäuble, W. Verhaltensmodifikation und Aktionsforschung: Argumente für eine lern- und personenzentrierte psychologische Forschung. In P. A. Fiedler & G. Hörmann (Hg.), *Aktionsforschung in Psychologie und Pädagogik.* Darmstadt: Steinkopff, 1978.

Watzlawick, P. *Die Möglichkeit des Andersseins.* Bern: Huber, 1977.

Watzlawick, P., Beavin, J. H., & Jackson, D. D. *Menschliche Kommunikation.* Bern: Huber, 1972.

Watzlawick, P., Weakland, J. H., & Fisch, R. *Lösungen: Zur Theorie und Praxis menschlichen Wandelns.* Bern: Huber, 1974.

Westmeyer, H. Verhaltenstherapie: Anwendung von Verhaltens-theorie oder kontrollierte Praxis? In P. Gottwald & C. Kraiker (Hg.), *Zum Verhältnis von Theorie und Praxis in der Psychologie.* Sonderheft I/1976 der *Mitteilungen der Gesellschaft zur Förderung der Verhaltenstherapie.* München, 1976.

The Problem of the Use of Cognitive Constructs and Cognitive Terminology

A Critical Analysis Exemplified by the Construct of 'Learned Helplessness'

EVELYN KRAUTZIG AND MICHAEL LINDEN

1. The Definition of Cognition

In his textbook *Cognitive Psychology,* Neisser (1974) includes under the term cognition

> all those processes, through which sensory input is transformed, reduced, processed, stored, called forth again, and finally used. . . . [The concept of cognition] refers to these processes even when they take place without the existence of corresponding stimulation, as in the case of images and hallucinations. Concepts such as sensation, perception, image, retention, memory, problem solving, and thinking, along with many others, refer to hypothetical stages or aspects of cognition. . . . One can say that cognition participates in everything that a human being can do. (p. 19)

Such very broad definitions of what is supposed to be understood by cognition can be found in a more or less modified form in all relevant survey works. Cognition thus becomes a hypothetical construct including almost everything that happens in man when a particular behavioral response follows a particular stimulus situation.

EVELYN KRAUTZIG • Institut für Psychologie, Freie Universität Berlin, D-1 Berlin 41, Bundesrepublik Deutschland.   MICHAEL LINDEN • Delbrückstrasse 13.17, D-1 Berlin 33, Bundesrepublik Deutschland.

Such a broad spectrum of meaning for a concept can be thoroughly legitimate and productive, if the point is to describe a particular professional philosophy and a particular methodological standpoint. Neisser himself says that

> every psychological phenomenon is also a cognitive phenomenon. But even if cognitive psychology has to do with practically all of human activity and not just with parts of it, it retains a very particular angle on this. (p. 19)

The breadth of this definition is no problem for cognitive psychology itself, because the concept takes on specificity as soon as the objective is to investigate specific cognitions. This means that, in cognitive psychology, cognition as such is not the subject matter of research; rather one deals with verbal coding, the recognition of patterns, problems of memory, speech perception, thinking, or problem-solving processes.

However, with increasing frequency one also comes across the concept of cognition outside the field of cognitive psychology, particularly in the field of clinical psychology and psychological therapy. Here, of course, the concept of cognition is no longer only the description of a professional approach, but a hypothetical construct which is made use of as an intervening variable in the explanation of behavior: cognition is cited as substantiation when the point is to explain differential causes of abnormal and normal behavior, cognition itself is described as being disturbed, cognition becomes the object of treatment, psychological disorders are supposed to become treatable through the modification of cognitions.

To make a hypothetical case, let us choose the broadest definition of cognition, and equate it with psyche. Then the sentences just formulated would state that the psyche is called on to explain abnormal behavior, that the psyche becomes the object of therapy, and that psychological problems can be treated through therapy by modifying the psyche.

Such sentences even have a certain informative content; however, it is quite obvious that the conceptual combination of cognition and psychotherapy does not readily offer more information about cognitive therapy than the use of the concept psychotherapy does by itself. Psychotherapy in all its variants has always dealt with sensations, memories, perceptions, and interpretations. Apart from a few exceptions, psychotherapy has always been the attempt to talk with patients about how they perceive their environment, how they interpret it, and how they react to it.

According to the definitions of cognition listed above, it is certainly correct also to apply the concept of cognition to such processes. However, it must be asked whether it is more productive to use concepts of cognition with increasing frequency, or whether concepts already in use, the concept of tranference in psychoanalysis, for example, or the concept of skill in behavioral therapy, could also continue to fulfill their function. This decision must be made to depend on whether it is possible by using cognitive concepts to reduce the number of theoretical concepts, and to improve the rules by which theoretical concept and observational level are brought into relation.

It is also necessary to examine the concepts of cognition now in vogue for their experimental grounds and their capacity for generalization. This is to be attempted in the following by way of example. Seligman (1975), on the basis of experimental findings with animals, introduced the concept of the helplessness syndrome into the literature. In the course of further research, he and his study group, as well as many other researchers, postulated the central disorder to be cognitive (Frese & Schöfthaler-Rühl, 1976). The various abnormal behaviors forming the helplessness syndrome appear when the individual has acquired a specific cognition of helplessness. This helplessness represents the theoretical link between various stimulus situations and behavioral responses.

The question is how this cognition can be observed, or, if it is not directly observable, how precisely it can be inferred. It must further be asked whether this concept makes it possible to predict reactions, or only allows a post hoc interpretation which ultimately does not say any more than that one cannot predict an individual's reaction from the knowledge of a specific stimulus situation.

2. The Use of Cognitive Concepts in the Paradigm of Helplessness

For a detailed presentation of the concept of helplessness, we refer to Seligman (1974, 1975). The initial experiment was performed by Seligman and Maier (1967). Learned helplessness develops when an individual is repeatedly exposed to unavoidable aversive stimulation. Seligman (1974) uses

> the term learned helplessness to describe the interference with adaptive responding produced by inescapable shock and also as a shorthand to describe the process [which he believes regulates the behavior]. So, learned helplessness in the dog is defined by two behaviors: (1) Dogs that have had experience with uncontrollable shock[1] failed to initiate responses to escape shock or are slower to make responses than naive dogs, and (2) if the dog does make a response that turns off shock, it has more trouble learning that responding is effective than a naive dog. (p. 86)

[1]Uncontrollable shocks are electric shocks whose appearance, intensity, and duration cannot be influenced by the behavior of the individual concerned.

Helplessness is, therefore, a hypothetical construct which is considered to be a cause of behavior. This construct, however, is not directly observable, but is inferred in retrospect when an animal has shown the described abnormal behaviors.

Subsequently, analogous experiments were also performed with human beings, and here too, in the opinion of the authors, they succeeded in finding evidence of specific abnormal behaviors allowing one to assume a helplessness in the individuals in question. The fact of whether an individual exhibits helplessness or not became a differential-psychological descriptive feature as an indication of an acquired personality characteristic. This abnormality of personality was topographically assigned to the field of cognitions.

If one asks what may be meant by a cognition of helplessness, then it is necessary to go into the numerous subsequent investigations in detail. In the following, only those subsequent experiments are discussed which used human beings as subjects. It is important to indicate from the beginning, however, that the construct of helplessness was first developed in an experiment with animals. If the description of helplessness in human beings as a cognition were to prove meaningful, this would imply that a cognitive disorder also existed in the animals which were investigated. While this is not particularly significant in the present context, it would at least exclude definitions of cognition which view cognitive processes as a typically human phenomenon, in contrast to animals.

If one examines the literature concerning the construct of helplessness, it is first of all striking that in almost every paper the attempt is made to reinterpret this cognition of helplessness, almost as an attempt to specify what it is supposed to mean.

In a survey work (1974), Seligman himself describes the cognitive effect of helplessness training:

> Learning that responding and shock are independent makes it more difficult to learn that responding does produce relief, when the organism makes a response that actually terminates shock. In general, if one has acquired a cognitive set in which A's are irrelevant to B's, it will be harder for one to learn that A's produce B's when they do. (p. 95)

Thus, helplessness is interpreted here as the resistance to change of a cognitive set.

According to one of the first works with human beings, by Miller and Seligman (1973), helplessness is a cognitive distortion relating to the consequences of one's own actions. This cognitive distortion is, in the opinion of the authors, obviously a perceptual disorder, because the subjects "tend to perceive reinforcement as more behavior-independent."

In a work by Hiroto (1974), helplessness is an expectation. Hiroto writes:

> Since uncontrollability of noise, externality [relating to the construct "locus of control" according to Rotter, 1966], and chance instructional set [in a problem-solving task] all impaired escape/avoidance in parallel ways, it was speculated that a common state may underlie all three dimensions—expectancy that behavior and reinforcement are independent.

Whereas in Hiroto's (1974) work this expectation is still looked upon as a "state," Hiroto and Seligman (1975) likewise speak of helplessness as an expectation that behavior and reinforcement are independent. However, they give this expectation the functional value of a "trait."

Helplessness is transformed into yet another concept in the work of Miller and Seligman (1975). The authors write that the model of learned helplessness makes the assumption "that a belief in independence between responding and reinforcement" is the central determining point. It can be speculated that the authors use belief and expectation synonymously; however, it could also be that belief refers to either an interpretation or an attribution, instead of an expectation. The authors themselves provide no help in this problem.

Klein, Fencil-Morse, and Seligman (1976) point out that the concepts they use within the framework of the theory of helplessness, including "the expectancy that responding will be ineffective" and "the perception that responses and reinforcement are independent" do not suffice, and further add "a decreased belief in personal competence," so that helplessness can no longer be interpreted with one concept, but is a construct which requires "constructs like attribution and personal adequacy" as "mediational cognitions."

In one of the papers of Klein and Seligman (1976) the subject of distorted perceptions is finally brought up again, as in the earlier contribution of Miller and Seligman (1973).

We believe that the preceding classification speaks largely for itself. Helplessness is interpreted as cognition. In the attempt at specification, different definitions are sometimes given even by the same authors in different papers. According to the studies in question, helplessness can denote the resistance to change of a cognitive set, a perceptual disorder, an expectation, an interpretation, an attribution, or several of these combined.

In the last decade, a great deal of effort has been put into proving experimentally that helplessness can always be found in various species of animals, accompanying the most varied stimuli, and in the most varied behavioral areas. All the authors who have set out to find helplessness have found it. However, if one keeps these quite varied definitions in mind, then the question must be allowed, whether the various authors have really dealt with the same phenomenon, or whether, in the last analysis, they have not classed various phenomena under a common concept, which is vaguely defined as a cognitive concept, and which finally masks the differences.

In the discussion of application, the problem becomes even clearer. The authors also rediscovered the cognition of helplessness in depressive patients, and they claimed that it was the etiological factor for depression. In the meantime, it was discovered in the case of heart attack (Siegrist & Weber, 1978) and, on closer examination, was found to have been postulated years before in the double-bind hypothesis[2] (Bateson, Jackson, Laing, Lidz, & Wynne, 1969) of schizophrenia. In this connection it is also interesting to note the existence of a great many studies which attempt to find evidence for the phenomenon of helplessness in ever new variations; though critical investigations are lacking which attempt to establish that the various phenomena that have been described may not really be interrelated.

The risk that an explanatory variable, such as, for example, the cognition of helplessness, can easily lead to pseudoexplanations may be illustrated by a brief example from the literature. Hiroto (1974) presented an investigation with the goal of proving that the decisive factor of the cognition of helplessness is the expectation that behavior and consequence—in the sense of an event which follows in time—are independent of each other. He used observations during an avoidance/escape assignment as a starting point for his considerations. The design was as follows: Subjects had the possibility of turning off a loud tone by manipulating a switch. Before the tone began, a light flashed. If the subjects operated the switch correctly during that time, they could avoid the aversive tone completely. If the correct manipulation had not been carried out after five seconds, the light went out and the loud tone began. It could still be turned off by the correct manipulation within the next five seconds; this means an escape reaction. After a total time of ten seconds, the tone was turned off by the experimenter and the corresponding experimental run was counted a failure. With this device Hiroto investigated, first, subjects who had previously gone through a typical training in helplessness in comparison with an untreated group, second, subjects, who had a high or a low value according to Rotter's (1966) construct of internality/externality, and third, subjects to whom it had been said either that the tone could be turned off according to a particular principle and that it was their task to discover this principle, or that the experimenter arbitrarily establishes from one time to the next how the tone can be turned off, but that the subject could *by all means guess* the solution and thus put an end to the tone. If the subject guesses incorrectly, the tone continues. Hiroto's re-

---

[2]Professor R. Cohen has pointed out the difficulty of separating the helplessness paradigm from the double-bind hypothesis.

sults show that subjects who had been made helpless took longer to turn off the tone than those who were not helpless, thus bearing out the hypothesis. Likewise, helpless subjects took longer to discover how the tone could be turned off.

Furthermore, the helpless persons had more frequent attempts in which they could not turn off the tone. For the sake of simplification, we wish to discuss only the third group in relation to the problem at hand. In this group, the effects of different instructions were investigated, and also differences were found between the chance group and the problem-solving group which appear at first glance very similar to the findings which were found in the comparison of helpless/not helpless. The chance group also took a great deal longer than the problem-solving group to turn off the tone, and more attempts to discover the principle according to which the tone could be turned off. On a closer investigation, however, differences can also be found between the results of the helplessness experiment and those of the instructional experiment. One difference, for example, is in the number of attempts in which the subjects were not at all successful in turning off the tone. In this aspect, helpless subjects differ in the helplessness experiment from nonhelpless ones. In the instructional experiment, the two instructional groups show no differences in this aspect.

A further difference between the two experiments is shown in the dependent variable of delay of response.

Whereas in the helplessness experiment the difference in delay of response between the helpless and the nonhelpless subjects is significant from the very first attempt, in the instructional experiment the differences develop only in the course of several attempts. According to these findings, two statements are valid for the instructional experiment. First, in the instructional experiment, the chance group and the problem-solving group were equally capable of the required escape behavior, only the chance group took a little longer for this. Second, in the course of several attempts, both groups learned how to do it; but the problem-solving group discovered it faster. The two statements do not hold true to an equal extent in the helplessness experiment. At this point it would be interesting to discuss the implications of these differences in greater detail. However, regarding the problem discussed here, it need only be pointed out that, in spite of these differences, Hiroto sees both experiments as belonging to a uniform theoretical approach, whereby the instructional experiment is supposed to serve to illuminate the mechanisms which underlie the helplessness experiment. Here Hiroto relies on the analogy in the results while ignoring the differences, and argues in a somewhat oversimplified way, which may be summarized as follows:

1. The theoretical assumption is that helplessness is the expression of an expectation according to which behavior and behavioral conse-

quences are independent of each other. One could also say that included in this expectation is the fact that the consequences follow the preceding behavior by chance.

2. Training in helplessness impairs achievement in a subsequent experiment, for example, in an avoidance/escape experiment.

3. If the subjects are given a chance instruction relating to their own behavior and its consequences, then these subjects likewise show poorer accomplishments in a problem-solving situation.

4. The chance instruction is accepted by the subjects, and generates the expectation of an independence between behavior and behavioral consequence.

5. Since the results are analogous in both experiments, the mechanism underlying helplessness is the same as the one in the instructional experiment, that is, an expectation about the independence of behavior and behavioral consequence.

As convincing as this chain of argumentation may seem at first glance, it turns out to be just as incorrect at a second look. Here it is necessary to consider the wording of the chance instruction given. Hiroto writes:

> The "chance" instructions emphasize that S had no direct control over the stimulus and that chance factors predicted success. [The instructions read]: "You will be given some trials in which a relatively loud tone will be presented to you at different intervals. Now here is the important part, and I want you to listen carefully. Whenever you hear the tone come on, there is something you can do to stop it. But I will be controlling the solution to the problem. In other words, the way to stop the tone is really up to me. As far as you are concerned, this is a guessing game. When you guess correctly, the tone will automatically stop. But if your guess is wrong, the tone stays on."

If one analyzes this experimental situation precisely, it seems evident that the independence behavior and behavioral reinforcers which were supposed to underlie this experiment are not given. Rather, the tone can in fact be stopped, when the correct guess is made. If this instruction can generate an expectation in the subject at all, then it is only that the various individual attempts are independent of each other. Therefore, the subject will, first of all, assume that he cannot apply what he experienced in a preceding attempt to a subsequent attempt. If a specific expectation is concerned, it certainly is not that described by Hiroto, "that behavior and consequence are independent." Possibly it would never have come to these interpretational fallacies, if one had only attempted to interpret the differences in the results of the experiments.

3. The Use of Cognitive Concepts

The preceding analysis of the use of cognitive concepts within the framework of the helplessness concept was not supposed to be primarily a critique of the helplessness approach. An analysis of this well-worked-out approach is worthy of a paper of its own. For an example, Levis (1976) has already taken the first step in this direction.[3] In this analysis we have been concerned only with pointing out, by means of an example, the degree of care necessary in dealing with concepts of cognition. The helplessness model lent itself to such an analysis precisely because it has been so well worked out experimentally (Linden, 1980).

As a rule, cognitive concepts designate constructs which can only be inferred indirectly. In order to be able to make inferences from one situation to another, or from one person to another, generalizing analogical inferences are needed. As was shown, however, these generalizing inferences can very quickly become false inferences. Second, the use of these generalizing analogical inferences is precisely what makes cognitive concepts so popular. The helplessness construct, for instance, is in the meantime used with ever-growing frequency and freedom by clinical psychologists and psychological therapists as a diagnostic concept from which existing therapeutic interventions are allegedly supposed to be inferred. However, if the transfer, for instance, of a special concept of expectation from one narrowly defined laboratory situation to another narrowly defined laboratory situation is already burdened with the problems indicated, then—until the opposite is proved—it must first be concluded that the use of the helplessness construct in the everyday routine of clinical psychology is, as a rule, incorrect, and suggests a pseudo-understanding of behavior disorders.

Human beings think, plan, interpret, expect, and evaluate what they experience, and these cognitive processes indisputably influence the choice of behavior. Therefore, clinical psychology will never get away from discussing with clients what they think, expect, plan, etc. Applied clinical psychology certainly cannot wait until assured scientific findings are at hand. But this means that one must proceed very carefully and cautiously when using cognitive concepts. Cognitions are important; cognitive concepts can be misleading.

References

Bateson, G., Jackson, D. D., Laing, R. D., Lidz, T., & Wynne, L. C. *et al.*, *Schizophrenie und Familie.* Frankfurt: Suhrkamp, 1969.

Frese, M., & Schöfthaler-Rühl, R., Kognitive Ansätze in der Depressionsforschung. In N. Hoffmann (Ed.), *Depressives Verhalten.* Salzburg: Müller, 1976.

---

[3]In relation to this, we would particularly like to make reference to the article, which appeared after this work went to press, by A. M. Buchwald, J. C. Coyne, & C. S. Cole: "A Critical Evaluation of the Learned Helplessness Model of Depression." (*Journal of Abnormal Psychology,* 1978, *87,* 180–193.)

Hiroto, D. S. Locus of control and learned helplessness. *Journal of Experimental Psychology*, 1974, *102*, 187–193.

Hiroto, D. S., & Seligman, M. E. P. Generality of learned helplessness in man. *Journal of Personality and Social Psychology*, 1975, *31*, 311–327.

Klein, D. C., & Seligman, M. E. P. Reversal of performance deficits and perceptual deficits in learned helplessness and depression. *Journal of Abnormal Psychology*, 1976, *85*, 11–26.

Klein, D. C., Fencil-Morse, E., & Seligman, M. E. P. Learned helplessness, depression, and the attribution of failure. *Journal of Personality and Social Psychology*, 1976, *33*, 508–516.

Levis, D. J. Learned helplessness: A reply and an alternative S–R interpretation. *Journal of Experimental Psychology*, General, 1976, *105*, 47–65.

Linden, M. Depression und gelernte Hilflosigkeit. In H. Heimann (Ed.), *Neue Strategien der Depressionsforschung*. Bern: Huber, 1980.

Miller, W. R., & Seligman, M. E. P. Depression and the perception of reinforcement. *Journal of Abnormal Psychology*, 1973, *82*, 62–73.

Miller, W. R., & Seligman, M. E. P. Depression and learned helplessness in man. *Journal of Abnormal Psychology*, 1975, *84*, 228–238.

Neisser, U.: *Kognitive Psychologie*. Stuttgart: Klett, 1974.

Rotter, J. B. Generalized expectancies for internal versus external control of reinforcement. *Psychological Monographe*, 1966, *80*, (1, Whole No. 609).

Seligman, M. E. P. Depression and learned helplessness. In R. J. Friedman & M. M. Katz (Eds.), *The psychology of depression*. Washington: Winston, 1974.

Seligman, M. E. P. *Helplessness*. San Francisco: Freeman, 1975.

Seligman, M. E. P., & Maier, S. F. Failure to escape traumatic shock. *Journal of Experimental Psychology*, 1967, *74*, 1–9.

Siegrist, J., & Weber, I. *Forschungsplan und erste Ergebnisse einer Retrospektiven Studie von männlichen Infarktpatienten*. Vortrag auf der Sektionstagung Medizinsoziologie der DGS. Göttingen, January 1978.

Author Index

Subject Index